Publisher's Note

This new edition of Dr. Kazimierz Dabrowski's second English-language book, *Personality-Shaping Through Positive Disintegration*, has been faithfully reproduced in collaboration with the Estate of Kazimierz Dabrowski based on the original 1967 publication by Little, Brown and Company, Boston. The text has been digitized for joint publication in print and e-book form. It includes the original Introduction, written by Dr. O. Hobart Mowrer (1907–1982), Research Professor of Psychology at the University of Illinois from 1948 to 1975 and president of the American Psychological Association in 1954. Dr. Mowrer was a great pioneer in his field: he developed integrity therapy, and his ideas have had a great influence on the alcohol and drug rehabilitation field. Like Dabrowski, he recognized the connection between morality and mental health and illness.

This edition also includes three previously unpublished biographical essays written by Dr. Dabrowski on Kierkegaard, Beethoven, and Unamuno, to supplement those given in Chapter 5 ("Examples of Historical Personalities"). In addition, the Index has been updated with additional names and keywords.

Much of Dr. Dabrowski's professional terminology is no longer common in psychological or psychiatric literature, especially those written for a broad readership; e.g., words like cyclothymia, schizothymia, psychastenia, neurasthenia, etc. In addition, many of Dr. Dabrowski's terms are unique to his theory and not to be found in any common psychology texts (recent or dated). While those terms unique to the Theory of Positive Disintegration are defined in the text, many of the others are not. So, to aid the reader unfamiliar with these terms, we have also included a glossary compiled by Dr. Dabrowski and used in his 1972 book, *Psychoneurosis Is Not An Illness*.

While the professional terminology may have changed in the intervening years, the unique terms form the skeleton of Dabrowski's theory, and the process of personality-shaping continues, regardless of the terms used to describe it. In fact, the public focus has changed recently through popular books with titles such as *Quiet: The Power of Introverts in a World That Can't Stop Talking*, *The Introvert Advantage: How to Thrive in an Extrovert World*, *The Highly Sensitive Person*, and *The Underdog Advantage*. If anything this change is in line with the Theory of Positive Disintegration, even if such works do not approach Dabrowski's level of synthesis and comprehensiveness. Unfortunately, other trends go in the opposite direction, with titles like *The Wisdom of Psychopaths*, making clear the need for a more widespread familiarity with Dabrowski and his works.

The 2015 edition of *Personality-Shaping* is the first in a project that hopes to see all of Dr. Dabrowski's English works back in print, including three unpublished book manuscripts, and numerous published and unpublished papers.

Personality-Shaping Through Positive Disintegration

Personality-Shaping Through Positive Disintegration

Kazimierz Dabrowski

Red Pill Press
2015

Contents

Preface

Personality is not a ready gift but an achievement. This achievement is a very difficult, even painful, process. The aim of this book is to describe and to discuss this process.

Our personality is shaped throughout our lives; our inborn characteristics constitute the basis determining our potential for inner growth. The shaping of personality occurs under the influence of various external milieus. However, it is in the inner psychic milieu that the formative process takes place. The role of the inner psychic milieu is most significant in the accelerated development of psychically richer and more creative individuals.

This means that our personality cannot be created or shaped by some external influence or process without our inner participation. Such involvement is most clearly seen in the development of higher levels of personality. For this to happen we have to have an enhanced awareness, a sense of autonomy and authenticity of our own self.

It will be shown in this work, on the basis of the author's clinical experience and research, that certain psychic elements, such as various forms of overexcitability, germinal elements of the inner milieu, or nuclei of creative abilities, are essential for the formative process leading to the achievement of personality and must come with hereditary endowment. It is usually emphasized that the most important period determining the shaping of personality is the period when the infant "tries his own forces" against the outer environment. However, one must realize that a period even more important than that of early infancy is the period of "awakening" that brings about the development of the inner psychic milieu and its main dynamisms.

Conflicts play an extremely important role in the development of personality. Of all types of conflicts the *inner* conflict is particularly significant. The same can be said about nervousness and psychoneurosis. Without the disturbance and disequilibrium brought about by nervousness and psychoneurosis, the process of personality development cannot be realized. This is because the dynamisms active in these departures from psychic equilibrium also contain the primary elements of creative development.

The author's basic thesis can be stated as follows: Personality development, especially accelerated development, cannot be realized without manifest nervousness and psychoneurosis. It is in this way that such experiences as inner conflict, sadness, anxiety, obsession, depression, and psychic tension all cooperate in the promotion of humanistic development.

Those especially trying moments of life are indispensable for the shaping of personality. An effort to overcome and transform psychoneurotic dynamisms reveals the action of self-directing and self-determining dynamisms that make autopsychotherapy possible and successful.

The difficult moments that promote personality growth generate psychic tension. We cannot, however, advise one to seek liberation from psychic tension since this very tension is absolutely necessary for creative development. Neither can we advise certain forms of "treatment" of nervousness and psychoneuroses that aim at ridding the individual of the so-called pathological dynamisms. In our opinion, most of these dynamisms are not pathological but are developmental and creative. We should rather recommend a very early and repeatedly performed multidimensional diagnosis of the developmental potential of a given individual. Only in this way can one help in the development of personality – not by "treatment," but by explanation and awareness of the inevitable stages of growth.

One must clearly understand that, for an individual and for the society he belongs to, only such development is positive which takes into account the creative aspects of the difficulties of everyday life, pain, dissatisfaction, and discontinuities in the – superficially desirable – uniform process of growing up.

In our view, personality is the ultimate goal of individual development. Such development occurs through the process of positive disintegration; it is at the same time the result of such disintegration.

Personality-Shaping Through Positive Disintegration is intended for readers with a synthetic approach to the humanistic development of man and society. The author hopes that through this book psychologists, educators, social workers, and physicians active in the field of human development, who find around them and in themselves symptoms of positive maladjustment, will be aided in their work and personal striving toward higher values.

K. D.
Edmonton, Canada

Introduction

In the letter in which the author of this remarkable volume invited me
to write an introduction to it, he himself included a paragraph which
might serve as a short preamble. He said:

> This work is based on many years of clinical and pedagogical ex-
> perience. I am sure that I commit, here, numerous errors and
> imprecisions. But, at the same time, I believe this book points
> to, and brings out, the general human tendencies involved in the
> difficult road to creativity, to perfection, and to mental and moral
> health. This process of human development is, I believe, concomi-
> tant with the progressive adjustment of the individual to "what-
> ought-to-be" and to positive maladjustment in regard to the infe-
> rior primitive levels of development and to all that is wrong and
> incorrect in the psychic inner environment and in relation to the
> external environment.

At once it will be apparent, from these few sentences, that Dr. Kazimierz Dabrowski is no ordinary psychiatrist. Although educated as a
physician, he has developed a conception of man and his "existential"
vagaries which radically transcends the physical and biological realms;
and although later trained in Freudian psychoanalysis, he has a point
of view which, instead of denigrating morality and idealism, puts them
in a place of supreme importance.

Dr. Dabrowski has certainly been a pioneer in the development of the
kind of psychiatry that is set forth in this book, and he deserves great
credit for his originality and courage. But, at the same time, there is
nothing singular or eccentric about his particular orientation. It is, in
fact, part and parcel of a widespread and growing perspective in clinical
psychology and psychiatry which can only be described as revolutionary.
Although Harry Stack Sullivan and certain other "neo-Freudians" may
be said to have paved the way for this line of development, its most
vigorous and clearest contemporary formulations are to be found in the

work of Dabrowski, and other writers such as William Glasser, Willard Mainord, Sidney Jourard, and Perry London. Here there is a shift in emphasis from biology to sociology, from illness to ignorance, from the organic to the interpersonal, and from the "treatment" model of general medicine to the teacher-pupil or *educational* paradigm.

It will therefore be my purpose, in this introduction, to try to "brief" the reader for a quicker understanding and deeper appreciation of this book and the general point of view it represents than might otherwise be possible, if he came to it without prior knowledge or preparation. Not only is Dabrowski's conception of psychopathology highly unconventional and thus not likely to be immediately grasped in its true light, but it is also couched in a somewhat technical language which the author, over the years, has evolved for his own purposes; it takes a little while for the uninitiated to learn to make the necessary "translations" into more familiar terms and thought forms. Also, although Dr. Dabrowski's command of formal English is excellent, his expressions are not always idiomatic and sometimes they fail to convey his precise meaning if taken out of context. By the time most readers complete this book, they will have become familiar with and indeed fond of the author's style. But it is hoped that some advance familiarity with his special terms and basic concepts will make the perusal of this book both more enjoyable and more informative from the outset.

I

Dr. Dabrowski's name and work first came to my attention in the form of a monograph entitled *Psychological Basis of Self Mutilation* which was published in 1937. But it was to be exactly a quarter of a century until I met the man himself. This came about in the following way. Early in 1962 I received a letter from Dr. Dabrowski indicating that he contemplated a trip to this country and would plan to visit the University of Illinois. From a knowledge of my own writings he said he thought we perhaps shared some very similar views concerning the nature and correction of psychopathology, which he would like to discuss; he indicated a further desire to pay his respects, while here, to the widow of his late fellow countryman and friend, Florian Znaniecki, author (with W. I. Thomas) of the sociological classic *The Polish Peasant in Europe and America*. The letterhead indicated that the writer was a professor at the Polish Academy of Science and Director of the Institute of Child Psychiatry and Mental Hygiene, in Warsaw.

During our several conversations at the time of his 1962 visit, Dr. Dabrowski piqued my curiosity with respect to what he was then calling "self-education." By now, I too was convinced that in the condition ambiguously called "neurosis" the afflicted individual has more responsibility both for having gotten into such a state *and* for getting out of it than we commonly suppose. So the concept of "self-education," or "autotherapy," was very congenial to me. But I had not at this point read any of Dr. Dabrowski's recent writings and my ability to grasp the full import of what he was saying was somewhat limited. Therefore, I was delighted, in 1964, to see the appearance, in English, of a book by him entitled *Positive Disintegration*, with a special introduction by Dr. Jason Aronson of Boston, and under the imprint of Little, Brown and Company. I read this book with great interest and subsequently reviewed it for *Contemporary Psychology* (10, 538–540, 1965).

Then, a few months later, another letter arrived indicating that Dr. Dabrowski was now in Canada on a research fellowship at a hospital in Montreal. Immediately I arranged for him to come again to Urbana and this time to deliver a number of lectures. During this visit I venture to say that our acquaintance began to ripen into friendship; but I was nevertheless surprised, and certainly much honored, to receive recently a typescript copy of this book and the author's request for some sort of introduction. Because it is my conviction that Dabrowski's general approach, although highly unorthodox by conventional standards, is basically sound and because I would like to see it widely understood and accepted in this country, I am happy to have this opportunity to write a commentary. I may say that Dr. Dabrowski is presently associated with the Department of Psychology at the University of Alberta, in Edmonton, Alberta, Canada.

II

Because it is my belief that this book is best read against a background
of some knowledge of the earlier volume entitled *Positive Disintegration*,
to which I have already alluded, I am taking the liberty of reproducing
here my review thereof. It will afford the reader of the present volume
an introduction, in some depth, to the author's central thesis and to
some of the many powerful ideas and subtleties.

"In contrast to integration, which means a process of unification of oneself, disintegration means the loosening of structures,
the dispersion and breaking up of psychic forces. The term *disintegration* is used to refer to a broad range of processes, from
emotional disharmony to the complete fragmentation of the personality structure, all of which are usually regarded as negative.

"The author, however, has a different point of view: he feels
that disintegration is a generally positive developmental process.
Its only negative aspect is marginal, a small part of the total
phenomenon and hence relatively unimportant in the evolution
or development of personality" (p. 5).

Thus does Dabrowski set forth, in general terms, his seemingly
paradoxical conception of "positive disintegration" and its role in
personality disturbance and growth. More specifically he says:
"In relating disintegration to the field of disorder and mental disease, the author feels that the functional mental disorders are in
many cases positive phenomena. That is, they contribute to personality, to social and, very often, to biological development. The
present prevalent view that all mental disturbances are pathological is based on too exclusive a concern of many psychiatrists with
psychopathological phenomena and an automatic transfer of this
to all patients with whom they have contact" (p. 13).

And later Dabrowski states his hypothesis even more baldly
when he says: "The recovery of numerous mental patients results
in not only their return to their previous state of health but also
the attainment of a higher level of mental functioning. Patients
often manifest a development of their creative capacities even during the climax of their illness" (p. 95).

Although this author does not always succeed in avoiding medical language, his concepts are not basically disease-centered. For
example, he says: "The theory of positive disintegration places a
new orientation on the interpretation of nervousness, anxiety, neurosis, hysteria, psychasthenia, depression, mania, paranoia, and

schizophrenia" (p. 14). And elsewhere, in speaking of a particular patient's disturbance, he says: "It indicated deep dissatisfaction with his internal and external milieu and a tendency with very high emotional tension to resolve this on a higher level of synthesis. His symptoms could be diagnosed as 'mixed depression and anxiety neurosis' or perhaps 'borderline schizophrenia,' but such a label is merely psychiatric etiquette" (pp. 31–32).

Dr. Jason Aronson, in his very useful Introduction, says, even more explicitly: "Like Thomas Szasz, author of *Myths of Mental Illness*, Dabrowski rejects the medical model of 'illness' for psychiatric disorder" (p. xvii). Not only does he reject, at least in a general way, the medical model, but he is also anti-Freudian. Although originally trained (in Vienna, under Wilhelm Stekel) in psychoanalysis and quite restrained in his direct criticism thereof, Dabrowski takes a position which can only be described as antithetical. Freud saw "neurosis" as caused by a superego, which is making unrealistic and too severe moral demands on the individual. "Conventional morality," Freud asserted, "demands more sacrifices than it is worth." And therapy, in this frame of reference, consists of trying to get the patient to "choose some intermediate course" (Sigmund Freud, *General Introduction to Psychoanalysis*, pp. 376–377).

On a scale of socialization or moral development, mental health, for Dabrowski, does not lie in the middle but at the high end. Unlike Freud, he holds that normality (or "therapy") consists of one's rising to the demands and challenges of conscience and the ideal community life it reflects, not in ignoring and trying to belittle them.

Dabrowski thus takes very seriously the possibility that, in so-called neurosis ("identity crisis" is a much better term), we are dealing with *real* guilt (which has been kept carefully hidden) rather than with mere guilt feelings. The following statements typify Dabrowski's position in this regard: "Guilt has a tendency to transform itself into a feeling of responsibility, which embraces the immediate environment and even all society. As has been mentioned, it seeks punishment and expiation. These latter factors play a major role in relieving the feeling *and in beginning the ascent of the individual to higher levels of development*" (p. 37, italics added). "An appraisal of the mental health of an individual must, therefore, be based on the findings of *progressive development in the direction of exemplary values*" (p. 113, italics added).

"Mental health is accompanied by some degree of ability to *transform one's psychological type in the direction of attaining one's ideal.* ... The transformation of psychological type, the deepening and broadening of personality, is directly related to symptoms of positive disintegration" (p. 116, italics added).

And what, more specifically, *are* "symptoms of positive disintegration"? They are "feelings of guilt, of shame, of inferiority or superiority, of the 'object-subject' process [obsessive introspection and self-criticism], of the 'third factor' [self-system], and of so-called psychopathological symptoms" (p. 22), "an attitude of dissatisfaction with [oneself] and a sense of shame, guilt, and inferiority" (p. 122). "Sadness, depression, discontent with oneself, shame, guilt, and inferiority are essential for development, as are also the experience of ... joy and creativity" (p. 119).

And *when* do these feelings, symptoms, signs of positive disintegration arise? At this point Dabrowski's analysis begins to show some of the vagueness and ambiguity which Aronson mentions in his Introduction. At several points the author alludes to puberty, menopause, and periods of "external stress" as the common instigators of positive disintegration. Here individual responsibility is not necessarily indicated. But at other places in his book Dabrowski takes the position that psychological stress arises from dissatisfaction "with regard to [one's] own conduct" (p. 36), "awareness of 'infidelity' toward the personality ideal" (p. 47), "an acknowledgment of having acted incorrectly" (p. 108), and "dishonesty" (p. 113).

Thus it is not unfair to say that for Dabrowski "symptoms of positive disintegration" arise when one violates his own highest standards (conscience) and those of the reference group (or groups) to which he "belongs." And the *capacity* to be thus disturbed, although undeniably the source of much suffering, is also the hallmark of our humanity and the wellspring of moral and social progression. The sociopath, as Dabrowski repeatedly observes, is deficient in this capacity and is, accordingly, less "healthy," less "normal" than are persons who are able to react to their own shortcomings ("sins") with active discontent and self-administered "correction." Here, incidentally, is a good place to say a word concerning the author's emphasis on what he calls "self-education" (or "autotherapy"). Whereas Freud saw conscience and guilt feelings as largely negative and something to be opposed, Dabrowski regards them as "an indispensable factor in development" (p. 39), "the basis of the creative tension that moves [us] toward a stronger process of self-education" (p. 49), which "will admit no retreat from the road ascending to a personal and group ideal. The growing realization of a personality ideal is the secondary phase of self-education and is unique to the formed personality" (p. 63).

But not *all* personal dissatisfaction, guilt, or "disintegration" is "positive," "self-educative." Dabrowski admits that it is sometimes "negative," "genuinely pathological," and conducive to personality "involution" (e.g., chronic psychosis or suicide) rather than growth. How can one "diagnose" the difference? Dabrowski takes the (scientifically and practically not very satisfactory) position that such a differentiation is actually not possible; one can only infer retrospectively that a given instance of "disintegration" was positive or negative. "From the point of view of the theory of positive disintegration, we can make a diagnosis of mental disease only on the basis of a multidimensional diagnosis of the nature of the disintegration. The diagnosis may eventually be validated by observation of the eventual outcome" (p. 17). "Even when suspecting psychosis, the psychiatrist must refrain from judging the case to be pathological disintegration until the end of the process. The so-called psychopathological symptoms – delusions, anxiety, phobias, depression, feelings of strangeness to oneself, emotional overexcitability, etc. – should not be generally or superficially classified as symptoms of mental disorder and disease since the further development of individuals manifesting them will often prove their positive role in development" (p. 103).

It thus becomes apparent that Dabrowski would be happy if he could avoid all reference to disease in the psychiatric context; but it is also clear that he does not entirely succeed in this regard. The difficulty, I submit, arises from a too global interpretation of the concept of "symptom." Two orders of phenomena are involved here, not one. The first comprises reactions of a purely *emotional* nature: guilt, depression, inferiority feelings, etc. The second has to do with the *behavior* a person manifests as a means of resolving these affects, i.e., the voluntary, deliberate, choice-mediated *responses* one makes in an effort to deliver himself from his emotional discomfort, disturbance of "dis-ease."

If a person has a conscience (i.e., is well socialized) and behaves badly he has no choice but to feel bad, guilty, "sick." His reactions, at this level of analysis, are automatic, reflexive, involuntary, "conditioned" and are neither positive nor negative, but *equipotential*. However, one does have a choice as to how one then responds to such emotional states, whether with "symptomatic" behavior designed to make oneself merely more comfortable or with what Dabrowski calls autotherapeutic, self-educative actions (viz., confession and restitution), which will be temporarily painful but ultimately and profoundly stabilizing and growth-producing. Here – and only here – can we confidently and meaningfully make a distinction between positive and negative trends, decisions, "strategies."

Thus there is no necessity to wait until "the end of the process" to determine what is positive "disintegration," or crisis, and what is negative. It is entirely a matter of how the individual *handles* his automatic (autonomic) guilt reactions. And in neither case does it contribute anything to our understanding or practical control of the situation to postulate the presence of a "disease" or "pathological process," any more than it does in any of thousands of other human situations where there is the possibility of making both good and bad choices.

Having in this way gotten the problem safely out of the realm of "disease" and into the area of decision theory, we can now take the further useful step of specifying, with considerable precision, the conditions under which one is likely to make good (wise) vs. bad (impulsive, foolish) decisions. Evidence from many sources indicates that individuals who live openly, under the judgment and with the counsel of their fellows, make, on the average, far better and better disciplined decisions than do persons who operate secretly, evasively, dishonestly. If we are committed to the practice of hiding certain of our actions and thus avoiding the consequences they would have if known, we are inevitably weak in the face of temptation, in that now impulse is easily dominant over prudential concerns. Willpower, it seems, is much more a matter of being "in community" than of having a special faculty or strength within oneself. Hence the great virtue and effectiveness of group therapy: it provides the occasion for a "return to community" and recovery of order, stability, realism, and joy in one's life.

But what if the community, group, society is itself wrong? Isn't it then folly to submit to its values and discipline? This is not the place to explore this issue exhaustively. Suffice it to say that groups can indeed be in error – and certainly one of the worst errors – a group can make is to assume or teach that secrecy, isolation, "independence" on the part of individuals is a good thing. Today our society is commonly called "sick" and much attention is being given to "community mental health," on the assumption that our way of life is *still* too demanding, strict, rigid, moralistic. This, in my judgment, is not our problem at all. Is it not rather that, as a people, we have accepted, as necessity if not an absolute good, the habit of compromise, deceit, and double-dealing? We shall, I think, vainly continue to seek "psychological integration" (or so-called "mental health") until we recognize, once again, the central importance of *personal integrity*.

Dabrowski's book *Positive Disintegration* usefully directs our attention away from the stultifying notion of disease and "emotional disorder" toward a way of thinking which, if not yet fully explicit and precise, is at least pointing in a new direction which we need to explore with all seriousness and dispatch.

III

Having considered this synopsis and critique of Dr. Dabrowski's conception of so-called "psychopathology," as developed in his earlier book, we are now in a position to examine, in proper context, the salient features of the present volume. For ease and compactness of exposition, I propose to list and briefly comment on these, somewhat didactically, as follows:

1. Basic Issues

The reader, as he gets into the body of this work, should not be surprised if he encounters concepts which are not entirely free of ambiguity and superficial inconsistencies. The author would, I think, be the first to agree that his thought in these matters has not entirely crystallized and is still evolving. However, what is important is that he is here asking the *right questions*, and struggling with absolutely central issues, in an honest and creative way. Psychological stresses and disorder are recognized, the world over, as one of mankind's great unsolved problems; and it is also increasingly evident that the more conventional theories and methods of treatment and prevention leave much to be desired. Therefore, originality and innovation should be applauded and actively encouraged, despite manifest imperfections and minor issues not yet fully resolved. As far as the general thrust and thesis of his argument is concerned, Dabrowski writes with courage and conviction, tempered only by personal modesty and scientific caution and restraint.

Although he does not often use the term, it is clear that Dabrowski is centrally concerned with what is commonly called human "socialization." Here are some pertinent quotations from the text that follows:

> The appearance of the feeling that one is committing a sin ("sin phase") foreshadows the turning point in the moral development of man. This is a period during which one passes from a full instinctive integration to a gradual multilevel disintegration (feeling of guilt, shame, responsibility). (p. 122)

> The pain and suffering of a child, his failures, his experiences of shame, and his feelings of inferiority or guilt are the fundamental dynamisms that reshape his primitive structure. They are positive dynamisms if, at the same time, they are offset by pleasant experiences: joy, satisfaction, ambitions, the feeling of superiority, the feeling of having fulfilled one's duty well, the experience of praise, and the like. This alternate action of unpleasant and pleasant stimuli is indispensable for the gradual "awakening of the inner milieu" ... (p. 158)

> Skillfully controlled exposure of the child to the difficulties, in the environment, of his peers is one of the important sources of refashioning the child's attitude, for his equals are considerably more direct in behavior, and often considerably more objective, than older people, even parents. The environment of peers becomes, therefore, an environment creating conditions for reshaping the egocentric, egoistic, imperious, and other attitudes. (pp. 160–161)

> The building of social and friendly relations in harmony with a moral responsibility for oneself and the environment, based on the one hand, on the development of social feeling, and on the other, on the injunctions of the developing inner milieu [is essential] in the method of positive disintegration and secondary integration. (p. 169)

And later the author epitomizes the forces making for human development as a "great creative tension" (p. 193).

One will at once sense here more of Alfred Adler than of Sigmund Freud. The latter took the position that psychopathology arises from oversocialization, from an educational and moral excess, from a superego or conscience which has been too highly developed and which, by virtue of its too great rigidity and strictness, "obstructs the stream of life," that is, destructively and pathogenically blocks natural gratification of the instincts. And treatment, in this context, requires that the therapist align himself with the patient *against* conscience on the inside and the supporting moral and social environment on the outside.

Dabrowski, like Adler and an increasing number of contemporary writers, takes the point of view that much of what is perceived as psychopathology is really just "growing pains" and thus healthy, normal, and inevitable. And when there is an arrest or reversal in this process of personal maturation, therapy, if properly conceived and directed, is not subtractive but positive, additive, educative, in the sense that it involves helping the individual to continue to *grow up*, to *advance* in socialization and personal integrity, rather than to reduce, undo, or scale it back. Therefore the aims of "therapy" – a term, incidentally, which Dabrowski rarely uses – are fully congruent with those of education, and not opposed as in the conventional psychoanalytic frame of reference.

Thus, if Dabrowski and others who are today taking a similar position are right in this contention, what they are calling for is indeed revolutionary and warrants our very thoughtful and urgent consideration.

2. Three-Factor Framework

One example of inconsistency which is more apparent than real arises from the fact that, in this book, the author seems repeatedly to shift his basic emphasis. Much of the time he stresses personal responsibility and the possibility of self-education and reeducation. But then he will write at length about hereditary determinants of personality structure and function or about important environmental influences. The key to understanding this seeming inconsistency is the fact that the author has a three-factor conception of personality; and what he calls the "third factor" or the capacity for *self*-determination – Harry Stack Sullivan often spoke of "the self-system" – is only *one* of three basic parameters or determinants, but one which Dabrowski, very correctly, feels has been badly neglected in the recent past. On this score he says:

> Self-education is the highest possible process of a psychological
> and moral character. It begins at the time when the individual
> undergoes changes which permit him to make himself partially
> independent of biological factors and of the influence of the social
> environment. At this stage a process, thus far not explained by
> psychology, takes place, as a consequence of which the individual
> becomes the resultant not only of inheritance, of factors acting in
> the womb of a mother, and of his biological and social environ-
> ment, but also of one more, ever more powerful factor, namely
> that of defining oneself and of acting upon oneself (the so-called
> third factor). (pp. 36–37)

Thus, what may at first appear to be inconsistency turns out to be
comprehensiveness, a well-rounded rather than one-sided understanding
of and approach to human personality and its determinants.

3. Some Essential Definitions

At this point I think it will be useful to look at certain of the special
terms which Dabrowski employs and make sure that their meanings
are fully explicit. Throughout this work the reader will find reference
to *primary* and *secondary integration*. These expressions correspond
rather closely in their meanings to what Freud, in his 1911 paper entitled "Formulations Regarding Two Principles in Mental Functioning,"
called the Pleasure Principle and the Reality Principle. For Dabrowski,
primary integration is a life style that is instinct dominated, pleasure-
oriented, primitive. And secondary integration means a higher, more
mature personality structure. Thus, *primary* and *secondary*, as here
used, have nothing to do with importance or desirability. They have a
purely temporal reference, implying what comes first and what comes
second – but not secondarily.

The reader may also at first be puzzled by Dabrowski's use of the
terms *unilevel* and *multilevel disintegration*. First it should be noted
that as this author commonly uses the term, *disintegration* means what
is often implied by the term *conflict*. Thus unilevel *primary* conflict
would be conflict between two or more instinctual drives or impulses.
Unilevel *secondary* conflict would be conflict between higher, socialized,

moral considerations. And multilevel conflict, or "disintegration," is conflict *between* levels, lower and higher. Multilevel conflict occurs first of all externally, between the child and his parents and other socializers, and then internally, between ego and superego or conscience.

As previously noted, therapy for Freud involved an attempt to get the superego (and parents) to soften their demands, modify their expectations. Dabrowski, on the contrary, feels that the problem is not usually one of too high expectation but of helping the individual move toward greater maturity and responsibility, toward learning to meet obligations rather than abrogating them. This is a considerable part of what Dabrowski has in mind when he refers to the "hierarchical psychological structure" (p. 22).

When one stops to think of it, one sees that much of what presently passes for therapy or treatment, psychological or otherwise, involves an attempt to lessen, arbitrarily and artificially, the pain of multilevel conflict. This is what sedation (as well as intoxication) is designed to do temporarily. It is probably a big part of the "effectiveness" of electro-convulsive shock therapy, which acts more protractedly. And it is what is more or less permanently accomplished by brain surgery, which involves an assault on the frontal lobes, where foresight and other higher mental functions are lodged. Also, this is what is attempted, functionally, in psychoanalysis, by "reducing the demands of the superego." Dabrowski's position is that the higher side of man is essential and cannot be repudiated except at enormous cost. And for him "therapy" consists of helping another individual fulfill his highest destiny, not escape from or compromise with it.

As one moves through the present volume, it will be apparent that the author makes more use of the term *instinct* than do most American writers. This tendency may arise in part from the fact that Dr. Dabrowski is not as conversant with contemporary learning theory as he might be, and he also seems relatively unfamiliar with sociological and anthropological work on culture and culture-transmission procedures ("education," "socialization," and the like). Thus, when he uses the term instinct, it is often merely an elliptical expression for phenomena or processes which can be more fully and satisfactorily interpreted in terms of learning and culture theory. But the tendency to revert to this term does not seriously detract from the overall value of this treatise, nor does it greatly lessen the cogency of the author's main argument.

4. "Positive" and "Negative" Disintegration

We come now to what I regard as the most serious – but by no means fatal – weakness in Dabrowski's entire approach: his distinction between positive and negative disintegration, or conflict. As indicated in my review of the earlier volume, *Positive Disintegration*, it seems to me that conflict, as such, is neither positive nor negative and that it only confuses matters to so regard it. Conflict, or "disintegration" in Dabrowski's sense, is itself "neutral" – or, as I suggested earlier, "equipotential." The positivity or negativity, goodness or badness, normality or "morbidity" lies rather, it would seem, in the nature of the response made thereto, the manner in which the conflict is resolved. Surely the essence of a "neurotic" or "morbid" solution to a conflict, of the multilevel kind, consists of one's trying to ease the pain of the conflict directly, instead of letting the pain motivate one to grow and develop as the situation demands. It now appears that much would-be professional therapy has mistakenly involved essentially the same strategy, of trying to relieve the individual's suffering in some artificial rather than natural way, that is, of trying to help the individual become comfortable without making the necessary effort which the situation logically requires. (Cf. the emphasis in a self-help group known as Recovery, Inc., on what its members call the Will to Effort rather than the Will to Comfort; that is, they do not try to feel better but to be, act better.)

Dr. Dabrowski acknowledges the difficulty which arises when one tries to distinguish between positive and negative conflict. He says:

> The distinction between positive and negative disintegration seems to be most difficult to draw. We say that we are speaking of a positive disintegration when it transforms itself gradually or, in some cases, violently into a secondary integration, or when, without passing into a clear and permanent, morbid, secondary or involutional disintegration, it remains a disintegration which enriches one's life, expands one's horizons, and produces sources of creativity. (p. 70)

> We call a disintegration negative when it does not produce effects

which are positive in relation to development or when it yields
negative effects. In the first case a man returns to a primary
integration, with negative tendencies of compensatory experiences,
connected with a short-lived disintegration ... (pp. 70–71)

And elsewhere the author speaks of a "truly morbid structure" (p. 33)
and "involutional mental disease" (p. 48). "We encounter permanent
disorganizations," he says, "principally in severe chronic mental diseases
and in acute chronic somatic diseases" (p. 70). Thus far the argument
seems to be largely circular and therefore lacking in cogency.

With respect to the more specific question of whether disintegration
will be positive or negative, the author says:

> Whether a man disintegrates positively or negatively is indicated ...
> by the more or less obvious presence of a factor which organizes
> such a state of slackening or of dissension, organizing it in the
> sense of ordering, evaluating, and purposeful utilization in build-
> ing the structure of a higher level. (p. 33)

This kind of theorizing is made unnecessary if one adopts the simpler
hypothesis that conflict, as such, is neither positive nor negative, but
that the reactions thereto necessarily are. If this position is adopted,
then one can ask the highly relevant and practical question: What can
one do to increase the likelihood of positive rather than negative conflict
resolution? At one point (p. 76), citing Janet, Dabrowski says that
intelligence is a factor here. But I would suggest that the transcendently
important consideration is whether an individual chooses to live secretly
or "in community." If a person resolves to keep his behavior hidden,
he is weak in the face of temptation, since he does not now have to
deal with the moral and interpersonal consequences of his irresponsible,
self-indulgent behavior. Therefore, he is likely to "solve" a conflict in
a shortsighted, primitive, ultimately self-defeating way; whereas, if he
subjects himself to the discipline of openness, he will have the benefit of
the negative sanctions which others provide for wrong action and will
thus be more likely to behave "integratively."

Although this is not a position which Dabrowski explicitly espouses, it
is, I believe, congruent with his basic assumptions and would, if adopted,
go a long way toward eliminating the problems which arise when the
terms *positive* and *negative* are used to qualify conflicts as such.

5. A Special Conception of "Personality"

What may at first escape the reader, and is quite important for full comprehension of this volume, is that the author is using the term *personality* in an extraordinary way. Usually we assume that everyone has, or is, a personality; but Dabrowski rejects this view. To everyone he attributes what he calls *individuality*; but, *personality*, or full *person-hood*, is a state of higher evolvement of which many of us fall far short and none of us attain completely. The following quotations, taken together, give the essence of the author's position in this regard:

> Such qualities and experiences, connected with the feelings and senses mentioned above, are signs that personality is developing. For this development is not possible without experiencing a feeling of veneration for the hierarchy of higher values and without the feelings of inferiority, sin, guilt, and shame. These feelings are a sign of the first step toward diminishing the evil, toward overcoming it. On the other hand, humility permits us to appraise the level at which we are, the distance which we still have to go, and the resisting forces which we will have to conquer. (p. 25)

> [The developing person] must leave his present level, lift himself to a new, higher one and, on the other hand, must, as we have said before, retain his unity, retain the continuity of his psychophysical life, his self-awareness, and identity. The development of personality, therefore, takes place in most cases through disintegration of man's present, initial, primarily integrated structure, and, through a period of disintegration, reaches a secondary integration. (p. 45)

> The process of personality building, therefore, is characterized by a wandering "upward," toward an ideal, of the disposing and directing centers and the gradual acquiring of a structure within which, besides individual qualities (the main trend of interests and capabilities, lasting emotional bonds, the unique set of the emotional and psychic structure), general human traits appear – that is, the high level of intellectual development, the attitude of a Samaritan, and the moral and social and esthetic attitudes. (p. 49)

> The new total organization is achieved painfully. (p. 59) This drama often gives way to a state of peace and internal harmony ... (p. 28)

In this frame of reference the normal person is one who has achieved "personality," that is, maturity, responsibility, integrity. And the so-called neurotic, far from being one in whom these attributes are overdeveloped, is an individual who has not yet achieved them – *but who has the capacity, the potential to do so.* Sociopaths ("psychopath" was the older designation) are, by contrast, less fortunate. Of them Dabrowski says:

> Such people are incapable of internal conflicts, but often enter into conflicts with the environment. ... A psychopathic individual usually does not know the feeling of internal inferiority, does not experience internal [multilevel] conflicts; he is unequivocally integrated [at the primary level]. (p. 51) They are not able to assume an attitude regarding time from a distance, nor are they able to make themselves mentally independent of it. They are constrained by the present moment, by the reality of flowing experiences, by their own type, and by the influences of the environment. (p. 52)

Although the sociopath does not hurt in the way a neurotic or psychotic person does, by the same token he lacks, or is at least seriously deficient in, the capacity for full normality, real "personality." Thus, he is the "sickest," the most "forsaken" of men. And it is a great misfortune, on the assumption that neurotic individuals are oversocialized rather than undersocialized, that many of them have been *pushed* toward sociopathy, rather than toward genuine normality, by misconceived forms of therapy. As a result of this mistaken conception of neurosis and its treatment, there is in our culture today a pervasive sociopathic drift and loss of "moral fiber." It now appears that much "therapy" has been directionally mistaken by exactly 180 degrees. And Dr. Dabrowski is patiently and persistently calling our attention to this tragic error and trying to right it.

6. Self-Education and the Concept of "Help"

The reader may be perplexed by the fact that Dabrowski emphasizes self-education and autotherapy but also believes that there is a place for "help" from others. The more traditional medical model has put a preponderant emphasis upon "treatment," which must be obtained from others, and a correspondingly smaller, sometimes almost negligible emphasis upon what the "neurotic" individual can do for himself. One of the truly exciting things about this book is that the author repeatedly asserts his belief that self-help is an ever-present possibility for disturbed persons and that it occurs in a highly effective and crucial way in far more individuals than we ordinarily realize.

But Dr. Dabrowski also thinks that others may usefully enter into the therapeutic or growth process as "advisers." The selection of this term is not, I believe, an inadvertence on the author's part. He definitely wishes to deemphasize the notion of disease which has to be "treated" by a physician; and what he stresses instead is the *educational* model, in which there is not only a place, but a necessity, for both a pupil (learner) and a teacher. There are many indications that the medical conception of illness and treatment is in the process of being replaced, in this total area, by the notion of *ignorance* – not only in the sense of one's not knowing but of ignoring certain important considerations, i.e., *ignor-ance* – and education, counsel, advice from others.

But there is still the apparent inconsistency between the notion of *self*-education and education by others. If one can and should educate himself, why does he need "outside" help at all? I believe Dabrowski fully recognizes and satisfactorily resolves this paradox. He is certainly well aware that in the beginning, that is, in the parent-child relationship, education is other- rather than self-directed; and he is also aware that in the strictest sense of the term, education never becomes self-directed. So-called self-education really involves a division of the personality into two parts – the "subject-object relationship" Dabrowski calls it – one of which is teacher and the other pupil. The most obvious, and most logical, candidates for these two roles are what Freud called, appropriately, the superego and the ego.

That I have represented Dabrowski's thinking in this connection correctly can be substantiated by a number of passages, two of which follow:

> Self-education is the highest possible process of a psychological and moral character. It begins at the time when the individual undergoes changes which permit him to make himself partially independent of biological factors and of the influence of the social

environment [i.e., the time at which external moral authority is "introjected" and conscience formation takes place] ... (p. 36)

In order to educate himself a man should, as it were, split himself into a subject and an object – that is, he should disintegrate [which I interpret to mean the development of a difference of opinion between superego and ego, as a result of which the latter learns a lesson]. (p. 37)

Now a person (self, ego) can obviously take either of two attitudes toward this type of process: he can resent and resist it, or he can trust, welcome, seek it. And at this point Dabrowski pertinently refers to the practice of *meditation*. He says: "This reaching out, through meditation and contemplation, to one's educational ideal usually contains in itself the elements of a religious attitude." (p. 38)

And then the author goes on to speak of the New Testament emphasis upon the ideal of "losing yourself to find yourself." He says:

We have repeatedly emphasized that the "birth" of personality by which we mean a decisive turning point in one's life – is a drastic experience for an individual. He senses the advent of something "other" in himself, he feels that the hierarchy of values thus far accepted by him undergoes changes, and that he is becoming much more sensitive to certain values, and less to others. (p. 40)

Self-education presupposes experiencing of the dualistic attitude by an individual, the attitude of incessant divisions of oneself into subject and object, into that which lifts and educates and into that which is lifted and educated. This is the already mentioned "subject-object in oneself" process. (p. 94)

To be very literal, as we have already seen, self-education is an impossibility. But each of us has to make a choice, the choice to be *open* or *closed* to the importunings of conscience and the external community (or what Sullivan called "the significant others") which it represents. A son cannot educate himself – that is his father's responsibility. But the son can and must choose either to accept or reject his father's tuition, and he must later exercise the same option with regard to the inner surrogate of the father and other "authority figures," namely conscience.

Even in folk wisdom, conscience is recognized as a great educator, or at least potentially so. We commonly speak of it as "punishing" or "rewarding" us, and these are the two great "reinforcing agents" of modern learning theory. Says Dabrowski:

> It is an active conscience, as it were, of the nascent personality in its process of development, which judges what is more and what is less valuable in self-education, what is "higher" and what is "lower," and what is or is not in accord with the personality ideal, what points to internal development and perfection, and what leads to a diminution of internal value. (p. 99)

> As the personality develops, punishment and reward become increasingly more introverted, internal, and become ever more independent of external sanctions. More and more often, punishment takes the form of "pangs of conscience" ... (p. 123)

Then the author asks the salient question: "Who is qualified to help in the development of personality?" Here we shall make no effort to review his answer, which is sagacious and subtle. But it is pertinent to note that the literature of another lay self-help group – Recovery (of Australia, not to be confused with Recovery, Inc., which is an American institution) – also puts stress upon the use of an "adviser," as does Alcoholics Anonymous in its sponsorship system. Although these are the purest forms of self-help groups, they see no inconsistency between this philosophy and the use of teachers. For if a teacher is to teach, he must have a pupil, and the pupil must do the pupil's work. He must be open and he must study, meditate, *listen* both to the "voice" within and the voices without.

How different all this is from the distrust of conscience and of "education" generally which characterized classical Freudian psychoanalysis!

7. Two Neglected Processes: Confession and Modeling

In a book which takes the moral dimension of life as seriously as this one does, it is remarkable that so little attention is given to confession as an essential measure in dealing with certain forms of guilt. At one point the author says: "With the feeling of guilt there usually rises, simultaneously, the need for self-accusation, penalty, and expiation. ... guilt calls for penalty and expiation." (p. 90) But reference to the factor of confession, specifically, is curiously absent. Much later the author alludes to a 6-year-old girl who, when she had engaged in some misdemeanor, usually took "many hours to confess." However, this is the only place I can recall seeing the word, although in one other place there is reference to an individual who took part "in the process of 'disclosure.'"

By contrast, much emphasis is put upon self-examination. To what has already been quoted on this score, I would here add the following passage:

> Meditation and contemplation are forms often preparing an in-
> dividual for secondary integration. Meditation makes one learn
> internal observation, to reflect on the essence of one's spirit, on
> the complexity of one's psychic structure, and on the transcenden-
> tal world. Contemplation is a process of bringing oneself in touch
> with the transcendental values, of separating from the instinctive
> structure, of gathering psychic and moral strength for one's inter-
> nal reshaping. In contemplation a process of knowing the higher
> reality, through love, sets in. (p. 121)

But is it not equally important for the "neurotic" individual to work at *being known*, at giving up his secrecy and alienation and destructive "privacy"? Only rarely, I believe, do guilty persons deal effectively with their problems without self-revelation to the important people in their lives. Self-observation and inner "listening" are obviously of great value and should not be neglected; but they will not, I think, entirely take the place of self-disclosure and "speaking."

There are many places in this book where the author makes state-ments such as the following:

> The feeling of guilt, as we have already pointed out, is an indis-
> pensable developmental element for every moral individual and

is strongly manifested in persons capable of accelerated development. It forms an indispensable creative tension, which lies at the root of true self-educational work. (p. 91)

But isn't the guilt-ridden individual usually also a person who has been in hiding? And what more appropriate action, in response to his guilt, than to bring himself back "into community," into honest and authentic relationship with the persons he has cheated or wronged?

And this leads us to a related consideration. If a therapist or "adviser" feels that confession and social reintegration are importantly related processes, the question arises as to how he can most effectively induce estranged, secretive, "neurotic" persons to become more honest, first of all in the therapeutic relationship, and then more pervasively so? Mere explanation of the guilt theory of neurosis is sufficient to permit some persons to begin to unburden themselves. But in most instances things go much faster if the therapist, sponsor, adviser will himself exemplify the behavior which he wishes the other person to develop, namely, deep candor and truthfulness about himself. Toward the end of the present volume, the author draws extensively upon the autobiographical accounts of five famous or near-famous persons who have experienced "positive disintegration" and written in some detail about it. Should this be the procedure which all psychiatrists and psychologists follow – to report or "analyze" the case histories of other persons but to say nothing intimate or revealing about themselves? In light of recent experimental work (by Albert Bandura and others) on the great aid to learning which is provided by modeling on the part of the teacher, it seems that we professionals in the field of personality alteration may need to take a second look at our own roles. And it is perhaps not without significance, also, that in such successful lay self-help groups as Alcoholics Anonymous, modeling is of the essence. Typically an AA speaker "qualifies" himself by giving his first name and admitting that *he* is an alcoholic. Perhaps the best way to help another admit who he genuinely is, is for the would-be helper to "go first" in the process.

Modeling and an increased emphasis on confession would, I think, be entirely consistent with the general point of view taken in this volume and would, I venture to say, be a very natural extension of methods already used and recommended by the author.

8. Scientists as the New Moralists

Not long ago I heard a remarkable lecture at a Unitarian-Universalist church, in the course of which the speaker pointed out that many liberal clergymen have today become so liberal and broad-minded that they have no strong or settled convictions about anything and thus have nothing very substantial to say to their congregations, whereas the dilemma of conservative ministers is that, although they may still have some "beliefs," these are often couched in a language which is no longer meaningful or appealing to 20th-century men and women. And the speaker then went on to point out that, somewhat paradoxically, it is today scientists who, although they are supposed to be "ethically neutral," are actually approaching the problem of morality from an empirical basis and thus developing some confidence in what they are saying in this area – and saying it in such a way as to make it relevant and plausible to modern audiences. The author of *Personality-Shaping Through Positive Disintegration* is, I believe, such a person. If his qualifications on this score are not already evident, perhaps the following excerpts from the book will make them so:

> As we have seen ... this "normativeness" of our approach is broadly based on empirical data. We may say that these "norms" are a logical necessity because of our subject matter and the method we use for its study. They serve us in everyday life, and in our study we apply them to prominent historical personalities and to living observed or investigated individuals, ascertaining their place in the adopted scale. (pp. 39–40)

> Knowing his son's capabilities and the somewhat exceptional and original character of the boy's development, he encouraged his son to develop in himself some critical attitudes in relation to the "laws" of man's developmental cycle in the period of maturation, and not to submit himself to these laws uncritically. (p. 173)

A few months ago my own teenage son and I were traveling together, and in a hotel one evening we happened to see a somewhat "primitive" revival meeting on television. There was the usual buildup of singing and high expectation, and then the evangelist himself started speaking. His topic was a familiar one, namely *sin*, but he approached its consequences in a new way. Not once did he allude to or threaten his audience with punishment in an afterlife. Instead, he made the connection between sin and personality disorder, and supported his thesis with "case histories" not unlike those which a psychiatrist or psychologist might use. Here is surely the heart of the matter, that sin is sin because it is personally and socially destructive, and this is something that can be empirically studied and verified and is not dependent upon myth or revelation. The fact that scientists, with their empiricism, do not now hold themselves above considering moral problems and that at least some ministers, with their moral concern, are willing to look at these matters pragmatically are developments which one can only welcome; and they point, at least tentatively, to the possibility of an era in which the present "conflict" between science and religion will be harmoniously and creatively resolved.

It has been a privilege and a challenge to read this book in manuscript and to set down here some of my thoughts concerning it. Others will, I know, also find it theoretically intriguing and practically suggestive. It will reward their careful study and I commend it to them heartily.

O. Hobart Mowrer, Ph.D. (1907–1982)
Research Professor of Psychology, University of Illinois (1948–1975)

Chapter 1

The Definition of Personality

Various terms that denote man as a unit are used in common language, literature, philosophical and ideological studies, as well as in scientific works, dealing particularly with psychology, sociology, and economics. Thus we hear or read such expressions as *human being, person, individual, individuality, personality,* and *self (ego)*.

This work does not intend to provide a systematic and comprehensive study of these concepts. The author will deal only with the problem of personality, as he views it, based on his own experiences, meditations, and ideas. As the above-mentioned conceptions obscure the problem of personality, which is in itself very complex, some, at least general, definitions are required.

The concept of self (ego) is of a metaphysical character. It is not clearly defined, has many meanings, and is used in various senses. Generally speaking, it denotes the distinctness of the existence of a human being, the source of his mental activity, and the individual substratum of his mental structure, which can be only vaguely known.

Common language frequently employs the terms *person, individual,* and *human being.* These terms do not possess any deeper psychological meaning. They are used chiefly to indicate that in a specific case we are thinking of a single man or representative of mankind, of some indefinite human creature. The general definitions of these terms are sometimes given more precise meaning by adding various adjectives, as in the expressions *a noble person, a disagreeable individual,* and so on.

The terms *individual* and *human being* may also have specific meaning; they may indicate some significant qualities of a given person, such as his rights, or his distinctness, coming clearly into view against the background of generally accepted customs, aspirations, and the average cultural level of the society. So conceived, *individual* brings us closer to two other concepts: that of individuality and of personality. Contrasting the individual with the society, we emphasize, first of all, the qualities represented by individuality and personality.

We understand the term *individuality* to mean a distinct human being, differing from other individuals of a given society in such aspects as mental qualities, talents, particular interests, way of behaving, ambition, and strength of pursuing his aims (regardless of moral injunctions). There may be more or less of such specific qualities present in an individual, some less, others more marked in strength, but all usually closely interlinked and possessing some tonality of their own, a feature peculiar to a given individuality. Strictly speaking, this peculiar tonality, connected in most cases with the temperament and character qualities, with the specific approach to matters at hand, with the exertion of will, and with the force of external appearance, is the gist of individuality.

A great actor who performs each of his roles in his own peculiar way, differing from all other actors in his approach to the subject, will possess this individuality in our eyes.

The concept of individuality sometimes concurs with the concept of personage. The latter term, however, is usually used to denote a person of high rank or significance in political, economic, social, or other life.

Personality, in the context of this work, is a name given to an individual fully developed, both with respect to the scope and level of the most essential positive human qualities, an individual in whom all the aspects form a coherent and harmonized whole, and who possesses, in a high degree, the capability for insight into his own self, his own structure, his aspirations and aims (self-consciousness), who is convinced that his attitude is right, that his aims are of essential and lasting value (self-affirmation), and who is conscious that his development is not yet complete and therefore is working internally on his own improvement and education (self-education).

These introductory definitions of individuality and personality will help the reader to distinguish the two concepts.

When we speak of individuality we refer to both positive and negative qualities, while personality has only positive constituents. Individuality is not necessarily involved in various general human problems, but if a person possesses personality he embraces with his intellect, sensitivity, and activity all the truly essential problems of mankind. The person possessing individuality may not possess the capability for deeper insight into his own self and consequently may lack the conscious urge for shaping and improving himself, but for the person characterized by personality the work upon himself, upon his mental and character traits, is of paramount importance. While the person possessing individuality, in enhancing his personal values, capabilities, and knowledge, usually has his own egoistic aims in view, the person characterized by personality enhances his qualities and powers in order to offer them in the service of mankind.

There are various definitions of personality, each differing in meaning and scope. Scientific psychology speaks for the most part of the empirical conception of personality, understanding by it the totality of psychical and physical dispositions of an individual (Stern, Kreutz, and others). So conceived, personality is identical with the conception of a mere human being without differentiation, evaluation, or hierarchization.

When we isolate the conception of personality from that of the human being, as such, and from that of individuality, we obtain a standard conception which visualizes personality as a composition of all the qualities which an ethic or an ideology expects from a given human being (Kerschensteiner, Bradley). We see that this normative conception of personality is relative in character. It depends on geohistorical and religious factors, on differences in customs, morality, ideology, and so on. So conceived, personality is identical with the concept of an ideal personality. This ideal is changeable, as are the factors determining it, depending on the epoch and environment. As the change may be fundamental, this ideal personality reveals itself as relative.

Besides the empirical and normative conceptions of personality there are other definitions which regard a human being as a personality if he possesses certain peculiar characteristics. For example, there are those who equate personality with the existence of particular moral characteristics. Others feel that personality is the attainment of self-control, overcoming biological instincts, with the aim of realizing individual ideals. Both of these definitions are incomplete and one-sided; they do not include a universality of positive values.

In this work, as our definition of personality indicates, we seek to give a possibly all-inclusive conception of personality and at the same time to free it from mutable and consequently nonessential qualities. We endeavor to base our conception on standards and on human values of a lasting character, on values accepted and realized by man since the very beginning of his culture, on values regarded as absolute. They have found their expression throughout the history of mankind, coming together in varying degrees in known historical personalities.

So visualized, the problem of personality requires a comprehensive study and cannot be exhausted in a short, sketchy monograph. The task undertaken, therefore, is limited to the introduction of certain delineations and definitions, which may contribute to a fuller and clearer formulation of the problem of personality, to a general explanation of the fundamental qualities characterizing personality, and – what may be of prime importance – to a presentation of the process and methods of its shaping.

Human Qualities and Their Lasting, Universal, and Unique Character

From the point of view of individual and social values human beings may be divided roughly into positive, negative, and mixed types, the latter with a predominance of positive or negative characteristics or with an unsteady balance of these characteristics.

There are very few human beings whose personal character is wholly positive. Also there are not many people of primitive, negative, expressly psychopathic character, people who are a burden for their immediate social group, such as their family, school, or place of employment, and whose influence on it is destructive and who detain and obscure its development.

The majority of human beings belong to the mixed type. They form the most interesting and "live" segment of humanity. In such individuals the positive and negative characteristics exist – various intensities – almost side by side, penetrating each other or conflicting in an incessant antagonism, the one or the other group winning temporary or permanent domination.

However, in general, positive characteristics grow in strength, importance, and domination. The fact that humanity survives and develops serves as evidence that the advantage is on the side of positive qualities. True, there are periods in the lives of individuals and epochs in the life of communities in which the domination of positive characteristics is disturbed, in which the negative traits of man awaken, mobilize, come to power, and reveal their destructive influence. This happens when an individual finds himself, or the community finds itself, in conditions liberating or even intensifying the most primitive driving forces of man, such as the brute instinct of self-preservation, instincts of fighting, cruelty, primitive sexual drive, aspiration for power, and a desire to subdue other individuals or societies by force. However, the periods of downfall usually do not last long. Man's instinct for development, which in the broadest meaning of the word is a tendency to mental and moral perfection, sooner or later gains power and reinvigorates and enhances the positive values. These values, sustained, consolidated, and developed by tradition, legal order, and moral and customary standards, may undergo jolts and perturbations, may be driven back to the level of potentiality, but can never be eradicated. Even in periods of collapse they survive in us in the form of moral readiness and yearning for their revival and full realization. As they constitute the foundation and prerequisite of the cultural and moral existence of humanity, these values are indestructible; they have existed from the beginning of man's history, and are unchangeable in their essence, though revealing various degrees of development and richness.

The concept of the domination and permanence of man's positive values is associated with the problem of the perpetuation of his negative traits, of the relationship between them, and of the evolution of both kinds of characteristics. The durability of positive values and their increasing domination, although often disturbed, obviously diminishes the scope, strength, and quality of negative traits. The latter are suppressed, ousted, sublimated as a result of individual or social action. Their drastic manifestation stimulates mankind to counteraction. The society becomes ever more sensitive to primitive, brutal symptoms of evil that endanger its standards, customs, and ideals, and the society endeavors to fight these evils by destroying their very foundations. The individual and the society strive to separate themselves from the bestial elements of human nature, to put a stop to them, and to enter on a road to humanization. Brzozowski states: "Man is not a continuation of evolution but a rupture in its thread, an opposition against it. When man emerged all that preceded him became his enemy." It seems, therefore, that the day of maximum control, of the sublimation of negative characteristics of man, will finally come, even though it may not be soon.

The lasting positive values of man may be classified into universal and particular, the latter occurring less frequently. The universal positive values that dominate societies of different epochs and cultures sometimes form a general positive characteristic of these societies. Decisive in this area is the frequency with which they appear. Such positive universal qualities include, for example, religiosity, the sense of individual and social responsibility, training in citizen's duties, fidelity to principles and people, a sense of justice, courage, honesty, and discipline. These particular qualities, or groups of some of them, appear relatively often among human beings.

We encounter among people less often such qualities as sensitivity and subtlety (moral, intellectual, and esthetic), emotional maturity, a faculty for self-knowledge and general knowledge and, what is entailed by it, open-mindedness, belief in the value of one's ideology, ability for unremitting work upon oneself, for constant perfecting of oneself.

The ideal of personality, conceived schematically, should embrace the fundamental positive qualities of man, not only those that are universal but also those appearing less often, such as open-mindedness, the highest possible sensitivity to human affairs, the faculty for conscious and effective working upon oneself along the direction accepted as one's own. The ideal of personality may, in the most general way, be formulated as follows: Personality is a synthesis of the most essential human values embodied in an individual.

A thorough psychological analysis of great figures of history – to whom we may apply the term *personality* as here understood, and in whom we find the faculties of self-consciousness, self-affirmation, and self-education – reveals that the final aim of their internal struggles, abounding in breakdowns, adjustments, and attainments of ever higher levels, was to realize in themselves the above-outlined ideal of personality. This shows that it is a universal ideal, an ideal answering the most essential needs of man.

Attitudes and Qualities of Personality

We shall shortly discuss some of the above-mentioned human qualities, both the universal and those encountered less often, since they may be treated as traits and attitudes constituting a human personality. In this connection we shall refer to those mental, social, and religious domains of human life without which the development and perfection of man is impossible.

We shall begin with mental traits, possessed in various degree and scope by particular human beings, which are prerequisites of personality.

Mental Qualities

Multilateral knowledge

In the sciences, even those which have departed most remotely from philosophy, such as the experimental sciences with a definite scope, methods, and aims, two different attitudes of scientists are observed. Some scientists, in their efforts to achieve a deeper understanding of fundamental problems in their special fields, seek solutions not only within the narrow scope of a given branch of knowledge but also outside it. Others, desiring to keep their methods free from extraneous influences so as to avoid dissipation of attention, do not move beyond the scope of their particular fields of study. The first attitude is characterized by a tendency toward broadening the horizon of thought, and the second to its narrowing, with the hope of obtaining a deeper insight into a particular subject matter.

History records that at different periods one or the other attitude won domination and that there has been considerable fluctuation in this respect. The periods characterized by the tendency toward the isolation of exact sciences and fields of study with their peculiar points of view and special methods follow periods in which the tendency toward a universal approach has been dominant. For instance, in medicine, after a period in which physicians were concerned with the whole of medical knowledge there ensued a period of specialization. New specialists appeared, such as surgeons, gynecologists, specialists in internal diseases, neurologists, psychiatrists, and others. In particular divisions of medicine new special branches evolved, limiting their scope of concern to stomach, lung, heart diseases, to allergy, to endocrine glands, and even to diseases of the thyroid gland alone.

It was evident in time, however, that a broader approach to a disease is necessary, that a too-narrow specialization is in fact harmful to a given field of knowledge and gives neither the proper deepening of medical knowledge nor satisfactory help to the patient, whose loss because of this excessive specialization is the greatest. For example, failure to consider infant neuropsychiatry, psychology, and pedagogics in pediatrics, or failure to consider neurology and endocrinology as well as psychopathology in psychiatry does not permit a correct assessment of pathological phenomena and a proper application of remedies. It is also a known fact that infant neuropsychiatry and mental health began to make progress and have attained their present higher level after the advent of close cooperation between the physician, psychologist, pedagogue, and even the sociologist. And pedagogics, as a science and art, appreciating the importance of social, economic, and religious influences on the development of individuals and groups, begins to depart from the attitude of half-automatic and half-conscious reactions to some partial groups of dynamisms in the development of a child. The fundamental educational requirements cannot be satisfied either by the best family, the best school, the best mental life, or by the most moral environment; they can be satisfied only by all the factors of direct and indirect education combined into an organic whole.

Scientific research in a given special field should be linked to related fields as well as to the broadest aspects of knowledge considered as a whole. Such research should be conducted at various planes and should give special attention to the hierarchy of phenomena. It should proceed from basic premises to knowledge wider in scope, to a point at which we pass from an unidimensional "I know" to a multidimensional "I understand." Knowledge is usually unidimensional and understanding multidimensional; knowledge is based on perception and judgment, understanding involves also experience and intuition which add depth to the perception and judgment.

Independent value judgment, feeling, and action

We usually perceive only that portion of reality which the quality and organization of our receptors of external and internal stimuli, and of our transmission "stations," permit us to perceive. The structure of our senses, natural impulses, feelings, and "mental powers" confines us usually within our volitional, emotional, and cognitive framework. We are imprisoned within a stereotype of our individual properties. For instance, we know from our own experience that one may associate with a person for years without noticing his striking and even most important character traits.

Our judgments and opinions also depend on the influence of various "constellations." Of great significance here is the suggestive influence on the part of our environment, whatever emotional or aspirational connections we have with it, and circumstantial bonds "for life" with this or that person or social group. The diversity of forms of our relations and mental attitudes is conditioned by our general sensitivity. Our judgments, emotions, and aspirations depend also on the condition of our organism and on our disposition, on our states of depression and excitability, on whether our mind is open or closed, on the level, readiness, and extent of our faculty for the internal transformation of what comes to us from the outer world, and on other factors.

Observation of everyday life and of environments at various cultural levels leads to a conclusion that self-dependency in feelings, judgment, and action is a very rare faculty among people. There are very few people among us who are consciously independent of the external environment and of the lower layer of their internal environments. To make oneself independent of both these environments one must go through the process of disintegration, which develops the faculty of using the moral judgment by resorting to a true sense of morality, and instills in one the readiness to act accordingly. A moral judgment not backed by the sense of morality and by the ability to effect its realization is nothing but conformity and reveals our superficial attitude toward a given phenomenon. We can point to many cases of such a deficient moral attitude. We disapprove, for example, of this or that egoistical deed, though we ourselves are ready to act in just the same way. School pupils and students consider the practice of informing by their mates and lying by their teachers as the most immoral acts but themselves inform and lie, to a smaller or greater extent. All indiscreet persons and meddlers agree during a discussion that meddling and indiscreetness are blemishes, but they themselves will continue to be indiscreet and meddling.

Sometimes the lack of a synthesis of intellectual, emotional, and volitional elements is considered a positive quality in pronouncing an opinion. Supporters of such a view say that this is a sign of mental cautiousness, an assumption of an intellectual attitude in pronouncing opinions, a right attitude of intellectual dubiousness. It seems, however, that it is nothing less than a sign of deficiency in cognitive faculties, a sign of weakness and vacillation in intellectual and moral dynamisms.

Many persons considered independent in thought and action disclose unsteadiness in their independence; an independent attitude assumed toward a phenomenon lasts for some time, then loses its strength, giving way to hesitation. This points to a lack of internal harmony in a person, to a wavering in the balance of his various tendencies. Of course, we are not here considering a wavering caused by the fact that a case is particularly difficult to handle but a wavering arising out of the fact that one has not made himself sufficiently independent of the lower external and internal environments.

The process of making oneself independent of the superficial estimates of other people goes hand in hand with the process of making oneself gradually independent of the necessities of a lower level that are not closely connected with the uniform line of feelings and actions of a personality. In a further part of this work we shall discuss in greater detail the process of making the personality independent of these factors. This process leads to a development of the psychic structure, which becomes increasingly more sensitive to various external and internal stimuli.

Such a structure includes a great number of receptors, organized into a harmonic, unique, individual whole. The person is sensitive to social, religious, esthetic, and scientific matters and tendencies, and has the capacity to encompass every problem in an organic, all-embracing, universal way.

After one attains the level of personality, suggestion in judgment, feeling, and action is replaced by conscious yielding only to those environmental influences which harmonize with one's distinct and firm convictions, and by a conscious rejection of those influences which act upon one's subconsciousness and uncontrolled drives (jealousy, conceit, and the like). Thus, at the level of personality, there occurs a weakening of susceptibility to various environmental influences – that is, to impulses stemming from the lower nature of man, to multidirectional, discordant stimuli, influences of public opinion, and so on. It should be clearly stressed here that the attitude of constant refashioning and of selectiveness in relation to external stimuli is opposed to instinctive and stereotyped mechanisms. Such an attitude requires the controlling of our own internal environment, and principally control of its instinctive and habitual level.

Man as a personality accepts, therefore, only such stimuli as are in harmony with his developing structure; he conditions himself to an ideal and makes himself independent of all he overcame in himself while struggling along the road of evolution, from the level of primitive and civilized man to the level of personality.

Self-knowledge and knowledge of others

The basic Socratic thought, "Know thyself," is always actual for everyone who consciously realizes his ideal of personality. It goes hand in hand with a fundamental query: "Who am I, and where am I going?" Learning to know oneself consists in seeking an answer, through experience and meditation, to the questions: "What is it in myself that is not 'me'? What is it that I am becoming, although it is not yet crystallized? And what should I strive, with persistent will, to make myself, although it is not yet myself, through meditation, contemplation, and continuous effort?"

Self-cognizance requires deep, hard thinking with the aim of arriving at the limits of self-knowledge. As the result of such thinking one develops a sense of humility as he begins to realize that wisdom is infinite. Finally, self-cognizance requires learning to know one's inner self within the structure of parallelism between somatic and psychic actions, as well as in their interaction; one should try – using all his experiences – to grasp the correlations between these actions.

In instances when self-cognizance is not a purely intellectual act but an act involving also elements of higher intellectualized emotions, then we are concerned with personality-cognizance and not only with intellectual self-cognizance. Personality-cognizance involves elements of strong internal experiences and is connected with the dynamisms of a simultaneous transformation of oneself as one reaches ever higher levels of self-knowledge.

Self-knowledge is positively correlated with the knowledge of others. For knowledge of one's self is not possible without association with other people, without orientating oneself to the content and motives of their behavior, which again implies the necessity of orientating oneself to one's own behavior, motives, and attitudes toward the environment. Self-knowledge and knowledge of others must be both analytic and synthetic in character; that is, it must embrace all the various traits and their integration.

Of course, when learning to know ourselves we must keep our awareness directed to our own and other people's ever-changing actions. We thus catch ourselves and others in fragmentary dynamisms, and also in wider and narrower integrations, remaining in the changing current of internal and external experiences. In any case the common measure of learning to know oneself and others consists in the continuous registration in consciousness of similarities and differences in our own and other people's behavior and action, within the scope of their intellectual, emotional, and volitional aspects.

Realization of personality must be based on the knowledge of various social phenomena with consideration given to their multitude and gradation. For the personality may neither judge the environment nor assume an emotional attitude toward it in an insufficiently differentiated, mood-conditioned, unidimensional way. Such an attitude is detrimental because despite good motivation the results are often bad. All symptoms of group evil, of the primitive character of human needs and smallness of aims should then be known and treated as actual, factual structures, and at the same time as structures containing nuclei of smaller or greater developmental possibilities. A proper attitude in respect to reality should be shaped in accordance with the principle that knowing all is not only forgiving all but also being ready to give a hand to those struggling with difficulties on the road to perfection, and developing in oneself the attitude of syntony and cooperation.

Knowledge of others and the attitude of empathy involve limiting our demands on the reality around us, to an extent indicated by our diagnosis of the kind and level of this reality, arrived at with an unperturbed mind and emotions, when viewing reality's actual state, its kind, and possibilities of development.

Moral and Social Qualities

Truthfulness and honesty toward oneself and other people

Truthfulness and honesty are closely related to independence of judgment and action, to a sense of justice, to courage, and sometimes to heroism. These qualities are based on one's own convictions, founded upon a wide objective knowledge of human nature and ideals. They lead one to personality and are realized in an internal struggle between the self-preservation instinct and the instinct to propagate the species; they point to the shaping of one's moral structure, to a conviction that the chosen direction is right, and to a will determined to remain at the attained level.

We sometimes imagine the personality as a harmonic structure, within which the "lower" qualities are subordinated to "higher" ones and to the personality ideal, and are canalized and mentally controlled. In truth the personality is not a definite creation, immutable in its structure. On the contrary, although it possesses most important and fundamental features, personality is, to a great extent, a pliable set of traits, sensitive to evolutional crises and environmental reactions. Therefore, if one is to take up the task of shaping his personality, he must be morally vigilant at all stages of development, so as to prevent dependence upon such factors from exceeding admissible limits, even in moments of physical off-balance. One should at all times guard against self-deception, autosuggestion, the inclination for self-justification, the attitude of pretense, convenience, and egoistic motivation.

Moral vigilance develops when it is based on the capacity for objective judgment, on the principle of demanding from oneself more than from other people, on an increasingly sharper examination of one's thoughts, feelings, emotions, and actions. However, the most important component of such vigilance would be the faculty for decrying in oneself il-

lusory moral progress, which expresses itself in barely noticeable transformations or in transmutations of certain conspicuous and negative
character traits into camouflaged ones.

An illusory progress may, for example, express itself in curbing one's
inclination to be vexatious, aggressive, and impolite when dealing with
strangers at the cost of increased bad treatment of one's own flesh and
blood. Such a curbing of negative inclinations is dictated by awareness
that strangers would not tolerate improper demeanor, while one's next
of kin may bear it and even conceal it from outsiders.

This example points to a growth in self-preservation tendencies at
the cost of social feelings. Another instance of illusory moral progress
is suppressing sexual drives and finding compensation in the form of
increased erotic phantasies.

Similar phenomena of the compensation mechanism are observed in
overcoming the tendency to torment people and in transferring it into
a covert or overt tormenting of animals, sometimes under the guise
of pseudoscientific aims, or in a formal attack on egoism accompanied
by increased self-admiration stemming from a successful attack on this
moral defect.

When we eliminate false appearances with respect to ourselves and become truthful in thought and action, we build the foundation for honest
treatment of the environment. We shall be able to treat other people
just as we treat ourselves, applying a proper measure when estimating
them, and to build up righteousness in our actions after we rid ourselves of the tendency to allow our own selfish interests to govern our
judgments and behavior. The measure of stability in a moral attitude,
so conceived, will be how benevolently we treat and how prudently we
judge our enemies.

So understood, honesty and truthfulness toward ourselves and others
reflect the principle "Love thy neighbour as thyself." By aspiring to
honesty and truthfulness we strengthen our attitude of love and raise
it to a higher level; such aspiration shows that we are mature enough
to become a personality or have already arrived at its threshold.

Courage

There is much controversy among thinkers about the conception of courage. One must distinguish very clearly the capacity for action, daring, aggressiveness, and speedy reaction to various stimuli, from true courage. For such traits may be the functions of primitive drives, of the fighting, possessive, or sexual instincts. Therefore we should distinguish various levels in the attitude of dynamism, energy, powerful striving, "strong character," and so on. The lower levels of courage may be characterized by a lack of thought about the sense of one's action, a lack of apprehension that one may possibly do wrong to other people, and an improper estimation of danger, or a lack of moderation. We should clearly distinguish, therefore, pseudo coinage from true courage. Many people who fought with courage in the war and who are bold and uncompromising in dealing with people and matters in their everyday life, belong to a category of men aggressive by nature, often displaying a tendency for bursting out in anger, and sometimes even for pronounced cruelty. Their courage is one of the primitive forms of the fighting instinct or may be an indication of sexual perversion. Besides, pseudo courage may indicate an improper estimation of the situation (belief that the other side is weaker).

Only a man who, conscious of the danger threatening him and of the changeability of fortune, of the consequences which his attitude may bring him, such as the loss of esteem, position, influence, decides, being true to his ideal, to take up a given action is truly courageous. True courage, and more so true heroism, have their foundations in experiences gained over a period of many years or even through one's whole life, during which has taken place a slow process of harmonization of the impulsive forces with personality dynamisms, the latter formed from one's experiences of life, in which suprapersonal, suprabiological tendencies play an increasingly more important part.

Dynamism, energy, power of striving, "strong character" may then be based on one of two centers, a primitive one attained through the processes of disintegration, or a secondary center where "vital interests" cease to be decisive with respect to dynamism, energy, and "courage" and are replaced by "vital interests" of another dimension.

Spiritual heroism is not possible without continued preparation, for it is evolved by means of the internal elaboration of experiences. The shorter or longer states of meditation and uplift which interrupt the current of our impulsive and habitual life are a prerequisite for making common-sense decisions in impersonal matters, for the ability to persist in a given position despite the greatest difficulties, and for the daily performance of assumed tasks. In such states we leave our biological self to attain higher levels of our inner feeling of self, where fear vanishes, and where interest in the present moment and the events of everyday life disappears or abates, giving way, after we are "filled up" with new energy, to a feeling that our capacity to organize matters of vital importance in accordance with the established hierarchy of aims has gained strength.

The greater our experience in life, the greater our sensitivity; the more intensive and thorough our elaboration of experiences, the clearer our ideal of personality; and the more we are apt to sacrifice, to subordinate our instinctive needs in favor of personality, the stronger is our disposition to the attitude of courage and heroism.

Love

When we speak of love we usually have in mind the sexual drive and the feeling of sympathy for an individual belonging to the other sex. There are various kinds and levels of a feeling of love so understood, from the distinctly sexual form, in which the need for having an emotional union with the other person either does not exist or is hardly noticeable, to a form which the higher emotional needs move out in front, subordinating primitive drives, and in which the emotional union survives despite a weakening or disappearance of the factors that caused the beginning and the development of the sexual drive (old age, loss of good looks, and soon). In the first case we are dealing with a scarcely differentiated drive, an uncomplex drive for lust and preservation of kind, while in the other case we are concerned with the subordination of the sexual drive, even if strong and natural, to higher feelings permeated with a finer love and finally with perfect love, at which stage the sexual drive is completely controlled and replaced by higher elements of the emotional union.

Writing of love, Bertrand Russell states that whether it lasts does not depend on us.[1] This opinion would be correct in connection with the more sexual forms of love. If, however, we consider love based not only on sexual drive, but love in which even strong sexual drives are harmonized and subordinated to the whole personality, love that makes both parties penetrate each other in a perpetual desire to improve themselves and perfect the union, then such love and whether it lasts depends on our consciously shaped personality and not exclusively on our sexual drives. The reasons why such love is a very rare phenomenon, why we can speak of it as of an ideal, are that the decision of two people to enter into a marriage contract is usually based on a semiconscious sexual drive, that in the majority of cases both parties do not know themselves deeply, that the decisive factors are material in character, that the influence of parents is not always positive, and that the parties believe it is good to get married in order to create for oneself the conditions for an "aversion-free" sexual life.

Marriage based on qualities of a personality "union" in which the sexual drive is subordinated to higher feelings permits the couple to assume a correct attitude about the question of procreation. The sexual drive becomes therefore not a blind force, but a dynamism controlled by sets of sublimating tendencies. The attitude of concern, responsibility, devotion to, and esteem for the future human being probably contributes also to the child "inheriting" the positive qualities of the parents and is certainly decisive in regard to his proper education.

One of the essential qualities in the structure of personality is an attachment on the part of humans, and especially children, to the worthy points of tradition, family, region, and nation, an attachment to parents and siblings, to worthy principles and habits prevailing at home. Such attachment plays a great role in deepening the feelings and in developing the sense of moral duty. Besides, it is a foundation on which grow values of lasting character, and the attachment permits the person, in relations with people and in dealing with problems, to distinguish between lasting things and those of fluid, temporary character.

Attachment to family relics, passed from generation to generation as symbols of our lasting memory of those who once lived with us,

---

[1] B. Russell. *Education and the Modern World.* New York: W. W. Norton and Co., 1932.

attachment to family graves and good care of them serve to show that an individual is shaping his character positively. For such an attitude, such a desire to extend the memory of deceased close relatives points to lasting feelings and to a transcendental attitude toward our next of kin.

The eternal commandment to love one's neighbor reveals the tragic dichotomy between the ideal and the reality. When we observe more closely just ourselves, our kinsfolk, and the circle of our friends, we see only some slight reflexes of love for our fellow creatures, while the chief preoccupation of most of us is with our own personal interests. If we ever wish to sacrifice something for other people it is almost exclusively for our closest relatives, those with whom we are most tightly bound, and therefore we cannot consider our action as an expression of love toward our fellow creatures in the full sense of these words, for such "love" results from our own personal interests. We manifest our love for a neighbor only when we sacrifice in his favor something that we ourselves need.

Love of our fellow creatures should also be extended to our enemies. By looking at a man, not as someone who is our personal enemy, but as someone who acts erroneously because of inherited inclinations, environmental influences, and low level of self-educating consciousness, we assume an impersonal attitude toward that man. Such an attitude toward an enemy is a clear sign of one's advance toward the ideal of personality.

The love of our fellow creatures cannot be the kind that ends within the bonds of our family and individual relations with our neighbors. We should embrace with it the society in which we live and the whole of humanity. This, as it were, social love of our fellow creatures finds its expression in various social, religious, and ideological organizations, whose aim is the perfection of entire groups of people through execution of specific and obviously important social tasks.

The desire to perfect ourselves and others

All educational systems recommend self-education and self-remolding before one takes on the task of the moral remolding of a society. Of course, some degree of internal preparation must be possessed by everyone who takes up social work. However, the recommendation that one should refashion himself before starting to work upon others does not appear right to us. Awareness of one's imperfection, anxiety with respect to oneself, longing for an ideal, accompanied by a perception that one must work upon his own remolding, should go hand in hand with the work of raising the level of society.

We can change and improve the group in which we live, therefore, only if we know how to develop ourselves. Otherwise we vitiate the social work, it turns into a pseudo work, a cover for attitudes and aims which often have nothing to do with real social work. Thus the reservations made with respect to the social work of individuals possessing no ability for the internal reshaping of themselves, for the realization of the ideal of personality, are fully justified. Such people become only "social servants" or "social benefactors" and never engage in real social work.

Among so-called social workers one may distinguish several groups. One group is comprised of people with small capabilities or "complete indolents," whose inclination to social work is based on an unconscious tendency to seek care for themselves. Another group consists of individuals for whom social work is just an embellishment of their professional work or an opportunity for easy gratification of vanity and ambition. From this group are recruited various types of "presidents," "chairmen," and "members of the board," whose activity consists mainly in venting their ambitions through make-believe actions requiring no particular exertion.

I shall not deal here with the problem of consciously and purposely organized social work that is harmful.

Whoever wants to realize social work carried on at the level of personality must internally remold his own apparent, artificial, temporary, habitual attitudes; he must acquire the capacity for recognizing the same in a given social group, so as to overcome, in his work upon and with that group, all those mechanisms in which the self-preservation instinct, or the instinct of power, the feeling of fear, or the feeling of "living in peace" are hidden behind a label of "social welfare."

Religious Qualities

Religious attitude

Realization of the religious ideal calls for renunciation and denial of our impulsive nature, thus introducing in our everyday life an attitude of adaptation to suffering and death. Love of God dictates the love of one's neighbor, love of the truth, and readiness to do good, and vice versa. When a religious ideal is cultivated there gradually develops a proper religious atmosphere, or religious feeling, which enhances the feeling of love and ultimately leads one, through contemplation, to a union with the Infinite. Therefore a sound religious attitude includes the feeling of humility and dependence on God, which, filling us with a feeling of power and elevating us to the level of true human beings, arms us morally and permits us to attain the independence and freedom both from our lower self and from certain forms of environmental reactions. Such an attitude is based on an intuitive feeling that the meaning of life depends on higher values, and on the integration of our human qualities of the highest moral value with the hierarchy of those supreme values at the pinnacle of which exists the Deity. The religious attitude is therefore understood as the attitude of cultivating these highest values.

We may distinguish several kinds of religious attitudes. One religious attitude arises from man's realization of how small, helpless, and ignorant he is. Such an attitude may be accompanied by the desire for realizing an ideal, by the desire to enter the supersensual world, in which one finds consolation, happiness, and infinite knowledge; but it may also be a label, a name, a superficial attitude, the "attitude of consent," assumed in order to get rid of an unpleasant feeling. In the latter case it is the most convenient form of a seemingly satisfactory solution to everyday difficulties which one wants to brush aside; this is an attitude without "internal elaboration," an attitude of pretense.

The source of another kind of religious attitude are the internal controversies – an attachment to life and an awareness of death, the feeling of love for our next of kin and the feeling caused by a threat that we may lose them or by actual loss, the need for sacrificing oneself and the strong self-preservation instinct, idealistic aspirations and strong sexual drives. Conflicts, breakdowns, suicidal inclinations, and other symptoms of psychic disintegration often lead to a secondary harmony when one creates within oneself new tendencies strong enough to win domination over other tendencies. Such harmonization is done by way of gradual transformation, "inner elaboration," or by way of revelation; but it proceeds, almost always, in connection with a search for support in the religious life.

There exists also a constitutionally conditioned religious attitude, which knows neither struggles nor difficulties, is characterized by an internal harmony, and is based on a belief that mundane life should be devoted to perfecting oneself internally, to approaching the supersensual world, to seeking a communion with God.

Yet another religious attitude is characterized by giving priority to intellectual elements. A given individual seeks a justification of his beliefs by rational proofs, by external experiences, and by sufficiently reliable historical evidence. Such an attitude usually indicates that the intensity of one's religious life is slight. It may also point to the existence of contradictory tendencies such as a strong religious yearning along with a no less strong tendency to explain it by reasoned thinking; it then contains the germ of tragic internal conflicts.

The best religious attitude, as far as the shaping of personality is concerned, is the one that draws knowledge from many sources. Given this attitude, the aspiration to enter into the supersensual world and to approach the Deity is realized in a person both through emotional tenseness and contemplation and through the intellectual and volitional faculties that drive one to the realization of the dictates of the personality and social ideal. Such an attitude protects one against unilateral mysticism, against quietism, or an excessive retiring into one's internal life, and, on the other hand, against a unilateral, formalistic, and dogmatic attitude characterized often by intolerance and a lack of love; finally it guards one against an excessive dissipation of one's mental energy into pseudo asceticism and superficial social work.

A religious attitude may, in many individuals, not manifest itself externally; it may be consciously or unconsciously suppressed. It may manifest itself in a sphere having apparently nothing to do with it, but its significance for man's life and development is always of a fundamental character. The conscious religious attitude constitutes one of the most powerful means of safeguarding ethically high-standing individuals against breakdowns in the most trying moments of life. It also belongs to the qualities possessed by an individual of high moral culture.

As for the question of the religious attitude in the development of historical figures, it should be noted here that religious inspiration was for most artists and philosophers of genius one of the most important and sometimes the only factor that led to the great successes they achieved in their creative work. Even among scholars devoted to strict sciences we observe many who are deeply religious or interested in religious problems, and not only from the scientific point of view. It seems that the multidimensional attitude in every field of life, including creative work, induces and forces man to overstep the scope of his limited field of knowledge and to explore what is not only outside it, but also above it. When one adopts the multidimensional attitude one begins as a rule to understand and experience religious life and all that goes with it.

The strength and universality of religious experience show that the internal attitude of man corresponds to a supersensual Being, transcendent as an object of these religious experiences and at the same time constituting a necessary condition for the very fact of the existence of this experience in our consciousness. This Being is a requirement of our hierarchical psychological structure, a requirement for its highest level, for it seems more convincing to assume that this hierarchy reaches into transcendency than to take it for granted that it ends in and with us. Furthermore, in the spiritual evolution of man, in his universal development, or universal outlook, the religious experience constitutes a domain which cannot be eluded, and its acceptance is a prerequisite of the multilaterality of development and of outlook that has just been mentioned. This fact also manifests – not only on the intellectual but also, in a way, on the existential plane – the objective existence of a transcendental object of religious experience.

In order to be able to receive and grasp the supersensual reality we may need special organs and functions, a kind of "transcendental sense," allowing us, through inner experience, to perceive the reality of the supersensual world. It may safely be assumed that this inner sense, the experience of which would possess convincing power for the experiencing individual, arises and develops in the course of multidimensional realization of the ideal of personality.

At any rate, the fact that among psychically and culturally sound individuals heightened religious life very often enriches their creative power, increases the scope of their interest and their capability of devotion and sacrifice should lead us to a positive evaluation of religious experience, apart from the question of the real and objective existence of the supersensual world.

The feelings of reverence, inferiority, guilt, and humility

Our capability of experiencing the feelings of veneration and esteem is one of the fundamental criteria of the development of personality. Without the feeling of a hierarchy of values above us and without an emotional attitude of esteem for these values, there would be no yearning for an ideal and, consequently, no action of dynamisms permitting the discrimination of various levels within our inner environment. The capability of experiencing the feeling of reverence is as a rule linked with the process of disintegration. The sensing of our own inner environment, the participation of consciousness and emotions in the dynamics of inner transformations, the feeling of the frequent wandering "up and down," associated with experiences of weakness, unsteadiness, breakdowns, difficulties in elevating ourselves to and stabilizing at a higher level – all these are causes of distinct experiences of higher values, more or less personified and transcendent; we seek help and guidance in these values and we unite with them.

The faculty of experiencing the feeling of veneration is closely related to the alterocentric attitude. Highly egocentric individuals – at the level of primary, primitive integration – are not capable of experiencing the feeling of reverence; on the other hand they easily assume the attitude of domination and tyranny toward weaker people, and that of fear and external subordination toward stronger people.

We distinguish two kinds of feelings of inferiority, one with respect to the external environment of an individual, and the other with respect to the hierarchically more valued structures of his own inner milieu. The latter kind of feeling of inferiority consists in experiencing one's own possibilities at various levels. Such experience is usually accompanied by conflicts of great dynamism, and by difficulties in attaining a distinct domination of higher values in one's inner environment, and consequently also by seeking help and support from those who, in our opinion, are standing at a higher level of development. Of course, the feeling of inferiority appears with respect to such people; there is no envy in it, however, but rather a feeling of reverence.

The sense of guilt is closely related to the feeling of veneration and sense of inferiority; it usually arises when one is dissatisfied with one's own deeds, if they prove to be contradictory to the level of personality that the individual considers he should have reached. It points to some disharmony between the appraisal of one's own tendencies before and after they are set in motion, to an insufficiently elaborated prospection, to an inadequate participation of imagination in the actions with which one is faced. Pointing to shortcomings in our own education, this sense of guilt often makes us dissatisfied with ourselves and anxious about the level of our actions.

The sense of guilt develops when one is highly sensitive to moral injunctions. The awareness of a distance between the ideal and one's achievements, of the constant wrecking of the level which one deemed to have been built already, may result in a permanent sense of guilt. The sense of guilt is also nourished by a sense of responsibility – not clearly discernible, as it is inherited and usually associated with a given trend of religious education – for the evil-doings of all humanity, groups, and families.

The feeling of sin experienced by a man is a result of a more or less distinct departure from the responsibilities placed upon one by a given religious, social, or moral code, responsibilities with respect to one's own or collective aims, or with respect to transcendental values. Sin, as an internal experience, is then a more or less conscious offense committed by a given individual in conflict with the principles accepted, recognized, and affirmed by him, and a transgression for which his conscience holds him responsible. Of course, the feeling of sin is not a measure by which one can establish the extent of the evil done. The objective evil as assessed by social measures may not be great or even may not exist at all, but a man may experience his sin very deeply and that experience may even assume a dramatic character. Thus what is significant here is not an external judgment but the content of the drama taking place in the internal milieu during the process of disintegration. One's exoneration from blame may be achieved only by internal expiation and not by purely external sanction.

The sense of shame which arises after one has committed some morally questionable deed is a somewhat weaker form of the sense of sin, and it contains a strong component of sensitivity to the judgment of the environment. In its coming into existence the fundamental role is played by a sense of the moral and ethical impropriety of a discovered deed, while in the arising of the sense of sin the main element is the feeling of a downfall and of failure to keep oneself at the attained level of development.

Humility is awareness of one's smallness and reflects the appraisal of one's level of development, considering all one's deficiencies, such as the changing and fluctuating values of our internal life, ease in committing sins, the frailness of our knowledge and of our moral forces. The sense of humility includes also recognition of and respect for those who morally and intellectually are closer to their own educational ideal and to transcendental values.

The sense of humility reflects one's multidimensional world outlook, in which a man realizes the existence of higher values and at the same time soberly appraises his own level and possibilities of development. The indeterminism of the laws, needs, and reality of our spiritual development is encumbered here by the sense of determinism of our somatic, instinctive, and material side, the sense which assigns us a definite point in appraising ourselves, a point from which we can lift ourselves higher only through very hard internal struggle.

Such qualities and experiences, connected with the feelings and senses mentioned above, are signs that personality is developing. For this development is not possible without experiencing a feeling of veneration for the hierarchy of higher values and without the feelings of inferiority, sin, guilt, and shame. These feelings are a sign of the first step toward diminishing the evil, toward overcoming it. On the other hand, humility permits us to appraise the level at which we are, the distance which we still have to go, and the resisting forces which we will have to conquer.

A strong Christian component in the development of the feeling of humility is based, not only on the above qualities, but also on the awareness of dependence upon the Infinite Transcendental Wisdom. The experience of the sense of humility – as conceived in a Christian frame of reference – constitutes a source from which springs a sense of power when we act in accordance with moral and religious injunctions, and a sense of weakness when our deeds are not in accord with them.

Adapting oneself to suffering and death

It is widely believed that the fundamental and strongest drive of a living being is the tendency to preserve himself and his species. To preserve oneself as a physical organism one should avoid to the extent possible all injuries and sufferings, one should keep oneself psychically balanced and widely enjoy all pleasures which are not detrimental to health.

The instinct of the preservation of the species moves, however, along other routes and is often contradictory to the self-preservation instinct. For example, excessive fertility and excessive care in bringing up her children lead to the devastation of a mother's organism. Hence the preservation of the species calls for sacrifices on the part of an individual.

We may also say that the paternal generative instinct introduces an element of opposition, struggle, and limitation with respect to the instinct of self-preservation. In opposing each other, these forces, on practically the same level, take part, among others, in forming the nuclei of conflicts of a higher order. These conflicts are conditioned by the splitting of the self-preservation instinct into biological and suprabiological levels (longing for immortality, the need for influencing the society by one's own ideas and conceptions even after one's death) and by the splitting of the generative instinct into several levels (sexual drive, the generative instinct proper, and social instincts of ever higher levels).

In the world of cultural values sacrifice plays a momentous role. Cultural injunctions are often realized despite natural tendencies. Suffering and even death may, as it were, give birth to higher values; this is a manifestation of the law of conservation of energy, of the law of the transformation of one value into other values. Hard experiences do not always dissolve psychic life, they often strengthen and improve it. Fasting, exercise in controlling oneself, and ascetism create resistance, strengthen one's moral vigilance, and increase one's readiness to enter a conscious struggle for the sake of principles one holds. Suffering, if we experience it correctly, makes us sensitive to the suffering of others, awakens in us a new awareness, and creates a breach in our excessively egocentric attitude toward the surrounding world.

In general, however, the reaction to suffering may vary from man to man. In some people suffering evokes the need for external projection, the desire to vent the accumulated energy in the form of vengeance or aggression. In other people, as the suffering grows, there arise states of gradually increasing weariness, of yielding to the suffering, of resignation and the sighing away of energy. In still other people there arise tendencies for reshaping themselves and for replacing the shattered forms of life by other forms. The latter reaction is, in most cases, characteristic of individuals with a fluctuating system of tendencies, lacking biopsychic stability, tending toward disintegration, and in whom cultural needs dominate the instinct of self-preservation, which finally leads to gradual harmonization of their inner life and to a development of personality.

Suffering and resignation may lead to the emergence of an attitude characterized by setting the ideal of absolute truth against the falsehood of human relations, and the temporary nature of emotional bonds against the permanence of these bonds. When one assumes such an attitude one's activity within the framework of the new system of values need not necessarily be transferred to the world of absolute truths or to the sphere of an ideal. However, when one possesses an active nature, prepared for and adapted to reformatory work in the real world, one may devote oneself to educational work in which one can gradually pass along to a social group the values gained through suffering.

With respect to death, individuals with a deeply developed process of disintegration, with a clear personality ideal, with a broad experience of life, and possessing a strong tendency for retrospection and prospection, prepare themselves for it, almost from childhood, in the world of the imagination. The thought of their own death often conditions the direction of their work, their deeds. Hence, in the actions of these individuals the foremost place is occupied by supersensual aims and by aspirations for immortality (fame, greatness, perfection). Such men are usually capable of unselfish, sacrificial, and heroic acts. Their attitude toward life includes the need to work for a better future, the tendency to create imperishable, everlasting works; it also includes the belief that deeply felt individual bonds will outlast death; and, finally, it includes the pursuit and realization of lasting cultural goods, in which the "eternal or universal man" comes to be expressed.

In attaining the level of personality, man's attitude toward death is, as it were, the result of two attitudes, one rational, objective, and critical, and the other emotional and dramatic. The first regards death as a universal process, which affects the given individual as "one of many," whereas the second expresses a drama, in which the negation of biological life is associated with the need and sometimes even with the necessity of supersensual life. This drama often gives way to a state of peace and internal harmony, which is connected with the supersensual Being, through meditation.

A correct attitude of humility, arising from the realization that we are infinitesimal creatures in this endless universe, from the tendency to assume an objective attitude toward reality, and from the survival of our individual spiritual beings and a sense of union with the Supreme Being, helps us to overcome the fear of our own death and to attain peace of mind.

Contemplation and mysticism

The capacity for contemplation is evidence of personality coming into existence. Contemplation is the stage of development at which a man passes from superficial judgments, from the attitude of consent, to conscious feelings and to a working out of the principles of one's action. It then implies a passage from sensual to mental life, from external to internal experiences, from reactive emotional life to deepened emotional life coupled with the intellect, and from unrelated experiences to integrated experiences. But, above all, it is a sign that a man is becoming harmonized at a higher level. The state of contemplation implies a level of development at which a man begins to appraise his own behavior, to confront it with the demands placed on himself, and at which he enters the world of higher values, from which he may draw inspiration and power, both of which are of great help in life.

Contemplation harmonizes in us the biological level – at which most of our everyday experiences take place – with the suprabiological level; it alleviates the drama of our experiences by enabling us to resign certain values and tendencies clinged to thus far, in favor of other, suprabiological ones.

Contemplation is also a sign of one's passing from a merely active life to a life in which action combines with moments of solitude. The capacity and need for isolation observed among normal people usually indicates progress in the development of personality. People who do not feel any need for solitude, or cannot bear it, are wholly extroverted and unprepared for psychic transformation. Dostoevsky is right in saying that solitude in the psychic sphere is as necessary as food is for the body. Moreover, the capacity for contemplation and solitude points to the spiritual independence of an individual.

Exorbitant need of continuous contact with a group may even point to certain maladies. Many individuals suffering from states of anxiety are not able to lead a solitary life; such individuals, when deprived of the possibility of living in a group, fall into depression. It is also possible that many hypomaniacal states arise with a pathological background tendency for compensation, caused by a lack of sufficiently frequent and satisfying contacts with a group.

When practiced by active individuals, full of energy, contemplation may evoke states of elevation, tension, or readiness for the greatest sacrifices. Short-lived states of elevation are experienced by the majority of people in certain exceptional circumstances (for example, in the moment when one learns that a beloved person was saved from death). These states are of a different order, however. The elevation of which we speak here is based on harmonized higher psychic sets gradually growing more independent of instinctive tendencies.

The contemplative characteristic of a universally developing individual not only does not interfere with his capacity for active social work but, on the contrary, improves and purifies it of superficial elements, of impulsive tendencies, makes a man capable of assessing himself critically, facilitates insight into his own personality, and helps him make a clear projection of the way toward an ever higher level of individuality.

The term mysticism derives from Dionysius the Areopagite and denotes a kind of union of man's soul with the Supreme Being. This is not only a kind of cognition but also a kind of coexistence, of living together. A mystic attains the utmost degree of such cognition and coexistence in the states of ecstasy invoked by a complete detachment from the outer world. But mysticism is not limited to ecstasy alone. The mystic transposes his ecstatic experiences to everyday life and shapes it in accordance with attained knowledge. He does this by constantly improving himself, by leading an ascetic life, and by helping other people.

Ever more frequent and deeper ecstatic states fill a man with increasingly greater energy, thus enabling him to win ever stronger control over his instinctive nature.

Esthetic Qualities

Art in the life of personality

It appears that the higher the level of personality the greater the sensitivity to truly inspired art. One may say that the esthetic component is, to a lesser or greater extent, one of the fundamental elements in the structure of every personality.

In three historical figures whom we shall discuss in this book – St. Augustine, Michelangelo, and Dawid – the artistic structure was a dominating structure (Michelangelo) or one of the main structures (St. Augustine). A relatively weaker artistic component was possessed by J. W. Dawid and this may have been one of the reasons for his too rapid unilateral internal "burning away," his too abrupt breakdown, and for his too strong and rapidly increasing instinct toward death.

To a personality within which the artistic component is dominant art allows the highest intellectual, religious, and even moral revelations. Beethoven said: "Music is a greater revelation than wisdom and philosophy."[2] Through their great love of beauty Socrates and Plato imparted an individual, emotional character to their science of impersonal general ideas, of the impersonal "essence of the thing," and thereby broadened it by adding a more human element. The poems of St. John of the Cross, endowed with a distinct though subtle sensuality, weakened his extreme attitude of denying all human spiritual unions in life.

The history of Indian, Egyptian, Greek, and Christian art strongly speaks in favor of the thesis that the highest art is born in a temple and belongs to the domain of the initiated. When, however, it is experienced by the masses it loses its "sacredness," its "mystic elevation," its level. Nonetheless it is a fact that some kinds and some elements of truly great art – for example, religious hymns – stir the latent and damped personality bonds of the majority of people.

---

[2]R. Rolland. *Vie de Beethoven.* (*Life of Beethoven.*), 18th ed. Paris: Hachette, 1913.

It appears, therefore, that truly inspired art contains strong intellectual, religious, and moral elements, that it pictures the drama of man's development, its process of disintegration, the dynamics of its relation to the personality ideal, its changeability and its developmental conflicts, its progress from sensualism and materialism to mysticism, from rationalism to intuitionalism, from instinctive to suprainstinctive attitudes and from the biological to suprabiological dimension. Such elements are found, in various configurations and intensities, in the works of Phidias, Socrates, the great Grecian tragedians, and in the works of Michelangelo, Dante, Shakespeare, Mickiewicz, and others.

The drama of man's attitude toward life

During the period of germination of the "seeds" of personality and during the later period of its realization, there occur fundamental convulsions in the internal life of a man – spiritual crises resulting from the struggle between sets of various tendencies. In the consciousness of the individual this struggle contains in itself the basic element, namely the struggle between good and evil, with the tragedy-swollen feeling of the necessity of selecting and deciding. This is the Shakespearian "to be or not to be," the Kierkegaardean "either/or," or J. W. Dawid's individual striving for salvation.

Kierkegaard stated:

> I fight for freedom, for the future, for either ... or. One selects oneself not in one's immediacy, not as this incidental individual, but one selects oneself in his eternal silence.... A man possesses his own self as determined by himself, as someone selected by himself, as a free being; when he comes to possession of his own self in this way, there emerges the absolute difference between good and evil. As long as he has not vet selected himself this difference does not show up.... The absolute selection of my own self is my freedom ... The moment of my own selection has remained for me as a solemn and venerable moment, though when I made my choice, I was under the influence of others....[3]

According to Kierkegaard man should be:

---

[3]S. Kierkegaard. In R. Bretall (Ed.), *A Kierkegaard Anthology*. Princeton, N.J.: Princeton University Press, 1946.

fearless in the midst of dread, passions, and temptations of life, moving forward along the path of faith, a path which is steep and dangerous but which leads one safely to the goal. Furthermore, his faith should be silent, humble, ready for sacrifices, sufferings, and hardships. Silence, fear, and trembling, these are signs which point to genuine faith. To achieve such faith, however, one must go through the wild and ghastly forest, full of thistles and thorns, following the example of Dürer's knight, who knows no hesitation and places his trust in God, Whom he serves and Whom he loves.

Before one becomes a distinctly new man, before one passes to the "other side," there ensues a period of struggle, calling not only for the pleasant freeing of oneself from the activities of former structures, but sometimes also for the breaking of the bonds with the structure, which one no longer considers one's own, as it is no longer essential. During this period in which one ceases to be a former man, but has not yet become the present and future man, one falls into a deep critical tension.

"There comes a moment," writes Dawid, "when a feeling and thinking man says to himself: I can no longer live like this. I must find for myself a 'new form of life and not a new form of cognizance.'"

> In states of highest spiritual tension man feels that he himself must know something, decide something, do something, and that in this no one can replace him ... Some people think that the essential thing in mysticism is the ardent seeking of absolute truth. They are wrong. The first, deep motive is always personal and moral, namely the salvation of life, the problem of suffering in the spiritual order of things.... When a man suffers, feels his guilt, and worries about his own redemption, then the problem of being and its purpose becomes a personal issue for him.[4]

The internal, gradually growing maturity of a man, or the spiritual agitations which accelerate this maturity, lead him to a negative attitude toward his thus far pursued aims and ways of living, the value of which diminishes or dwindles. Simultaneously, he begins to seek fervently for the meaning of his own existence, not by philosophizing but by a deep experiencing which involves a struggle between conflicting powers in his

---

[4] J. W. Dawid. *Ostatnie Mysli i Wyznania.* (*Last Thoughts and Confessions.*) Warsaw: Nasza Ksiegarnia, 1935.

nature. The idea, in this seeking, is to find the new essence of existence, in another dimension, and this is accompanied by a personal drama which one must go through.

Some Individual Qualities of a Personality

Among the majority of maturing individuals and among some "average" adults, while experiencing states of great joy, suffering, or despondency, there arises the sense of loneliness, the sense of "otherness" with respect to the common, everyday, familiar states. This "otherness" in experiencing points to the activity of something thus far unknown to one, something coming "from outside," something unexpected, for which one lacks adjustors in his psychic structure. The less rigid this structure is, the higher the degree of its nonpathological disintegration, and while states of "otherness" are more frequent, they are also more acceptable to the person. They are the main characteristics of sensitive and more than normally excitable people.

This susceptibility to nonpathological disintegration is the main quality of a psyche capable of development. Such individuals are seemingly immature, often show psychic pseudoinfantilism, freshness, proneness to enthusiasm, tendency to idealism; they are "permanently maturing" as it were, unlike the majority of people who adapt themselves more quickly to a typical environment. People with such a weak coherence of their structure, provided it is not a truly morbid structure, show developmental disintegration which, in its nonpathological aspect, may be regarded as the chief diagnostic measure of development. Whether a man disintegrates positively or negatively is indicated, as we shall later show more explicitly, by the more or less obvious presence of a factor which organizes such a state of slackening or of dissension, organizing it in the sense of ordering, evaluating, and purposeful utilization in building the structure of a higher level.

What are the basic individual qualities in the structure of personality? One of these qualities is the fundamental trend of interests and capabilities. It is a capacity for grasping reality at its various levels, grasping it from a special side, or rather with a special emotional tone.

When we speak of the main trend of interests and capabilities, we mean those interests and capabilities which are distinct, self-conscious, and self-affirmed, imparting the dominant tone to one's psychic nature, interests and capabilities without which one cannot imagine a given individual as possessing certain essential traits. Various examples are the interests and capabilities of Socrates, without which, as he himself says in his "Apology," life would mean nothing to him; musical, educational, medical, architectural capabilities; or a desire to study nature, to travel, and so on. These interests and capabilities need not necessarily be at the level of talent, but even at the germinative stage they show such a peculiar structural quality, so strongly associated with a given individual, that they must be regarded as gifts of nature, gifts brought into the world with life, and inseparable from the further actions of a man.

Another basic individual quality is represented by lasting emotional bonds of love and friendship, bonds symbolized by the Platonic myth of two halves of the same soul. The best example of such conjunction are the bonds between Christ and His Apostles, which lead to the highest degree of friendship, or the individual bonds between Christ and St. John, Mary Magdalene, and Lazarus. Such bonds are further exemplified by the spiritual bonds between Socrates or Pythagoras and their disciples, or by the brotherhood often entered into in religious orders (St. Francis and his three friars, the spiritual union between St. John of the Cross and St. Teresa, or that between St. Clara and St. Francis). A profoundly significant and even touching example of eternal individual union would be the love or friendship on the part of St. Augustine toward his mother, St. Monica. In common life we encounter such individual or group unions of a higher order of spiritual tension in the love between married people, in the fraternal or sisterly unions, and in the friendly unions between individuals not related who go side by side desiring the realization of a common idea.

The third basic individual trait of personality is a certain specific, unique tone of the spiritual life, specific expression or manifestation of which is observed in a man's countenance and eyes or felt in his movements, expression of voice, behavior, and personal charm, the latter being a kind of individual "magnetism."

Awakening of Self-Awareness; Self-Affirmation and Self-Education

A man usually distinguishes consciousness of his own self from awareness of the outer world. The main characteristic of the first consciousness is the faculty for distinguishing oneself from the external world and especially from other persons, having a sense of one's own activity, one's identity in time, and a sense of singularity.[5] When our consciousness of ourselves is more or less filled with a distinct content, we may speak of consciousness of our own person.

Changes in the consciousness of our own person take place primarily in the period of maturation, in which we begin to sense these changes and to feel that we are becoming something else; moreover, these sensations are accompanied by states of temporary depression (something is passing away) and excitement (something new is coming to us), as well as by alternately arising feelings of inferiority and superiority, of contradiction between our feelings and thoughts and of the strengthening of their unity. This state is a symptom of disintegration, but of a psychic rather than a moral character. An infantile individual vanishes and gives way to an adult individual; tendencies existing up until then become weaker and wane or take on a different color; and in their place arise other tendencies, partly foreign and unpleasant, and partly attractive because of their newness.

In some so-called morbid cases (psychoneuroses, schizophrenia) we face symptoms of a similar kind, namely a sensation of something foreign in us, something uncommon and of higher value, the lack of a full sensing of oneself as something that is wholly integrated. In the process termed here the awakening of self-awareness, which arises in connection with moral crises and with efforts to transform oneself (birth of personality), there occur symptoms analogous to these but not identical with them. This is the process of becoming aware that there exists in us the higher and the lower, the spiritual and the instinctive, structures. This is the process of becoming aware of the distinctness of the new structure which emerges from the former one, wherein the active, directing part is played by the separating structure, which is conscious

---

[5]K. Jaspers. *General Psychopathology.* Manchester, England: Manchester University Press, 1963.

of being spiritual, suprainstinctive, and realizing that the evolutionally lower qualities must be subordinated to the nascent, or an already more clearly visible ideal, and reshaped to serve it.

Awakening of self-awareness is usually accompanied by an emotional component, symptoms of which are the sense that something is passing away in us, that something departs from us, and by depression, by the sense of nascency, affirmation, excitation, and, sometimes, ecstasy. There is, however, a fundamental difference between analogous symptoms occurring in the period of maturation and in morbid states, on the one hand, and those occurring during the emergence of personality, on the other. For in the latter case one's consciousness is not diminished; on the contrary, it is strengthened and shows great intensity. The everyday life of the individual is marked by consonance despite inward concentration and isolation. In the process of the awakening of self-awareness a man subordinates himself to a strong dominant, which is a supreme, prevalent, distinct idea; through retrospection and prospection he perceives the line of his life more clearly than before. We shall call this supreme idea – this pattern of life – the personality ideal.

This state, which is characteristic of the awakening of self-awareness, disintegration, separation, and the throwing over of a part of our structure, may take a sharp form, may last for months, years, and even throughout one's entire life.

Scrutiny of one's structure in its diverse dimensions, on its various levels, and in its various conditions, brings forth, again and again, a state of feverish tension of consciousness, of continual and frequent questioning of oneself and of uncertainty and depression. Finally there ensues an act of clear awareness, connected with the factor of will, which accepts the transformation that has set in, affirms its aim and sense, affirms the newly created state and the isolation of man's own and essential set of qualities: one reaches the state of self-affirmation.

Self-education is the highest possible process of a psychological and moral character. It begins at the time when the individual undergoes changes which permit him to make himself partially independent of biological factors and of the influence of the social environment. At this stage a process, thus far not explained by psychology, takes place, as a consequence of which the individual becomes the resultant not only of inheritance, of factors acting in the womb of a mother, and of his biological and social environment, but also of one more, ever more powerful factor, namely that of defining oneself and of acting upon oneself (the so-called third factor).

In the light of introspection we see that this new structure – which consciously takes part in matters concerning its own evolution and which acts as a "third factor" in the shaping of the personality – clearly rises in conflict with the fundamental instincts of our biological "I" and in conflict with the common forms of reaction of a social group, and creates its own extrabiological and extrasocial aims. When a man rises against the most important instinctive forces, both those springing from generic and those springing from personality sources, and against social suggestions that strengthen these forces, then it is evident that he has become self-dependent.

In order to educate himself a man should, as it were, split himself into a subject and an object – that is, he should disintegrate. He must be the one who educates and the one who is educated and he must isolate in himself the active entity and the one which is subordinated to it. The structure, or set, of the higher level must continuously react upon the structure, or set, of the lower level, and the higher feeling must react on the lower feelings. Of course, in this process a vivid picture of one's own personality ideal, made dynamic in the processes of disintegration and self-education, plays a fundamental role.

A child may possess some self-educational nuclei but their existence is only weakly manifested. Among the majority of adults, standing at a normal intellectual level, self-education is a sectional, periodic phenomenon, possessing no conscious character and not isolated from other educational methods. As a matter of fact, true self-education starts when the personality comes to life – that is, from the period in which the process of self-defining and self-cognizing becomes marked, the process in which a man begins to be strongly interested, intent, and sees the need of isolating in himself that something which constitutes his true self. He then attempts to understand the biological and extrabiological character of this self, its hierarchical values and its purpose.

The process of self-education consists in admitting to consciousness all that may stimulate and educate. In doing so we should adopt an attitude of constant differentiation and selection of these stimuli, partly or wholly rejecting some of them and admitting others. In this process there are moments of interruption of one's daily activities, moments of withdrawal from the daily routine and of breaking contact with the external world, in order to enter, with a fully relaxed body and mind, into communion with one's ideal, and to charge oneself, as it were, with subtle spiritual energy. This reaching out, through meditation and contemplation, to one's educational ideal usually contains in itself the elements of a religious attitude.

The process of self-education consists in reflecting upon and controlling the impulses, derived from the grasp of one's own personality ideal, which are eventually expressed in action. The daily separation of our true self from that which does not belong to it but may only serve us as material for the building of our personality, separation of lasting values from fleeting values and appearance from reality, is the function of this method.

The daily routine of self-education consists in the realization of particular educational aims, stemming from one's personality ideal. It is a way of developing in oneself sublimating habits, of sane rejection of compensatory mechanisms which fade and cease to be educational methods for a personality. Furthermore, this is a method of one's own realization through devoting oneself to helping others, by remaining open to their difficulties, conflicts, shortcomings, and faults. This is a way of educating oneself within the daily experiences of life, by forgetting oneself and apparently losing one's personality in the service of the ideal of duty to one's neighbor. In the evangelical paraphrase this process finds its expression in the words of Jesus, "He that loseth his life shall find it."

Further Remarks on the Definition of Personality

Having acquainted the reader with the definition of personality given at the outset of this work, and with its fundamental, general, and individual characteristics; and having established the fact that personality possesses a distinct hierarchical structure of values, which is attained through the dynamic development of the nuclei inherent in it, we think it proper to turn the attention of the reader, at this point, to two aspects of our approach, namely:

1. The multidimensional component, specifically, the empirical and the normative

2. The durability and immutability of certain qualities and attitudes of a personality with their permanent "quantitative" development

Let us present these two components once more, in a synthetic way.

The empirical and normative aspects

In the practical field of mental health we broadly apply empirical methods, among others, in studies of persons possessing the nucleus of a personality or who are personalities in the making. These are, in most cases, individuals with an increased capacity for development, and in studying them empirically we come into contact again and again with the problem of the hierarchy of values and the realization of these values. When investigating such individuals, therefore, we must apply a certain scale of already existing values, and observe how these values arise and how they are developed.

We ascertain these changes, through, among others, catamnestic examination of persons who attain ever higher values in this or that accepted scale or hierarchy, who realize their program and aims and who realize, in a way, their own "personality standards." The shaping of personality is, therefore, an empirical and normative phenomenon. Hence our studies are, on one side, of an empirical character, and, on the other, of a teleological character, or, in other words, of empirical and normative character.

The conclusions we obtain from empirical studies of the structure of personality we try to transfer and apply to historical personalities, which we place in certain more or less determined scales of values, according to biological, social, and individual (personality) conceptions. At this point the empirical and the normative points of view come together.

Both actually investigated individuals with a developing personality and historical personalities considered from the point of view of realized or attained ideals call for a construing of personality standards and consequently we conceive the personality in normative terms. As we have seen, however, this "normativeness" of our approach is broadly based on empirical data. We may say that these "norms" are a logical necessity because of our subject matter and the method we use for its study. They serve us in everyday life, and in our study we apply them to prominent historical personalities and to living observed or investigated individuals, ascertaining their place in the adopted scale.

In introducing the hierarchy of values in school teaching, in behavior, in qualifying people for various posts, in setting patterns for school youths and adults, we always make use, more or less strictly, of empirically accepted moral standards, from the average to the highest.

Of course this point of view and these methods may arouse some reservations; nonetheless they are of vital necessity in common practice and in research work.

The durability of certain qualities, and their enrichment

We have repeatedly emphasized that the "birth" of personality – by which we mean a decisive turning point in one's life – is a drastic experience for an individual. He senses the advent of something "other" in himself, he feels that the hierarchy of values thus far accepted by him undergoes changes, and that he is becoming much more sensitive to certain values, and less to others. In this period the individual changes fundamentally, and at the same time there comes to power within him a new or a higher type of driving elements, a new system of internal environment arises, and he becomes more selective in his attitude toward external contacts.

There also arises the already-mentioned feeling of "otherness," a feeling that the meaning of life has changed. Self-awareness increases significantly and there develops the process of the segregation of values into central, marginal, less significant, or vanquished values. This transformation and the "otherness" of common and individual values find expression, or rather one expression, in a conviction that life would have no meaning without some concrete values.

There comes into view here the previously described individual traits of a personality, such as the main trend of one's interests and capabilities, lasting and exclusive emotional bonds, uniqueness of personal, impressional, and emotional elements, awareness of one's own individuality and the uniqueness of one's history of experiences and development, which are ingrained, as it were, in the common values of personality.

The lasting and exclusive character of these qualities is a fundamental clement of personality.

Of course, new values arise as the individual moves toward his goal of personality; however, these new values do not affect the central position of those thus far realized and affirmed by him. These new values may be important, they may enrich the whole personality, but they always remain marginal in relation to the central values.

So, with respect to the world of values, as shaped from the moment of birth of personality, we observe objectively and in the self-awareness of an individual "quantitative" changes of values, but we do not observe qualitative changes of those values which have already been accepted and experienced by an individual as central ones and which constitute for him a necessary condition for the meaning of existence.

The above considerations point to the need of stressing in our definition of personality this unchangeability of values, and particularly of central values.

Chapter 2

The Developmental Instinct, Primary Integration, and Disintegration

The Developmental Instinct

Its Role in the Shaping of Personality

The ontogenetic development of man possesses characteristic proper-ties, which appear, take on intensity, come to the highest point of development, and then abate or dissolve. The fundamental state of these properties, in their positive and negative correlative system, in their dominants, growth, intensification, and abating, may be observed in the aspirational, emotional, and intellectual structure, as well as in physiological operations and body structure.

A man comes into the world, develops, matures, and acts under the influence of basic instincts. As he gets along in years most of the in-stincts grow feeble, the sensual and mental functions deteriorate, the value of previously pursued aims becomes less and less conspicuous and the dynamism of the whole organism becomes weaker and weaker.

However, there are people, not few in number, in whom, besides the schematically described cycle of life, there arises a sort of a "sidetrack," which after some time may become the "main track." The various sets of tendencies tear away from the common biological cycle of life. The self-preservation instinct begins to transform and exceed its proper ten-dencies, attaching ever more importance to preservation of a man as a spiritual being, and to moral action, even to the detriment of man's physical side. The sexual drive is sublimated into lasting, exclusive, "non-species-oriented"[1] as it were, emotional bonds. The fighting in-

---

[1] "Nonspecies orientation" consists in the individual's sexual drive being rechanneled,

stinct shifts to the area of conflicts in the world of moral values, transforming and sublimating the conflicts into an attitude of fighting for a good cause and into an attitude of sacrifice and love.

These tendencies and their realization bring about a loosening and disintegration of the fundamental instinctive forces and lead to a loosening of psychophysical unity. This proceeds under the direction of a dynamism which we may call the developmental instinct, using a broad sense of this word, since under its influence there arises a higher, cultural personality. This instinct transcends the narrow biological aims and exceeds the primitive drives in strength. It is clearly in opposition to the limited, common life cycle.

The action that disintegrates primitive sets also disintegrates the unity of the individual's structure. The individual, therefore, develops, but at the same time loses his tenacity, his unity, which connotes the feeling of man's sense of existence. The developmental instinct, consequently, when disintegrating the present structure of an individual tends at the same time to reconstruct this unity at a higher level.

We observe then in this process three significant phenomena of a partly compulsory character:

1. A tendency for disintegration of the present, more or less uniform, structure, set by the determined life cycle of a man, which he begins to feel as limiting his further and fuller development, as wearisome, stereotyped, repetitious, and ever more alien to him.

2. A loosening and disintegration of a man's present structure with a simultaneous loss, to a greater or smaller degree, of internal unity; this is a period of man's preparation, as it were, for new, not yet fully realized and consolidated values.

3. A clear consolidation of new values, purposeful reshaping of the structure, the regaining of a shaken or lost unity – that is, integration of an individual at a different, higher level.

When a man oversteps the normal, common life cycle there begin to act such new tendencies and aims, and such attractive values, that,

---

from an emphasis on women in general, to a concentration on an individualistic and exclusive union with a partner in marital life.

without them, he sees no more meaning in his own existence. He must leave his present level, lift himself to a new, higher one and, on the other hand, must, as we have said before, retain his unity, retain the continuity of his psychophysical life, his self-awareness, and identity. The development of personality, therefore, takes place in most cases through disintegration of man's present, initial, primarily integrated structure, and, through a period of disintegration, reaches a secondary integration.

The Phases of the Developmental Instinct

The processes of transformation and sublimation of particular instincts will be discussed in the section of this work dealing with effects of positive disintegration. Here we shall relate the most general characteristics of the phases through which the developmental instinct passes, against the background, briefly presented, of the mechanism of the development of instincts in general.

Our considerations of the developmental process (positive loosening and disintegration of the instinctive structures and functions) are based to a considerable extent on the theory of the structure and functions of instincts presented by Von Monakow[2] with considerable modifications of our own. At the root of the instinctive dynamisms Von Monakow sees the mother dynamism of all instincts, namely horme (agitation, force, internal drive). "This is a tendency," writes Von Monakow, "for creative adaptation of oneself to conditions of life, in all its forms, in order to ensure oneself a maximum security, not only at the present moment, but also for the long, long future." According to Von Monakow, an instinct (of an individual possessing a nervous system) "is a latent propulsive force, a derivative of horme, which realizes the synthesis of internal excitations of protoplasm (introceptivity) and external excitations (exteroceptivity) in order to safeguard the vital interests of an individual and his species by means of adaptive activities." As for embryonic development, Von Monakow introduces the conception of a formative instinct, which is a dynamism determining this development.

---

[2]C. V. Monakow and R. Mourgue. *Introduction Biologique a l'Etude de la Neurologie et de la Psychopathologie. (Biological Introduction to the Study of Neurology and Pathology.)* Paris: Alcan, 1938.

According to Von Monakow, the most primitive instincts differentiate, under the influence of external factors, into hormeters (the instincts proper) and noohormeters (instincts coupled with the intellectual function). He distinguishes these two types in any formed instinct. For example, the self-preservation instinct of a newborn child possesses a very narrow range of needs (the need of warmth and food, "firstlings" of the vegetative life), which then gradually expands. Under the influence of differentiating emotions and on account of conflicts, the self-preservation instinct reaches beyond mere interest in oneself and the child begins to bind himself successively to his mother, then to inanimate objects and animals, to the family, to the closest social group, society, humanity, and finally to the universe. This tendency toward ever more extensive needs and ever more distant aims is connected with the intellect's gnostic functions. And in tendencies such as love of the poor, of the sick, and in expression of the religious instinct Von Monakow sees manifestations of the elements of the sexual drive in its higher forms (noohormeters).

Thus, according to Von Monakow, the development of drives proceeds by way of conjugations of primitive instincts with the orientational and gnostical sphere, with the sphere of exteroception. Moreover, to facilitate understanding of the developmental dynamisms, under whose influence the drives are reshaped, Von Monakow introduces the concept of syneidesis or biological consciousness, which is a force balancing various values of instinctive dynamisms.

Of course, the mechanism presented by Von Monakow possesses an unquestionable value, owing to his keen biological and psychological analysis, his dynamic approach, his valuable attempt to determine the phases of the development of instincts, and his stressing of the importance of the role of gnostical factors in their development. However, it needs to be complemented.

For one cannot without reservation accept the statement that in ontogenesis the orientational and gnostic spheres play a decisive role in an instinct passing from the lower form of development to the higher form. Of course, this conjugation plays an important role, but of no less importance for the proper functioning of orientational and gnostic factors is the dissolution of the cognitive, affective, and motor functions. At the lower levels of the animal kingdom this conjugation occurs in integrated structures, in which no particular member can be isolated. The proper, higher development of every one of these elements cannot take place without a phase of loosening, disintegration, and periods of conflict between them and between their component elements.

In the instincts themselves, therefore, there exist transforming dynamisms, for which the conflictive experiences and participation of gnostic mechanisms are fundamental factors determining the development of a man.[3]

Though they undoubtedly possess great value, the concepts of horme, formative instinct, and syneidesis present some difficulty; when they are used one does not clearly see the developmental, dynamic unity in a man. It would seem to be more advantageous to group all these dynamisms under the term *developmental instinct* and to study the mechanisms of the advent and development of instincts and of their regulation, within the area of the developmental instinct, through the phases of loosening and conjunction, disintegration and integration.

The basic, most general dynamism of a man, embracing all other more particular mechanisms, and revealing itself at the time of fecundation and differentiating itself in a particular way in every individual during his development, is the instinct of life. In various periods of development two groups of particular instincts are manifest in a man, and take a greater or smaller part in his actions. We call these instincts – possessing an egocentric or alterocentric, autotonic or syntonic component – autotonic and syntonic instincts. The first would include the self-preservation, possessive, fighting, and other instincts; the others, the "companion-seeking" instinct, sexual drive, maternal or paternal instinct, herd, cognitive, and religious instincts. The general separation of these two groups, in a sense the contradictoriness and the overlapping of structures of particular drives in both groups, already forms a fundamental basis for conflicts between instincts, for the collision of interests of particular instincts, and for new systems arising during the life of a

---

[3]"There is however no power in us that would make us wish to break the violence of any drive, similarly we have no influence on the choice of a method and on its successful result. In this process our intellect is, most obviously, only a blind instrument of some other drive, which competes with our 'tormentor': be it the desire for peace, the fear of disgrace, or another grievous consequence, or eventually love." F. Nietzsche. *Morgenrothe.* (*The Morning Star.*) Stuttgart: Kroner, 1921.

personality.

So far we have dealt with a decisive domination of innate and in-herited biological dynamisms, the role of which is to build a separate biological entity and to perform compensatory transformations of its biological structure in embryonic life (under the influence of damaging or useful stimuli of the embryonic environment). We are dealing here with a biologically determined developmental instinct, which largely corresponds to Von Monakow's formative instinct. One could say that this is the first phase of the developmental instinct, as understood here, the phase of distinct primitive biological integration, manifesting itself in embryonic life.

When the child comes into the world his innate dynamisms "mea-sure their strength" in relation to diverse environmental conditions, and this measuring of strength causes, in the majority of cases, the so-called adaptation to the often changing external conditions encoun-tered, and in a few cases it causes disintegration, involutional in charac-ter, of psychic structure (involutional mental diseases). In this process of "strength measuring" there may also occur the act of one subordi-nating, to himself, the external environment and treating it as a set of changing stimuli for the development of strong innate dynamisms.

Depending on the prepotency of the sthenic or asthenic tendencies connected with the dynamisms of temperament, on the health or weak-ness of the organism, on the prepotency of the autotonic or syntonic group of primitive drives, we will be dealing with the prepotency of adaptation to the changing conditions of life in the form of virtual sub-ordination or submission, or in the form of apparent subordination or submission. All these forms of behavior will, however, be in accord with the external as well as internal environment, and will be characterized by a lack of any major conflicts with these environments.

In the next phase of the manifestation of the developmental instinct, we enter into the region of the manifestation of the creative instinct. This instinct reflects a loosening or slow disintegration of the internal milieu, and a man's obvious failure to adapt himself in certain regions to the external environment. The above-mentioned conflicts between the two fundamental groups of drives (autotonic and syntonic), as well as between particular instincts in each group, lead to the formation of more or less distinct creative attitudes or attitudes aimed at exceeding the basic adaptative "norms," when a man becomes subtly sensitive to his own internal milieu and to the reaction of the external environment. He becomes weary of his present internal milieu, dissatisfied with himself, and often feels guilty. The monakowian *klisis* (movement toward objects) and *ekklisis* (movement away from objects) in taking an attitude toward the outer world gradually changes into *klisis* and *ekklisis* in relation to one's own internal environment.

In its further progress the developmental instinct passes into the personality "building" phase, that is, into the self-development or self-improvement phase. The internal environment becomes dominated by a "third factor" (a dynamism of conscious direction of one's development) which goes beyond the innate biological structure and beyond the reaction to the external environment. This phase is characterized by the expansion of the action of creative dynamisms over the entire psychic structure. The disintegration processes begin to act in a decisive way in the inner environment, the picture of one's own personality ideal becomes ever more clear, the cognitive functions are increasingly more strongly engaged in the work of realizing this ideal, which is connected with the attitude of a Samaritan sacrifice, social work, love, and with moral independence from the external environment. In the process of the loosening and disintegration of the primary integrated structure of instincts and in the process of their transformation and sublimation, there begin to appear moments of unification, which may lead the individual to a secondary integration at a higher level.

The process of personality building, therefore, is characterized by a wandering "upward," toward an ideal, of the disposing and directing centers and the gradual acquiring of a structure within which, besides individual qualities (the main trend of interests and capabilities, lasting emotional bonds, the unique set of the emotional and psychic structure), general human traits appear – that is, the high level of intellectual development, the attitude of a Samaritan, and the moral and social and esthetic attitudes. The intensive development of this phase retains the acquired essential traits, of which a man is aware, and which he fully affirms.

The various dynamisms presented here in their structure, action, and transformations we also call instincts. Our reason for including these forces among instincts is that, in our view, they are a common phe-

nomenon at a certain level of man's development, they are basic deriva-
tives of primitive instinctive dynamisms, and their strength often exceeds the strength of the primitive maternal instinct.

The principal difference between our conception of the instinctive
structure and functions and former conceptions (McDougall, Mazurkiewicz, and others) is that in our view: (1) the instinct evolves in phylogenetic development as well as in man's life cycle; (2) all three structures
of instincts – the aspirational and emotional, gnostic, and motor structure – are subject to development; (3) the instincts of a human being
are to a considerable extent subject to the principle of dynamic disintegration – that is, they create collisions between and within themselves
(multilevel disintegration), in order to unify within the process of development in a homogeneous personality structure; (4) man's instincts
differ considerably from animal instincts, in that they are more plastic, more easily lose their individual character and independence, and
are subject to changes; (5) the characteristic feature here is the duality
of behavior of an instinct not only toward external objects (toward an
object and away from an object activities) but also within one's own domain, where forces, negating and affirming certain levels of an instinct,
arise and act.

Primary Integration

In its early period the life of a child is enclosed within the framework
of the simplest necessities of life. At this stage the development of
particular functions or sets of functions in a small child is periodically,
and rather positively, subjected to such dominants as the need of food,
various forms of movement, a great need of sleep, and so on. The
reality function, dominating in the hierarchy of needs of an adult man, is
here at the service of simple, common instinctive needs or physiological
functions. These are, as it were, primary integrated functions.

Such structures occur also with adult people. The most frequently
occurring types of primary integrated structures are observed in individuals in whom unilateral narrow interests and unilateral driving tendencies are evident at early stages. As these tendencies dominate other
tendencies, the latter gradually undergo atrophy. The reality function

is here conjugated with those unilateral tendencies, and its task is to adapt itself to the environment that these dominating tendencies may, most easily and most widely, be realized. Such individuals usually do not react to stimuli other than those peculiar to their structure; they realize their own type, as it were, and remain insensitive to other aspects and levels of reality. Such people are incapable of internal conflicts, but often enter into conflicts with the environment.

Integrated structures are also encountered among psychopathic individuals who, believing their morbid tendencies are hierarchically superior, subordinate to them all other dispositions and functions, adapting them more or less adroitly to the environment. A psychopathic individual usually does not know the feeling of internal inferiority, does not experience internal conflicts; he is unequivocally integrated.

The kinds of integration just mentioned might be called, in the most general sense, primary, nonevolutional forms of integration. When an individual with a tenacious structure goes through typical, general biological phases, when unilateral interests develop in him, or so-called "normal" inclinations, or when possibly his psychopathological structure is "improved," this does not mean that he actually develops, but that he merely attains this or that kind of ability, this or that form of the "art of living."

An individual of a permanent primary integrated structure generally acts in the name of instinctive interests in an automatic manner, revealing the moderating functions within the narrow range of habitual experiences. He usually does not possess the feeling of his psychic individuality. Such individuality exists in him as a vague conceptual creation. He is generally unaware of the identity of his present self with the "self" of past periods of his life. The feeling of his activeness is but weakly marked. True enough, the above traits may be manifested in permanently primary-integrated persons, in moments of emotional tension, or when various unpleasant experiences evoke reflection, but such manifestations are temporary and ineffective.

Thus, with persons not burdened with a negative heritage and equipped with a simple psychic structure, there occur more or less long-lasting states of deviation in adaptation to the narrow actual reality, as a consequence of such things as misfortune, physical suffering, or, much less rarely, uncontrollable joy. In these instances one's psyche transcends the most common actual reality.

The death of a child weakens the sharpness of a mother's self-preservation instinct. Acute suffering crushes for some time the force and range of action of a limited, narrow function of reality; there begin to appear disintegration processes, a weakening of the process of adapting oneself to the present reality, and a strengthening of the retrospective and prospective attitude. Physical suffering often causes a widening of the sphere of experience, a greater understanding of the suffering of other people, a movement beyond the sphere of the self-preservation instinct, and a loosening of the thus far existing structure. The feeling of approaching death enhances the attitude of prospection in respect to near relations and friends, for whom one executes a will.

All these are manifestations of weak, transitory forms of disintegration. If their suffering passes the individuals discussed above return relatively quickly to their former attitude of adapting to the narrow sphere of actual reality. They are not able to assume an attitude regarding time from a distance, nor are they able to make themselves mentally independent of it. They are constrained by the present moment, by the reality of flowing experiences, by their own type, and by influences of the environment.

John Galsworthy lucidly pictured the deviations of transitory disintegration among representatives of the "society of possessors," in whom the possessive instinct ruled as the disposing and directing, superior and integrating center:

> For the moment, perhaps, he understood nearly all there was to understand – understood that she [his wife] loathed him, that she had loathed him for years, that for all intents and purposes they were like people living in different worlds, that there was no hope for him, never had been; even, that she had suffered – that she was to be pitied. In that moment of emotion he betrayed the Forsyte in him – forgot himself; was lifted into the pure ether of the selfless and impractical. Such moments passed quickly. And as though, with the tears he had purged himself of weakness, he got up, locked the box, and slowly, almost trembling, carried it with him into the other room.[4]

---

[4]John Galsworthy. *The Forsyte Saga*. ("The Works of John Galsworthy.") London: Heinemann, 1927–1929.

In the excerpt cited here we see that Soames was only able to go a little beyond his own fixed sphere of aims and experiences and beyond his own function of reality. Given his strong possessive instinct, if these experiences, so strange to his type and level, were not "flowing" experiences, if he had many similar experiences, they could have created internal conflicts, permanent dissatisfaction with himself, a tendency for transformations, for a loosening and disintegration of his type and a tendency for discord to arise.

The tenacity of a structure of a man integrated on a primary level is not always characterized by constancy and immutability; it may be disturbed not only transitionally. This is because the structure may include dispositions which, as a result of conditions and experiences, will disturb its tenacity and touch off the process of disintegration.

It should also be kept in mind that there are people, though rarely met, whose initial integration belongs to the higher level, whose rich structure, constantly improved by life's experiences and reflections, does not undergo the process of disintegration, but harmoniously and without greater shock develops into a full personality.

Disintegration

Its Definition and Kinds

The terms *integration* and *disintegration* were used by Descartes, and later by Spencer, Jackson, then by Sherrington, Pavlov, and others. Since the second half of the 19th century these terms have been rather systematically applied by various philosophical schools. Jaensch uses them in his attempts to classify people typologically. They were often applied by the Gestalt school. Presently these terms are commonly used in neurology and psychiatry. In the developmental process – from child to adult, and from primitive to cultural man – we come into contact every day with cases of disintegration of primitive, tenacious, instinctive structure due to obstacles being encountered and the experiences connected with them.

A child bringing various objects to his mouth meets with a contradiction between the feeling of pleasure (visual) and the feeling of unpleasantness (taste) aroused by one and the same stimulus. He is not clearly instinctively attracted to or repelled by an object. He must differentiate his relation to it by experience. When he touches the flame of a candle, the visual picture of which evoked a pleasant desire, there arises a conflict within him. More or less similar mechanisms occur in a primitive man. Observations of something that attracts and in some respect is a source of pleasure, but turns out to be unpleasant in another respect and becomes a source of displeasure, are numerous and varied. Passage through a period of such painful experiences gives rise to an attitude of inhibition, cautiousness, and reflection. But before this comes about, there dominates for a time the attitude of unordered stimulation and inhibition, fright and irritation, together with chaotic, unbalanced, and unharmonized reactions. Beginning with instinctive conflicts through ever more psychic conflicts, with an ever greater participation of our own reflexive acts, we are subject to the developmental process by means of "positive disintegration," attaining ever higher forms of adaptation through disintegration, unfitness, and "errors" of the lower forms of psychic acts. In the place of the former distinct uniform acts come indecisive, inconsistent acts; there appear therein instinctive acts which are deformed until new dynamisms arise, dynamisms ordered on the basis of another principle and new experiences. A long experience in new conditions of life, with the modifying system of the inner milieu, results in differentiation of stimulating and inhibiting acts. That which stimulated differentiates into that which further stimulates and that which gives rise to inhibition; that which was inhibited becomes uninhibited and may form a stimulating factor.

The primitive instinct loses its infallibility; within its structure individual and cognitive elements become isolated, both of which for some time act coordinately. There ensues a loosening or disintegration of instinctive structure into various actual structures, less strongly conjugated than before, hierarchically independent or coordinate.

Excessive tenacity of a structure is a factor checking psychical development. One might assume that the disintegrative process, while loosening the tenacity of psychic functions, makes them to some extent independent of itself. As a result their scope of activity expands, their receptors are more likely to be activated, they acquire greater elasticity and sharpness, and in the period of synthesis they penetrate and aid each other more easily.

The process of disintegration is usually accompanied by a greater or smaller participation of self-awareness, from very weak components up to a morbid intensification of it. A man whose self-awareness is dormant and who, therefore, is incapable of observing himself, and of reflection, does not feel any contradiction either in his own behavior or in its motives. Everything appears natural to him and as a matter of course. He commits acts which contradict each other but he is unaware of their divergence and, in this situation, does not aim at harmonizing them; in short, these acts do not create in him any basis for "remorse." Such a man succumbs passively, as it were, to his inclinations, which are not corrected by the experience which come from understanding that the results of one's behavior may be unpleasant and sometimes even injurious to the environment and to one's own development.

At the other extreme we have cases of excessive self-awareness. Such individuals deliberate at every step made. This "psychic operating" on oneself may help development, but sometimes may become an unfruitful habit, a mania, an aim in itself, which deepens the process of disintegration in an abnormal way. Of course, the fact that one is aware of his own internal disintegration does not by itself result in the tendency to remove it. An impulse in this direction usually springs from a nucleus of a newly arising, higher disposing and directing center.

The question arises as to what conditions and what dispositions facilitate the process of disintegration.

The influence of environment on a child often possesses a character of disintegrating action (bringing the child to shame, prompting in him the feeling of guilt, or a showing of anxiety with respect to his behavior). However, this influence does not penetrate deeply into the mind of a child, because he quickly realizes that it is only a verbal action, the essence of which is usually only partly experienced by parents and tutors.

Inherited dispositions, puerperal traumas, diseases, reaction of the environment, an unsuitable profession, violent experiences, all influence the dissolution of the tenacity of the disposing and directing center of a man. This loosening of the structure is particularly strongly marked during the period of maturation, when new forces, new tendencies, making their way more or less violently through the present system and disturbing its thus far existing balance, begin to acquire significance. A change in the system of forces in the inner milieu slowly pushes forward new dominants, which oppose the thus far existing ones.

Excessive excitability is, among others, a sign that one's adaptability to the environment is disturbed. These disintegration processes are based on various forms of increased psychic excitability, namely on psychomotor, imaginative, affectional, sensual, and mental hyperexcitability. Psychomotor excitability is basic in the development of functional hyperkineses, tics, and psychomotor obtrusions, as well as vagrancy. Imaginative excitability reveals itself in the form of daydreaming, in the intensification of night dreams, in illusions, in artistic ideas arising, which point to the tendency toward dissolution and disintegration of one's adaptability to the narrow actual reality. Affectional hyperexcitability produces states of agitation and depression, sympathy for or dislike of oneself and the world, dissatisfaction with oneself and the environment, strangeness in relation to oneself and the environment, and feelings of inferiority or superiority. Sensual excitability, with the cooperation of other forms of hyperexcitability, develops the complex receptors under the pressure of sensations and stimuli, making them sensitive (strengthening and refining the sensual and esthetic experiences, but leaving one with a feeling of their relative incompleteness), which, in turn, dissolves the tenacity of the structure. Finally, increased mental excitability causes the dissolution of its conjugation with the controlling set, makes itself independent, and dissociates itself from its too close relation with the aspirational and emotional structure; it discovers within itself and develops new directing tendencies, intellectualized to a great extent.

Any of the types of excitability, if too strongly developed, subordinates to itself the function of reality and often results in a limitation of other kinds of experiences. Habits and addictions occur usually, therefore, when the individual is unable to endure too excessive internal psychic tension at the existing excitability. Excessive smoking of cigarettes by people with sensual and psychomotor hyperexcitability, is symptomatic of a venting of passion in a substitutional, indirect, abortive form. This is often a palliative action where one lacks the possibility of proper action. The use of alcohol and other narcotics often signifies violation of the function of reality, whose inhibitions are too weak to control impulses aimed at splitting the individual from actual reality.

Excessive sensitivity, given its too unilateral or too weak conjugation with the disposing and directing center of a higher level and given the difficulty it has bearing tension, sometimes leads one to become uninhibited and to subordinate oneself to the center of a lower psychic level (primitive drives, such as aggressiveness, finding one's outlet in sexual life, and so on).

The self-awareness of an individual, with the accompanying process of self-education, plays an important role in the process of disintegration, as has already been mentioned. It is time and, so to speak, "space" that are connected with the dissolution and disintegration of the individual, through the discovery and singling out in oneself of that which is "more I" from that which is "less I," that which is more a "subject" from that which is more an "object," and through self-defining within the scope of "who am I and what am I really like?" This is a process of making dynamic one's own inner milieu, a process of humanizing oneself. Its development is connected with the general laws of evolution, perceived in the phenomena of mutation, which complicate the uniform development of organisms. In this process, with the growing participation of self-awareness, the aims of the individual expand and reshape, through the inclusion of the suprabiological elements (moral and social, such as the superstructure of the generative instinct, and metaphysical, such as the superstructure of the self-preservation instinct) into the instinctive structure.

In what manner does such differentiation occur? Within the very biological structure of the individual inheres the necessity of the partial resignation of one drive in favor of another drive (for example, the partial resignation of the self-preservation instinct in favor of the generative instinct), the necessity of periodically passing from certain dominants in a given hierarchical system to others through shocks and attitude of resignation (for example, in the maturation and climacteric periods).

Self-awareness – developing in connection with the mentioned processes and everyday-life conflicts, inhibiting processes, reflection, recesses in vital functioning – gradually participates, to an ever greater extent, in the reshaping of the primitive instinctive structure. Experiences, lived through, point to shortcomings in our actions, make us aware of them and of the wrongs done by us to the environment, not intentionally but through lack of adequate sensitivity, adequate prospection and retrospection, and adequate knowledge of ourselves. Estimating effects leads to a better knowledge of oneself; to gradual dissolution of the tenacious instinctive structure, to the control of direct reactions to stimuli, and to the formation of more highly complicated and less direct reactions. The participation of memory and anticipation expands awareness and permits it to transcend the actual reality.

The primitive structure, dissolved by unpleasant feelings, such as awe, fear, unrest, searches for new cognitive and emotional conjugations, for new solutions, by means of making particular elements more sensitive, by means of the method of trial and error. The shattering of the narrow actual reality leads to an even greater differentiation of instincts, to emotional ambivalence, to an increasingly more keen working of the consciousness.

In the process of psychic disintegration discussed here we may single out three characteristic types: (1) unilevel disintegration, (2) multilevel disintegration, and (3) disintegration with respect to scope, length of time, and effects (initial and total, permanent and impermanent, positive and negative and eventually pathological disintegration).

Unilevel Disintegration

Unilevel disintegration manifests itself in various forms not easy to delineate in their structure, functions, and reshapings. We shall deal here more closely with some of its forms.

Unilevel disintegration of the maturation period is marked by quite a number of distinct structural changes of the internal environment. The thus far operating dynamisms characteristic of a child in the period of infancy, such as objective interests of a total character, a friendly living together which is only vaguely selective, subordination of oneself to parents and tutors, adaptation to the environment, harmony between behavior and action, and a serene spirit, all begin to abate and to lose tenacity and harmony. Slowly they are replaced by special interests, a critical attitude toward parents and elders, a tendency to morally evaluate the environment and oneself, inadaptability, disharmony in behavior and action, uneven and depressive moods, more exclusive sentiments, and by slowly arising and increasingly more intense sexual interests and tendencies. Under the influence of new dynamisms attitudes toward friends, toward oneself, toward the other sex, and toward the so far binding standards, undergo change.

These transformations are accompanied by the advent and development of states of lighter or more serious mental unbalance. The life of the individual, during the period of maturation, remains under the influence of two controlling centers: the retiring former one and the oncoming new center. The operating dynamisms existing thus far do not retreat without fighting, without emotional shocks, and the oncoming dynamisms do not organize themselves and do not take over control too easily. Affectional conjugations from the period of infancy and conjugations arising under the influence of the pressure of new tendencies, with mutual regrouping, result in a considerable lability of moods. This state manifests itself in the attitudes of denying and affirming, feelings of inferiority and superiority, moods of agitation and depression, of joy and sorrow, and, finally, in tendencies to solitude and in the periodic intensification of the need for group life.

Prospective dynamisms struggle here with retrospective dynamisms; there is no harmony, calmness, or peace. The new total organization is achieved painfully. There are periods when one feels the need for holding on to the center which is losing its psychophysiological vitality but to which one is bound by emotional memory. What dominate in this period are the asthenic attitude, depressive moods, and "partial attachment" to often apparent values, to abortive actions.

The states of disintegration and fluctuation of dominants in the structure and dynamisms of an individual are rather distinctly reflected in experiences characterizing the moods of disintegration – suspense, sorrow, a weakening of confidence in the environment and oneself, depressions, the need for solitude, and, on the other hand, in the surge of the sthenic disposition, energy, ideas, and so on.[5]

The second characteristic form of unilevel disintegration is that taking place during the climacteric period. It is also characterized by a weakening or evanescence of certain dynamisms or certain values in favor of others, and general experience tells us that almost always these

---

[5]Unilevel disintegration of the maturation period may mark the beginning of disintegration of another kind, namely, of multilevel disintegration, which shall be dealt with later.

new elements are of lesser value compared to the retreating ones. In this period the sexual drive weakens or transforms itself into other drives, one's vital efficiency usually weakens, the interests pursued thus far are no longer as strong and one is not so vigorous in one's attempts to realize them; one's somatic side also undergoes changes which are biologically disadvantageous to the individual, changes that are reflected in the weakening of one's efficiency in action and in growing old. The individual is trying to substitute new or strengthened dynamisms in place of the retreating dynamisms, and this is usually more difficult to accomplish than in the preceding period (tendencies toward strengthening of family life, greater thriftiness in material matters, parsimony, not paying too much attention to one's dress, arbitrariness, egocentrism, and so forth). Nevertheless, the psychic state at the time of substitution is marked by the weakness of vital tension, an uncertainty in action, a feeling of inferiority, depression, retrospective tendencies and fear of the future, and a slackening of prospection.

Let us now pass to the problem of unilevel disintegration connected with external – fortuitous, as it were – events in the life of an individual.

In the first section of this chapter we quoted examples of temporary weak symptoms of the unilevel disintegration of individuals possessing uncomplicated psychic structures, who realize simple aims, strictly connected with rather primitive instinctive dynamisms. A catastrophe causes confusion in their set of main dynamisms and in their directional tendencies, or it causes an abatement and short-lived exile of the thus far existing dominants to a background position (exemplified by Soames in the quotation from *The Forsyte Saga*). This is, however, a temporary confusion and the weakening of one dynamism is compensated for here by the strengthening of other fundamental dynamisms, which are part of the already mentioned set (growth in the need of possession, increase in arbitrariness in relation to one's family, the need for external accentuation of these attributes, and so forth).

This kind of disintegration may be caused by the "breakups" an individual suffers such as a state of disability which does not allow the realization of his thus far pursued aims, loss of the chief field of activity, derision and defamation, and some forms of impairment and injury of the fundamental individual biological tendencies.

Let us now take another example. Picture a man with narrow mental horizons, with slight psychical sensibility, a strong, tenacious instinctive structure, a man aspiring to a position of power, desiring to "get ahead." This is a clever man, but fit only for a narrow field of operation. The "environmental" conditions cause the need for such a type of specialist to wane and our man faces the necessity of a new start. A shift to a kind of work not drastically different from the former one is possible, provided he completes his education, but this type of individual finds this difficult to achieve. This situation entails a period of dissension, breakdown, uncertainty, depression, a jumping from one conception to another, from mood to mood; it entails instability between excitation and inhibition – in short, disintegration. Due to a low plasticity and a narrow range of aims, and because of small compensatory and, even more so, sublimatory reserves, such individuals go through breakdowns more seriously, adapt themselves to changed conditions with greater difficulty, and this may lead to suicidal tendencies and even to a sharp outbreak of mental illness. A positive way out of such a situation consists in a slow transposition, in fact in a transformation, of one's attitude even if within a narrow field, in a slow realization of one's capacities and consequently a return to the former way of life which is usually just slightly expanded.

Above we touched on compensatory and sublimatory difficulties. In everyday practice we sometimes encounter quite contrary examples of exorbitant adaptability to the changing conditions of life. It is manifested often in the attitude of keeping up appearances, in the attitude of deceitfulness, ensuring a good opinion of oneself, success, special favors, and so on. An example of such compensation would be a white-collar worker who, while in his office, is composed, calm, friendly, kind, industrious, and at the same time is a brutal and inconsiderate egoist in his family life. This reflects disintegration into two forms of behavior: one, which is apparent, reflects the need for adaptation and is an expression of the self-preservation instinct; the other, inherent in a given individual, is primitive and brutal. Two mechanisms may occur here. In the first case the apparent behavior is dictated by one's desire to gain material profits, a favorable opinion, and the like, without which a given individual would not be able to realize his primitive drives. This is a cynical attitude. In the other case such an individual, though having the best intentions, may not be capable of fully mastering himself on a higher level, in living together with his family the way he lives at his place of work. Both these mechanisms, independently of their moral value, reflect superficial unilevel disintegration, in which there is not a more serious disintegration of the primitive instinctive structure.

Lying, which produces a feeling of constraint, shyness, apprehension, is also one of the forms of unilevel disintegration. In this area we are dealing alternately with appearance and reality, the desire to remain "oneself" and to appear to be someone else.

We will turn our attention for a moment to the problem of unilevel disintegration which characterizes the constitution, as it were, of a given individual or his type. It is a difficult problem. We will devote to it only several general remarks.

Individuals of the schizothymic type experience on the one hand coldness, difficulty in establishing contact, the need for solitude, and are excessively critical; on the other hand, they experience hypersensibility, even touchiness, and are refined in the reception of stimuli from the external and internal environments. These are, as it were, two separate structures, two kinds of dynamisms acting without harmony and without logical infiltration.

In cyclic-type individuals we deal with dispositions tending to intensified excitability and depression, to volatile associations and perseverations. Moreover, these cyclic states may follow each other, every now and then, in longer or shorter periods; they may produce a very frequent fluctuation of the entire psychic structure, or its particular sets so that we may have almost "simultaneous" states of intensified excitability and depression in very closely related psychic areas. It seems that in both polarized sets a third member is lacking, that *tertium quid* which would breach the split, synthesizing both structures, thus protecting man's mental equilibrium. This deficiency and the possibility of removing it characterize a phenomenon widely discussed in the psychology of feelings, namely the fact of experiencing, at the same time, fundamental mixed feelings – that is, the feelings of pleasure and displeasure. Dissolution and even disintegration of particular structures and sets allows the same individual to experience simultaneously various kinds of feelings in various realms. We will discuss this problem in detail in the chapter on the development of feelings in general. In the present consideration stress is laid on the typological, constitutional predisposition for the alternate, and often simultaneous, experiencing of sorrow and joy, sympathy and antipathy, enthusiasm and discouragement, exaltation and tragic depression. Because they coexist and at the same time oppose each other, these experiences introduce an element of dissolution, ferment, which often results in another form of disintegration – multilevel disintegration.

The basic characteristics of unilevel disintegration may be presented schematically. (1) Unilevel disintegration is a process taking place at one structural and experiential level. (2) It is principally an automatic process, in which self-awareness weakly participates at various times. (3) In this process distinctly dissociative dynamisms dominate the transforming and restoring dynamisms (with the exception of the disintegration of the maturation period). (4) New elements appearing in this form of disintegration usually do not possess moral value greater than existing ones. (5) Remaining long in this state leads, in most cases, to reintegration at a lower level, to suicidal tendencies, or to mental illness. (6) Unilevel disintegration is often an initial, poorly differentiated setting for multilevel disintegration.

Multilevel Disintegration

With multilevel disintegration, as with unilevel disintegration, loosening and disintegration of the internal environment occur, but they take place with respect to lower and higher layers. The course of multilevel disintegration is accessible to objective study and the experiencing individual is conscious of it. The process of evaluating one's own internal environment is essential for multilevel disintegration. The feeling of the separateness of one's own self increases and this is so not only in contradistinction to the external environment, but also, even primarily, in relation to one's own inner environment, which is evaluated, is made into a hierarchy, and becomes a subject of more precise cognition and appraising thought. A "subject-object" process takes place in one's own self. One's internal milieu is divided into higher and lower, into better and worse, and into desirable and undesirable. There appears here the feeling of "lower value" and the feeling of guilt when one "falls down" to a lower level, knowing that he actually has the capacity to raise himself up. He knows this as his memory tells him of the pleasant moments of past achievements.

Along with the feeling of the fluctuation of the disposing and directing center, "up" and "down," there appears on the one hand the feeling of inferiority and on the other the awareness of an ideal, the feeling of superiority, an aspiration toward a power of a "higher order," the desire for the realization of other aims of life, a prospective and retrospective attitude with a plan for perfecting oneself.

The feeling of higher and lower values in oneself is concerned on the one hand with the primitive drives, which one wants to reshape, and on the other with the structure of the ideal from which one draws creative forces for these reshapings. This is accomplished by means of acute fighting, which Ernest Hello has described in these words:

> The higher man, constantly tormented, internally torn by the contrast between ideal and reality, feels better than anyone else the human greatness and more painfully than anyone else the human misery. He feels himself carried to the realms of ideal sublimity, which is our final aim, and mortally affected by the eternal failure of our miserable nature. He infects us with these contradictory feelings which he himself experiences; arouses in us a love of existence and stimulates in us an incessant awareness of our nonentity.[6]

Multilevel disintegration is accompanied by the phenomenon of self-awareness and "enhanced consciousness," or self-cognizance. If within the structure and dynamics of consciousness we ascertain the existence of foundations such as the awareness of the unchangeability of certain elements and the changeability of other elements in the current of life, the awareness of one's present and past identity (Jaspers), then there must also arise the conscious feeling of development, a feeling of dissolution and of the shattering of old values and aims. Precisely these psychic states point to the fact that multilevel disintegration is in progress.[7]

---

[6]E. Hello. *Studia i szkiee.* (*Studies and Essays.*) Lwów: Ksiegarnia B. Poloniecki, 1912.

[7]The awareness of development and of disintegration leads to one's being pitted against oneself, as illustrated by Nietzsche's words: "Alone from this moment and suspiciously mistrusting myself, I have taken, not without anger, a position which opposed my own self in all that which gave pain and hurt me." F. Nietzsche. *Thus*

The principal differences between unilevel and multilevel disintegration are best shown, we think, if they are examined in the same areas. Let us consider the symptoms of multilevel disintegration in the maturation period. In the forefront here is the process of evaluation, both with respect to the internal and external environments. In both these environments one sees that which is worse and that which is better, the higher and the lower, the near and the farther, and what is familiar and what is strange to us. Thus one divides one's external and internal environments into certain layers according to their values. The association between the fluctuating disposing and directing center and certain levels of both environments becomes weaker. A considerable role is played here by consciousness, which takes an active part in the process of the loosening and disintegration of these environments. The retrospective and prospective attitudes, which grow increasingly important, also assist in this process. The first examines the "lower" environments taken in time and their changes which depend on time, and the other draws its energy for the analysis and reshaping of the external and, above all, the inner environment from the growing hierarchy of aims and dynamisms of one's own personality ideal, which is increasingly more distinctly shaped.

In this process the domain of instinctive life, particularly of primitive drives, is very often clearly regarded as a lower domain from which one should make himself independent in order to be able to realize a proper plan of development. Such an attitude is sometimes accompanied by a strong sense of the fundamental differences between body and spirit. This reflects disintegration in the domain of somatopsychic interactions, which captures the attention of a given individual and makes him sensitive to these problems and to their practical manifestations.

When one is aware of the existence of differences between particular levels of one's own psychic structure and attempts to control the domains he considers to be lower, then one experiences feelings of shame, guilt, of the inferiority of some levels in relation to others, and these feelings lead him to erect an increasingly clearer ideal for his own development. Lack of equilibrium in the internal environment, lability and

Spake Zarathustra: A Book for All and None; translated by Alexander Tille. London: Unwin, 1908.

inconsistency in the association of the disposing and directing center with a given level and its fluctuations afford increasingly greater joy as a result of attainments – and a state of depression and the feeling of inferiority, mentioned above, when one experiences failures. In experiences connected with multilevel disintegration of the maturation period, that which is new becomes a subject of evaluation, weighed in reference to total development and in the scale of moral estimation, and that which is new is usually estimated as better and morally more worthy.

In the process of multilevel disintegration of the climacteric period a man estimates "that which was" as more worthy and higher in the hierarchy, and more or less intensely seeks for new values which would not only compensate for but also exceed the retreating values. An estimation of thus far attained intellectual values, wisdom, temperance, richness of experience, and so on, shows that only a remaking and reshaping may form the basis for the elaboration of a new system of values which could, more than adequately, replace the values a man loses as he grows older and older. The process of the advent of the "new" in this period, with the continued existence and vitality of the "old," is accompanied by periods of exaltation and depression and, as multilevel disintegration correctly proceeds, an increasingly stronger feeling of peace.

Multilevel disintegration connected with external events and forced upon the individual by fate is most closely connected to the inner milieu which is sensitive to a certain type of external experience. These experiences "consolidate," as it were, the individual's psychical resources toward their activation for internal remaking, for the estimation of errors, for the program of transformations, for obtaining a new hierarchy of values, and for the reshaping of one's own type.

A man who faces life with a considerable fund of good will, theoretical knowledge, with a desire for right solutions to problems that may confront him, and with a conviction that he will actually reach a correct solution, comes, after countless experiences, to a conclusion which differs considerably from the original one, namely, that he is not prepared for proper behavior, that he is committing many errors and doing a great deal of wrong because of his shortcomings in his behavior toward people and because of a lack of knowledge or lack of anticipation of effects. These experiences and estimates lead him to the conclusion that he must enrich his mental, intuitional, and moral outlooks, along the principal course on which he is at present heading, loosen, and even disintegrate many schemes, many instinctive mechanisms and impulses, which are causes of his improper behavior. Slow adjustment to the "new" brings about the need to free oneself from undesired mechanisms, the need to widen one's horizons and to secure oneself against new errors. A man, when working to disintegrate the thus far existing stereotype, arrives at a point which allows him to draw energy from the disposing and directing center, which passes to a higher level.

Dwelling in the sphere of one's increasingly more distinct personality ideal facilitates the adoption of an alien attitude toward the abandoned levels, the separation of oneself from them, and even the act of contradicting them. Adequate intellectual and moral resources, life catastrophes, breakdowns, and personal defeats a man has experienced, may be the causes of a complete reshaping of his forms of thinking, behavior, and action (Dawid, Beers, St. Augustine, and others). In these circumstances a man often experiences mystical and religious states, states of strong psychic concentration, of creative improvisation, in which he experiences almost "tangibly" the realities of a "higher" order.

The most important characteristics of multilevel disintegration, taken schematically, would therefore be: (1) A loosening and often a disintegration of psychic structures and functions into particular more or less isolated types and levels. (2) These multilevel structures remain in more or less permanent conflict. (3) The disposing and directing center takes part in this conflict in different ways, but with a tendency to occupy a position in the highest of these levels. (4) An estimation is made by the disposing and directing center of particular levels and of one's place in the structure of the personality ideal in general – this is a differentiation into lower and higher total-development values and into higher and lower moral values. (5) The functions of multilevel disintegration are to a considerable extent volitional, conscious, and refashioning functions, in relation to lower levels. (6) These functions are based on the individual's analysis of his own psychic structure, and on his hesitation in yielding, even though it progressively decreases, to the higher-level aims and one's own personality ideal. (7) Multilevel disintegration embraces sublimating mechanisms.

The chief differences between unilevel and multilevel disintegration, besides the general differences indicated by the name, are weak volition in the course of the disintegration process in the first, and marked participation of volition in the second; the weakness of the tendency to reshape the inner milieu in the first and a marked, or even a very great, tendency to do so in the second; the dominance of the feelings of inferiority, guilt, and shame in relation to the external environment in the first and the marked dominance of the feeling of inferiority in relation to one's own inner environment in the second; the tendency for the conflicts in the first to be external, and in the second internal; the tendency in the second to attain, hierarchically, increasingly higher aims, up to the personality ideal; the dominance of partial disintegration in the first form, and the dominance of global disintegration in the second form.

However, despite these differences a strict temporal and spatial delineation of both forms of disintegration cannot be made, because the first is often the initial, poorly differentiated phase of the second.

Other Forms of Disintegration

These other forms include disintegration with respect to scope, length, and effects, or partial and global, permanent and temporary, positive and negative disintegration.

Partial disintegrations are those which embrace only a part of the structure and psychic functions of an individual. Unilevel disintegration is a partial disintegration, and multilevel disintegration is usually a global disintegration. We observe partial disintegration in the form of a disturbance of the tenacity and unity of some psychic functions as a result of injurious experiences within the sphere of these functions (for example, forms of increased excitability, explosiveness, some phobias, such as agoraphobia, tics, and so on).

These partial disintegrations are observed with people who behave quaintly. Their behavior does not disturb their psychic tenacity and is evoked usually by trying experiences, which have developed in them certain stereotyped, ineffective, and abortive forms of reaction. We also come into contact with partial disintegrations in some developmental periods. In order to illustrate this let us take the example of the disintegration of the sexual drive and feelings into two levels: one revealing the highest idealization of the object of the feelings, with total moderation of the sexual life, and the second (in relation to another individual) in which, at the same time, the sexual drive glaringly reveals itself.

We often come into contact with partial disintegration in infantile neuroses, in which, with adequate innate dispositions, pathological conjugation and "denaturalization" of certain physiological functions arise under the influence of fundamental educational errors (for instance, daily vomiting reflecting resistance or unsatisfied claims).

We come into contact with global disintegration almost exclusively in cases of very intense experiences which disturb or destroy the thus far existing foundations and aims of an individual. In such circumstances there occurs the loosening, disintegration, reshaping, and rebuilding of the whole psychic structure. Such phenomena usually occur with sensitive people, possessing high cultural feelings.

We may talk of a global disintegration in some psychoses of the cyclic or schizophrenic type, sometimes affording grounds for a good prognosis and representing the nuclei of fundamental transformations, leading to new foundations in life and development, and to a new hierarchy of aims (Beers). In the maturation and climacteric periods we may also talk of global disintegration, mainly in cases in which compulsory transformations are accompanied by a more conscious effort on the part of the individual attempting to guide himself by these modifications. Such transformations are usually thorough; they dissolve and disintegrate the thus far existing structure in all its aspects, causing in these periods the advent not only of "new" but of simultaneously "higher" structures and aims.

The distinction between permanent and temporary disintegrations is rather obvious. We have already pointed to the fact that, with the majority of individuals, who are called normal, both in particular developmental periods and when under the influence of grievous experiences and sufferings, there occur periodic changes in their principal attitude. Instances of such changes may be the psychic state of a mother after her child's death, or the state of the already cited Soames in *The Forsyte Saga*. The persons mentioned abandon, under such conditions, their tenacious structure for varying lengths of time, go beyond the forms of their everyday behavior and make the nuclei of their higher tendencies independent of a strict conjunction with the primitive instinctive structure, in order to return to it more or less quickly. These are both partial and temporary disintegrations. Such temporary disintegrations are encountered also in cases of disturbed mental equilibrium in somatic diseases, and also in transitory states of reactive neuroses or when a man passes through some form of severe psychosis.

We encounter permanent disintegrations principally in severe chronic mental diseases and in acute chronic somatic diseases (surgical tuberculosis, progressive, degenerative nervous diseases, grave disabilities).

In the case of so-called positive disintegration – that is, disintegration signaling and producing positive transformations of the psychic structure – which is a source of creativity, we may be dealing with permanent disintegration, which is decisive for the positiveness of the individual's transformation, throughout his entire life, and is responsible for ever-vital sources of creativity (Michelangelo, Dostoevsky, Zeromski, Weininger, and others). It characterizes the path of genius and the path to moral personality.

The distinction between positive and negative disintegration seems to be most difficult to draw. We say that we are speaking of a positive disintegration when it transforms itself gradually or, in some cases, violently into a secondary integration, or when, without passing into a clear and permanent, morbid, secondary or involutional disintegration, it remains a disintegration which enriches one's life, expands one's horizons, and produces sources of creativity. The first criterion is difficult to apply, since the disintegration as a positive process may last throughout the individual's entire life, without leading to a secondary integration. Sometimes we cannot ascertain whether the disintegration process is negative in the course of severe psychoses, and this is because only after they have passed and left some effects is it possible to estimate whether we were witnessing the positive or negative form of disintegration. Of course, an experienced clinician, very familiar with these problems, may, on the basis of a descriptive diagnosis and the course of the disease, not only give a good or bad prognosis for a given disintegrative disease; he may also often foresee the effects of disintegration. This is, however, not an easy task and one should be very careful with such foresight.

We call a disintegration negative when it does not produce effects which are positive in relation to development or when it yields negative effects. In the first case a man returns to a primary integration, with negative tendencies of compensatory experiences, connected with a short-lived disintegration; i.e., he merely substitutes one lower-level need for another.

Disintegrations which cause negative compensations for the life and development of an individual are observed in cases of serious disability. In these cases compensation may develop in the direction of ill will or hatred for the social environment, and the feeling of inferiority is compensated for by way of aggression or by taking the wrong approach to life.

Negative disintegrations occur in all cases of chronic psychoses leading gradually to the involution of a personality.

But, as has been already mentioned, we cannot pass a judgment that we are dealing with a negative disintegration based only on the fact that it lasts long and that we do not observe in it any sign that it will become transformed into a secondary integration.

Disintegration in Relation to Disturbances and Mental and Somatic Illness

Disintegration in Mental Disturbances and Illnesses

For lack of space we shall not discuss here the so-called standard and its significance in the notion of mental health and disease, and we will limit ourselves to the statement that, in our conception, a mental disturbance is, in many cases, a positive phenomenon, not only in the personality and social senses, but sometimes in the biological sense. The contrary conception, now current, is based on the analysis of serious dissolutional or involutional diseases – that is, of residual forms in the great developmental process. The symptoms of educational difficulties in life, nervousness, neuroses, psychoneuroses, mark, in the majority of cases, the process of development, the process of positive disintegration (creative inadaptability). This is true also of a number of cases of untreated and treated psychoses.

We shall discuss briefly the problems of disintegration in relation to general psychopathological symptoms and the problem of disintegration as related to isolated states of mental disturbances and diseases.

Let us consider first of all disturbances in the intellectual functions, primarily disturbances in the experiencing, perception, and comprehension of sensations. Hyperesthesia and hyperalgesia, occurring in many mental diseases, may reflect general sensitivity or periodic hypersensitivity, which, like depression, may play a positive role in development (objective, critical attitude). A feeling of estrangement and freshness of sensations in relation to various types of stimuli may have creative significance and is often observed among poets. Illusions are characteristic not only of the mentally sick but also of the majority of writers, painters, and people with highly developed emotions and capacity for phantasy. Furthermore, simple and conjugated hallucinations have often been observed in prominent people in the period of their mental diseases (Beers, Mayer, Kandinsky) and in other outstanding people who were not suspected of such disease (Wagner, Wladislaw Dawid). Many kinds of hallucinations reveal a mechanism similar to that of dreams. Regardless of the organic ground of hallucinations, we observe them in individuals inclined to eidetism, in people with a highly excitable imagination, in maladjusted individuals, in people with a high sensitivity to external stimuli and with a capacity for plastic memory.

The same holds true for disturbances in thinking and association. For example, the wild flight of thoughts occurring in maniacal states also characterizes the states of creative tension, with the difference that in the former states the associations are superficial, changing, subject to incidental influences, while in the latter states the associations are precise and ordered and profound. In the period of creative tensions we find three elements of the maniacal state, namely increased feeling of one's own value, an accelerated flow of thoughts, and motor excitation. The opposite state, inhibition, which is somewhat short of the melancholy state, is observed with creative people after their creative periods.

Perseveration of associations may reflect narrow-mindedness, the processes of thinking slowing down, becoming dull and stereotyped. It may reflect weariness, but it may also be a symptom of monoideism and lasting emotional attitudes (the perseverations and ideas Beers had during his illness gave rise, after his recovery, to a great social reform).

States similar to those of delusion as to one's greatness or to persecution mania, which point to the lack of harmony between the individual and the environment, and to the lack of a proper estimation of oneself, are not always morbid states. The so-called delusions of wisdom, reformatory tendencies, often characterize prominent people who, as history tells us, were not always estimated properly (during his stay at a hospital for the mentally ill, Mayer had ideas that led to the discovery of the great law of the conservation of energy).

It is difficult to speak of memory – for instance, of hyperamnesia – as a pathological symptom, for it can also be a symptom of development. A permanent weakening of memory is, of course, a pathological symptom and in most cases connected with organic disturbances. On the other hand, a periodic weakening of the memory, or gaps in the memory, is often a sign of self-defense on the part of the patient's organism and personality, or evidence of the liquidation of trauma.

Disturbances of consciousness and orientation, besides various mental diseases, are encountered in states of ecstasy and deep meditation. The main characteristics of the latter are the spontaneous, volitive surrendering of oneself to these states and the lack of injurious repercussions from them in the totality of one's life.

Taking the view that emotional life is a controlling structure in the personality, we now pass to disturbances in the emotional life. An intensified sad mood (hypothymia) or gay mood (hyperthymia) and the length of time they are experienced do not provide evidence that these experiences are morbid in character. Such moods are often connected with a strong experiencing of internal conflicts, with the shift of the disposing and directing center to an ever higher level, or they are, in other ways, of a protective, developmental character. Apathy, both in its conscious form (in psychoneuroses) and in its unconscious form (in schizophrenia), does not necessarily reflect indifference. In psychoneuroses, indifference is related to only some areas of reality and some internal structures; in schizophrenia apathy is caused mainly by the impossibility of expressing one's feelings in the period of a negative attitude toward the injuring environment and daily stimuli. In reality such individuals are excessively sensitive and crave love, warmth, and kindness. "Injury," failure in the gratification of these needs, results in negativity and in the mask of callousness. We meet with an essential lack of affectual sensitivity in moral insanity, which is characterized by psychic integration at a low level.

The changes of personality observed in hysteria (loss of the feeling of one's own personality, and so on) cannot be considered solely from the pathological point of view. Many changes of personality, many forms of its loosening and disintegration, are symptoms of developmental disintegration, which is most strongly manifested on the borderline between normality and abnormality, as found in the states of nervousness, neuroses, psychoneuroses, and in states of intensive and accelerated development.

The conception of a pathological weakening of volition is also very difficult to grasp. Decisions and action should be grasped multidimensionally. Individuals susceptible to inhibitions in daily life may be able to make a decision and to act energetically in difficult circumstances. The same may be said about excessive volition. One should also beware of the simplification of treating as exclusively pathological parafunctions or the so-called deformations of manifestations of will. Stereotypy (mental and moral) is often developmental in character.

Importunate drives and their realization may be manifested on various levels – from vulgar and aggressive attitudes and reactions, contradicting moral principles, to acts of the highest level, to inspirations. Distorted instinctive tendencies are not always rightly interpreted.

These short remarks tend to show that the classification of and generalization about symptoms of psychic disturbances are not an easy matter. "Pathological" disturbances of personality, mental functions, desires, or drives may on one hand be retrogressive symptoms, injurious to the individual and the society, and on the other hand they may be useful, improving symptoms, raising the individual to a higher cultural level.

We shall now give a short interpretation of some sets of mental disturbances and diseases, nervousness, and some neuroses and psychoses, from the point of view of the theory of positive disintegration.

The essential characteristic of nervousness is an increased excitability, symptomatized in the forms of sensual, psychomotor, affectional, imaginational, and mental hyperexcitability. It consists in an unproportional reaction to a stimulus, an extended, long-lasting, accelerated reaction, and a peculiar reaction to a neutral stimulus. This hyperexcitability is therefore a strong, uncommon sensitivity to external and internal stimuli; it is virtually a positive trait. Talented people, capable of controlling their own actions and fighting against social injustice, are characterized by a sensitivity to esthetic, moral, and social stimuli, to various psychic processes in their own internal environment. Each of the forms of psychic hyperexcitability mentioned is characterized by valuable, actual or prospective, properties. Sensual hyperexcitability is an attitude of being sensitive to external stimuli, such as the sense of color, form, and tone. Psychomotor hyperexcitability gives sharpness, speed, and an immediacy of reaction and capacity for action; it is a "permanent" psychomotor readiness. Affectional hyperexcitability is evidence of the development of a property which is the controlling dynamism of the psyche. Imaginational hyperexcitability gives prospective and creative capabilities, as well as those of projecting and foreseeing. Finally, mental hyperexcitability results in easier and stronger conjugations of particular forms of increased sensibility, which facilitates their developmental work and is a factor that controls and enriches the mentioned dynamism (creativity, psychomotor readiness, etc.). None of the forms of hyperexcitability mentioned above develops in isolation. As a rule these are mixed forms with predominance of this or that form. They are disintegrating factors and, in conjugation with mental hyperexcitability, permit preparation for higher forms of disintegration and secondary integration.

As for neuroses and psychoneuroses, we accept the view of such scholars as R. Brun, M. Bleuler, and others, who do not consider the terms *neurosis* and *psychoneurosis* to be synonymous, though they consider them closely related. There are certain differences between the two, such as the psychic dominant in psychoneuroses and the vegetative in neuroses, a wider range of the domain of the "pathological" in psychoneuroses and a narrower range in neuroses, and finally the fact that neurosis is so often located in just one organ.

Let us now pass to some psychoneuroses and neuroses. The many forms of hysterical syndromes present great difficulties in classification and in our attempt to set up a group unity. According to Kretschmer hysteria arises out of the difficulties in realizing the self-preservation and sexual instincts. Hysterical reactions, according to this author, are instinctive reactions with the selection of lower instinctive "old ways" (higher "new ways" are always mental in character). The actions of an hysteric are subordinated to impulses, and accompanied by hypobulia, dissolution of the will, and weakness and contradictoriness of purposes.

According to Janet,[8] hysteria is a form of mental depression characterized by the narrowing of the field of consciousness, a lowering of the
level of mental activities, susceptibility to suggestion, and dissociation
of personality. The most important characteristics – according to the
majority of authors – are vegetative stigmatization and infantilism. A
great difficulty with the points of view of the authors just cited is presented by the fact of the existence of many "hysterics" of intellectual
and moral prominence (religious leaders, diviners) who stand out with
respect to strength of decision and persistency (anorexia, asceticism).
Therefore the reduction of hysterical mechanisms to the lowering of
mental and volitional activities does not always agree with the facts. In
our opinion, the so-called "hysterics" are characterized, not by a lower
but by another kind of mental and volitive activities, not by a lower but
by different kind of moral ideals. Strong emotionalism and dissociation,
stressed by Janet as morbid characteristics (symptomatic of an arrest in
development), are, in our opinion, often positive properties. However,
in cases where there is a lack of sufficiently developed intellectual traits,
many hysterics do not arrive at secondary integration as do "hysteric"
geniuses and saints. Individuals strongly emotional and susceptible to
dissociation, with insufficient mental resources, remain at the level of
various forms of disintegration, which make adaptation difficult and
reflect uneven, often abortive, forms of syntony, with an external accentuation of the self-preservation or sexual instincts, although these
instincts are in most cases weakened. The results of studies confirming
the opinion that all emotional life has its neurological counterpart in
the extensions of the vegetative nervous system of the frontocortical
area which govern all psychophysical life will give, we think, the proper
foundation for an estimation of the role of emotionality and its positive
disintegration in the development of man.

Psychasthenia is, true to its name, characterized by psychic asthenia.
It should be noted at the start, that besides the psychasthenics under
treatment in clinics, sanatoria, and hospitals, there are many more psychasthenics who handle their difficulties by themselves. The asthenia
of the first group of people is more psychic, and the asthenia of the
second group is more physical (a weak organism). The latter group

---

[8]P. Janet. *The Major Symptoms of Hysteria*. New York: Macmillan, 1920.

yields writers, thinkers, and artists capable of doing at times very hard mental work. In general physical asthenics are creative, sensitive, and psychically rich. Who knows whether a certain involution of physical efficiency does not possess a subcortical character? Physical exhaustion is most probably connected with undue intracortical work, which compensates the work of subcortical centers. Therefore psychasthenics display undue inhibition, an inclination to hesitancy, reluctance to finish work started, interest in the realization of ideas, a lack of weakening of the function of reality, which is understood by them in dimensions other than normal. The feeling of the "blankness" and "otherness" of the internal and external world encountered in psychasthenics arises as a consequence of sensitivity to, as it were, his "own" subtle stimuli, and great reluctance and even a negative feeling toward alien stimuli flowing from the environment. This mechanism is partly explained by Pavlov's paradoxal and ultraparadoxal phases.

We will now comment on manic-depressive psychosis. Its inheritance points to the importance of those factors which are summed up in the experience of generations and to the explosion of cyclicity of maniacal or melancholic moods. These states are released often by psychic injuries. The melancholic image of inhibition, difficulty in action, timidity, suicidal thoughts is the picture of the disintegration of the inner milieu. In the conflicting attitude, therefore, the upper hand is gained by such inhibitory cortical factors as the analysis and criticism of one's own affectional attitudes, and the feelings of guilt and inferiority. The "laughing melancholies" are evidence of high tension in the conflict between depression, suicidal tendencies, and the disposing and directing center, which cause internal introspection and even the attitude of being an observer of one's own drama (the "subject-object" process). The developmental character of the melancholy phase is shown to some extent by the fact that these individuals frequently regain their health, after they satiate themselves with depressing matter, and by the partial participation of reshaping mental activities of the analytical type. The maniacal image consists of an increased feeling of one's own value, an accelerated flow of thought, motor and affectional excitation, and enhanced attention. Individuals in this state make decisions easily, easily carry them into effect, display a weakening of inhibition, and they may attain very good results in their work because of their increased

and indefatigable energy. Depending on the cultural level of a maniacal individual, he may be dominantly either quarrelsome, aggressive,
inclined to vexatiousness or syntony, to undue alterocentrism, to social
activeness, or have a tendency to help others and show empathy in relation to them. The capacity for differentiated syntony may lead to an
actor perfecting his performance, to increased creativity, or to a drive
to reform. In mixed states we come into contact with experiences of
unpleasant tension, with angry and depressive moods, and with manifestations of mixed feelings (pleasant and unpleasant). In manic-depressive
psychosis the material for reshaping is supplied by the changeability of
states (in maniacal states, depression; in depressive states, mania; and
in both states, the state of unrest).

Paranoia is often characterized by both an increased feeling of one's
own value and an accelerated flow of thoughts and psychomotor excitability. The basic difference between paranoia and the maniacal
phase of manic-depressive psychosis consists not so much in delusions
of one's own greatness or in persecution delusions as in their systematization. It is evidence of disintegration at a rather low level. This is an
attitude of a narrowed synthesis, which does not let the stimuli have
their say that would widen the sensations to allow a proper synthesis.
A paranoiac may be keenly attentive, may have great dynamism, may
make fortunate but primarily strong and violent decisions in his work,
but his structure is not developmentally integrated and does not subject itself to disintegration. He falls into external conflicts but not into
internal conflicts; he suffers delusions of persecution, yet he does not
display feelings of inferiority and guilt in the face of these delusions and
his intelligence is clearly at the service of his emotions and delusions.
A paranoiac is highly critical, but not self-critical, and he displays self-
feeling without the feeling of inferiority and humility. The paranoic
structure is related to psychopathy, as conceived by us; it is a structure
integrated at a low instinctive level, with intelligence at its service.

As for schizophrenia, the majority of psychiatrists recognize in its eti-
ology the basic role of psychogenesis. The psychogenetic point of view
is now clearly taken by newer movements – existential psychiatry and
the modified psychoanalytic method of so called "symbolic realization."
For a description of "schizophrenic worlds" one uses philosophical terms.
The schizophrenic ceases to be exclusively the classical pathological case

and becomes, in the first place, a man who suffers and feels as all other humans. The basic difference consists in the schizophrenic's constitutional difficulty in adapting himself to the world. It is, in the last analysis, a specific psychic constitution, consisting of excessive sensitivity (susceptibility to psyche injury) leading, in connection with it, to injuries and conflicts, frustrations, serious traumata, which, being often repeated, change the functioning of neurons, just as toxic factors or mechanical excitations do. According to Sechehaye, schizophrenics, when going through painful, profound experiences, guard themselves against contact with people in various ways, principally by way of external unconcern and negativity, and by way of impulsiveness and violence, evoked by the internal struggle between the need for contact and the dread of it; they guard themselves by passivity and the catatonic attitude, by running away from the environment, and especially from the doctor, and by absurd and grotesque behavior, if they have no other ways of covering themselves up. They avoid contact with the environment because of dread of emotivity, for fear of disturbing the psychotic equilibrium, of rousing one's own aggressiveness, of humiliation at the hands of other people, and in the internal injunction connected with the feelings of guilt and regret due to departure from the autistic attitude. This avoiding of contact may be overcome, according to this author, by convincing the patient that we wish to satisfy his essential needs. There are two ways of finding the patient's basic needs: an affectional approach to him during his "bright spells" and better periods of feeling, and the analysis of expressions. Here the external world should adapt itself to the patient, and since the world of symbols and magic is the only world that the patient may tolerate, one should organize this world for him in the least injurious way and permit its gradual reshaping into worlds more closely resembling reality. Schizophrenics are deeply traumatic people and therefore need more feeling and protection than other people.

In our opinion this "special constitution" in schizophrenia seems to possess two fundamental characteristics: (1) markedly increased psychic excitability and (2) a psychic immaturity, in the attitude taken toward the normal, and even more so in the improper reaction to the environment. These are, in essence, positive characteristics (high sensitivity, subtlety, and, not rarely, a considerable fund of capabilities), requiring, however, longer periods of development. In contradistinction to neuroses, we observe in schizophrenia a considerably lower resistance to external stimuli, higher fragility, greater infantilism, and a weaker instinctive structure.

It should be noted that light dissociative processes characterize, as a rule, hypersensitive individuals, and also individuals with a tendency for extended periods of development. Feelings of guilt, difficulties in contacts and in adaptability, an inclination to mysticism, mania, artificiality, and animism are observed in poets, painters, philosophers, and artists in general. Pursuit of an ideal, affirmation and negation of various values in oneself, suicidal thoughts and tendencies, the need for solitude, all these are traits of positively developing individuals. Schizophrenics are people possessing tendencies to accelerated development; they are hypersensitive, predisposed to disintegration. When the influence of the environment is abnormal, when instead of long periods, short periods of development are imposed, then, if we are dealing with a special constitution, the patient may not withstand the developmental tensions and fail into negation, with its pathological forms of dissolution. In the practice of criminal psychiatry one may often observe that in the course of observation the suspected schizophrenia transforms itself into reactive psychosis, with symptoms strongly similar to that of actual schizophrenia. This is evidence of the existence of tendencies toward adaptation to the conditions of life.

From the point of view, therefore, of the theory of positive disintegration we speak of mental disease on the basis of the exclusion from its description and mechanisms of those characteristics which are evidence of a marked participation of the process of positive disintegration (see chapter on positive disintegration) and on the basis of its final effect. We base our estimates of all the sets of "psychic disturbances" and diseases on ascertained, more or less distinct, signs of evolution or dissolution. The chief criterion for the estimation of a mental disease would therefore, be a lack or loss of the ability for positive psychic development, and, conversely, the existence of such ability would provide evidence of mental health.

Disintegration in Somatic Illnesses

Somatic disease causes disturbances in normal, everyday relations with the external world, as well as disturbances in the psychic milieu. It causes short or long, more or less global interruption in vital activities, disintegration of more or less integrated relations of one's own organism and psyche with its thus far existing world. Depending on the seriousness of the disease, it amounts to a characteristic intensification of the negative attitude to one's own state, to a feeling of some impediment, of some encumbrance, and of being imposed upon by something unexpected and unwanted. Many everyday matters lose their importance, the integrated conditions of life are shattered, there is a shift in the existing dominant in psychic life, and a compulsory process ensues "time must stop." Longer-lasting or chronic diseases (tuberculosis, tuberculous osteomyelitis, articular disease, serious chronic heart disease, and the like) require reshaping of the relations with the external world and changes become ever more "astereotypic." There results the feeling of impotency, excitement, depression, discord, concentration on the functioning of internal organs, on the difficulties of adapting oneself to life. This results in superfluous deliberation, prospection and retrospection, analyzing, and then, with the psychic energy accumulated by the summing up of particular inhibitions, in affectional outbursts.

Serious chronic disease, manifested in its dramatic stages when death approaches, and in the slow decomposition of tissues while one is still mentally efficient, undoubtedly constitutes a medium for the advent and development of the "subject-object" process in oneself. One's self-awareness ascertains that decay of the somatic side is taking place, while psychic functions are retained. In the same consciousness knowledge that disintegration of the "soma" is unavoidable produces a rejection of the body as an object of interest and integration concerns only the creation of a new, suprabiological whole.

Disintegration in Certain Spheres of Physiology and Psychophysiology

Cortical impulses strengthen or weaken the course of unconditional reflexes (Orbeli); that is, they loosen and disintegrate primary reactions, subordinating them to the activity of the cortex. The fundamental element of the new structure of disposition is the factor of inhibition, permitting one's adaptation to the new reality.

Sleep and the richness of dreams reflect processes which disintegrate the narrow actual attitude and actual adaptation (keeping the personality from "real" and "vital" experiences). These processes are accompanied by changes in the area of the vegetative nervous system. We deal here with the ascendancy of parasympathetic nervous system activity (a slowing down of heart action and breathing, a decreased body warmth, a contraction of pupils, convergence of eyeballs, and an assumption of a motionless position). On the other hand, excitation, lively interest in the external world, and contact with the environment cause excitation of the sympathetic nervous system, with quite contrary symptoms. These systems, acting antagonistically at lower nervous stages and in the area of particular organs, and synergistically at the highest cortical stages, reflect one and the same law of development, which, through disintegration at a lower level, prepares a man for integration at a higher level. Dystonia and amphotonia of the nervous system reveal themselves in a similar way in the psychic area, in the form of ambivalence and ambitendency (excitation and depression, sorrow and joy, inclination to solitude and to contact with the world), up to the synergy at a higher level (secondary integration).

As for the disturbances in the synergy of the endocrine glands characteristic of certain developmental periods, arduous situations in life, and conflicting experiences and neurotic states, these depend on, *inter alia*, the dynamic state of the cortex on its various levels, the relation of the cortex to the subcortex, the state of the centers of interests and the disposing and directing centers, and the capacity for psychic reshaping. An interesting fact is that the compulsory castration of a man results in deeper psychic and mental changes than voluntary castration. These facts and the phenomenon of anorexia nervosa point to the fundamental importance of psychic factors in the regulation of the activity of the endocrine glands. The activities of vegetative and endocrinological integration and disintegration (global, partial, periodic, and permanent) depend on many factors and the dispositional stage at which they take place (marrow, subcortex, cortex).

Of significance are operational experiments in lobotomy (prefrontal leucotomy) giving no positive results and even deteriorating the psychic state in cases where there is no interstage conflict or layer conflict (psychopathy, paranoia). On the other hand, they result in an improvement or remove the symptoms of depressions, obsessions, suicidal tendencies, changing the personality in the direction of extroversion, better adaptability to oneself and to the environment, but at the same time diminish the creative tendencies, the faculty of anticipation and of insight into oneself. A lobotomy operation changes a morbid disintegration, which is often developmental, into integration with a general hindrance of the psychic faculties.

The cerebral cortex also acts disintegratively on the subcortical centers. Typical cortices often display lower efficiency and even disturbances of psychomotor efficiency.

Chapter 3

Positive Disintegration

The Character of the Process

Our considerations so far have led to the isolation of so-called positive disintegration from the various kinds of disintegrations. The positivity of certain forms of disintegration is manifested by the fact that a child, a developing being, reveals in certain periods of his development many more disintegrative properties than a normally developing adult – traits of animism, magical thinking, an unwarranted flightiness of attention and difficulties in concentration, emotionalism, and capriciousness. In periods of intensive development, such as the period of contradictoriness and primarily the period of maturation, we come into contact with a particular intensification of disintegrative symptoms, which points to a close, positive correlation between susceptibility to development and certain forms of disintegration. The process of positive disintegration often manifests itself in the phenomenon of Rorschach's ambiequal types, in the period of contradictoriness and primarily in the period of maturation. Furthermore, we realize here the striking fact that these types, which, as Rorschach sees them, are the most harmonious, occur most frequently in periods characteristic of disintegrative processes.

With normal people we observe the symptoms of positive disintegration in moments of arduous experiences, or, less often, in moments of great joy, in moments of increased reflection, meditation, unrest, and dissatisfaction with oneself. The intensity of these symptoms is evidence that such individuals possess more or less marked resources for accelerated psychic development. With such persons we usually observe an above-average psychic sensitivity, and superior syntony – though not always displayed externally – and a greater subtlety of feelings.

On the other hand, enhanced psychic excitability is characterized by marked psychic frangibility, disharmony in the internal milieu of nervous individuals, and often by inadaptability to the social environment. The same phenomena are observed in a considerable number of neuroses and psychoneuroses, which are usually not treated, since individuals affected by them do not normally present themselves for treatment in a sanatorium or clinic.

Even in certain psychotic processes we may observe processes of positive disintegration, not only on the basis of the positive result of the final resolution of the psychosis, in the form of the shaping of a richer personality, revealing intellectual, moral, and social values higher than those before the disease, but also on the basis of an analysis of the clinical "picture," which, even at the stage of symptoms of dissolution, is characterized by such peculiarities as periodic tendencies to autopsychotherapy, manifestations of creativity, and the nuclei of secondary integration.

Positive disintegration is, therefore, a process, which, in our opinion, is the fundamental process in the development of an individual. In order to leave the lower developmental level and pass to a higher one, the individual must go through a greater or lesser disorganization of primitive structures and activities.

The normal disintegrative activities, which characterize certain developmental periods, such as the period of contradictoriness, maturation, and climacteric, enter as something basic to all phases of an individual's life, if he possesses dispositions for the development of a moral personality and for creative development, more or less universal in character.

The process of disintegration starts often with unilevel disintegration, which is characterized by weak participation of consciousness and volition, by a rather marked automaticity of these processes, by lack of evaluation – that is, by lack of "multilevelness" or "multilayerness." When it lasts longer such disintegration often passes into (positive) multilevel disintegration, in which fundamental changes take place in the organization and hierarchy of the psychic inner milieu.

What then would be the most important characteristics of positive disintegration? We shall limit ourselves to the description of only some of them.

The positive disintegration process is characterized in the first place by a predominance of its multilevel form over the unilevel form. Even if we deal with a marked predominance of symptoms of unilevel disintegration, still positiveness is manifested by the presence of self-awareness and coexisting symptoms of the creation of new values.

Positive properties of disintegration are manifested also by the predominance of global forms over narrowed forms – that is, with the disintegration process embracing the whole of personality. This process is also characterized by a lack of weakness, of automatisms, and stereotypes, and on the other hand, by the presence of plasticity and the capability for psychic reshaping.

The presence of retrospective and prospective tendencies and activities, with a simultaneous equilibrium of these dynamisms, would also be evidence that the process is positive. This attitude would be connected with abilities helpful in reaching a clear shaping of the personality ideal. The ability for consonance with the social environment would also be a determining factor as to the positiveness of the disintegration process.

In cases of nervousness, neuroses, and psychoneuroses, and sometimes also psychoses, positive disintegration would be reflected in the capacity for autopsychotherapy.

Another fundamental property of the positive disintegration process is the ability for a gradual realization of an ever higher level of personality. However, this usually can only be ascertained after long observation of a disintegrating individual.

The areas of the manifestation of positive disintegration given above and measures of ascertaining it nowhere near exhaust the whole complexity of its forms and areas.

The Major Dynamisms of Positive Disintegration

In the process of positive disintegration there come into play such experiences and dynamisms as anxiety over oneself, the feeling of shame and dissatisfaction with oneself, the feeling of guilt, the feeling of inferiority in relation to oneself, and the experiencing of the process of "subject-object" in oneself. These reshapings are connected with the advent and development of the so called "third factor," which consists in a conscious affirmation or negation of certain qualities in one's own inner milieu and of certain influences from the external environment. This process is connected with the upward moving disposing and directing center, and with an increasingly more clearly seen personality ideal and the dynamization of this ideal.

We will now briefly analyze these fundamental experiential sets and dynamisms, which are characteristic of positive disintegration.

Anxiety over Oneself and Dissatisfaction with Oneself

Anxiety over oneself differs essentially from anxiety about oneself. The latter reflects the irritability of the primitive self-preservation instinct, and the first reflects the experiencing of consciousness (with participation of moral dynamisms) connected with the exposure of the self-preservation instinct to primitive activity, or of other instincts of an already attained higher level of personality. Anxiety over oneself reflects an enhanced sensitivity of the feeling of one's responsibility for one's own development, as a result of coming to the conclusion that the participation of "reshaping" factors in concrete instinctive activities and affectional experiences is inadequate. Anxiety over oneself is, for emotional development, an element similar to that of astonishment in the area of intellectual activities. Both these dynamisms are creative, preparatory dynamisms, the first in intellectual development and the second in emotional development. Such anxiety indicates that something inappropriate is going on in the action of our psyche, in its reactions to stimuli of the external environment; all this inappropriateness is indicated, not from the side of low-level instinctive structures, but from the side of the disposing and directing center, which forms during the process of positive disintegration, and moves to the higher level. Anxiety is a sign of more or less marked fluidity and disorganization of the inner milieu, as a consequence of clashes between that which is primitive, instinctive, and integrated with that which is developmental, arbitrary, and still not stabilized. This is the first phase of the division into the "lower" and the "higher," that which is close to the instinctive level and that which is close to the personality ideal.

Dissatisfaction with oneself reflects an increasingly greater advancement in the process of positive multilevel disintegration, which is manifested, among other ways, in this feeling. It concerns the area of multilevel structures, of which some are subject, and others object, to the dissatisfaction, of which some "disappoint" the expectations of our disposing and directing center at a higher level and others "experience" this disappointment, of which some are "lower" and some "higher" in the inner milieu. Dissatisfaction with oneself is a frequent experience, based on affectional memory of many such "divisions" into subject and object in the inner environment. Dissatisfaction with oneself, therefore, is based to a great extent on the "subject-object" process in the inner milieu, of which we shall speak later.

Dissatisfaction with oneself reflects a loss of uniformity in behavior, a loss of the assurance which characterizes primitive instinctive action – it is a clear symptom of the process of positive multilevel disintegration. This reflects the advent and development of the process "I" and "not I" in the inner milieu, the process which participates in the upward movement of the disposing and directing center.

Feelings of Shame and Guilt

The feeling of shame reflects a marked stirring in the inner milieu of the sensitive, "unsteady" structure, on which the internal stimuli act, expressing dissatisfaction with their behavior as revealed to the external environment. This type of experience consists in realizing that one's behavior and action in relation to other people, and particularly in relation to those with whom one is closely affiliated, is inappropriate, and at the same time the character of these experiences usually entails a stronger "opinionative" than moral component.

Thus the experience of shame is concerned on the one side with whether our behavior and action does or does not offend moral principles, and on the other, and this to a higher degree, with the "face" of our action – that is, how it appears to a given environment.

In the content and form of the experience of shame we observe at times that we startle ourselves and others by the "awkwardness" and the "unexpectedness" of our behavior. We are dealing here with a content and form of experiencing other than that in the feeling of guilt and sin. This is primarily a reflection of an attitude which is sensitive to the judgment of the external world. Shame reflects, in a way, one's readiness to feel concerned about the harmony between one's own moral resources and their external manifestations. This is one of the first stages in the loosening and disintegration of the primitive instinctive structure in the process of multilevel disintegration, which is, however, not yet far advanced.

The conversion of experiences of shame into the vegetative nervous system is rather marked and reflects the predominance of sympathico-tonic reactions and sensitivity to the environment, manifested by such symptoms as flushing, a quickening of the pulse, and, psychically, by the need for hiding oneself.

The feeling of guilt reflects a considerably deeper engagement of one-self, with respect to oneself and to one's behavior, than does the feeling of disappointment with oneself. The experiential element is here much stronger, it more fully embraces the whole personality, binding itself more strongly with the affectional memory and with the retrospective attitude. In the feeling of guilt both dissatisfaction with oneself and, to a somewhat lesser extent, shame are strongly represented, but the feeling of evil or vice committed in relation to one's own development and to the human environment occupies the prime place. With the feeling of guilt there usually arises, simultaneously, the need for self-accusation, penalty, and expiation. The feeling of guilt is a poignant experience, and is connected with the experience of "fear and trembling." As we have shown, it has a considerably greater influence on the whole of personality than does simple dissatisfaction with oneself, or the feeling of shame. When this experience is accompanied by the process of consciousness, it reaches deeper into the subconsciousness than other experiences. On the one hand, it reaches with its roots into heredity and often into the phase of early-childhood injuries, and on the other, it is transposed into the feeling of responsibility for the immediate or more distant environments, or for the whole society.

As we have already mentioned, the feeling of guilt calls for penalty and expiation. At the same time, both the penalty and expiation become fundamental elements in the elimination or weakening of the feeling of guilt and in the preparation of the individual for a gradual passage to a higher level of development. The feeling of guilt is at the root of the process of multilevel disintegration, for it reflects a failure in meeting the demands placed on oneself, a failure in fulfilling the indication flowing from our disposing and directing center, which steers toward a realization of the personality ideal.

This feeling is, therefore, based on distinguishing between the higher and lower level of our structure, and at the same time the higher structure becomes responsible for the activities of the lower level. The feeling of guilt, as we have already pointed out, is an indispensable developmental element for every moral individual and is strongly manifested in persons capable of accelerated development. It forms an indispensable creative tension, which lies at the root of true self-educational work.

The Feeling of Inferiority in Relation to Oneself

In general there is no mention in literature about the feeling of inferiority in relation to oneself. Consideration is given to the feeling of inferiority as a reflection of a specific relation between the individual and the social environment. The essence of the problem of the feeling of inferiority in relation to the environment, the development of this feeling, its causes, its antisocial consequences, and sublimations, has been worked out by Alfred Adler.

According to Adler, a child, a weak and fragile being, has the feeling of inferiority in relation to adults, who are strong, "all-powerful," and "omniscient." The feeling of this weakness and inferiority is very early compensated by the child through the "will to power" attitude, through the feeling of fear, irritation, anger, and excessive subordination of himself.

Such facts as special feebleness, disability, ugliness help to form the feeling of inferiority. Uneven and unjust treatment of a child, doing wrong to him and humiliating him, the situation of orphancy or misery, all distinctly cooperate in the development of this feeling. On the other hand, the fact of being an only child, pampered by parents, develops in a child a feeling of his exceptional situation in life, with a consequent growth of his demands, which cause difficulties in adaptation to those environments which do not tolerate these extra demands. A passage from these pampering conditions to an environment such as a school may cause the advent and development of the feeling of inferiority.

According to Adler, the feeling of inferiority may be compensated by social attitudes – phenomena of positive compensations – or we may be dealing with antisocial attitudes – negative compensations. The first attitude is most widely observed in persons inclined to self-criticism on the one hand, and on the other bestowed with a strong developmental instinct and strong dynamisms, guiding them to an educational ideal. Many scholars agree with the following opinion of C. Macfie Campbell (1933): "None of the great human works appeared without a participation of this feeling."[1] It seems that general mental development, and also development of moral personality, would not be possible without participation of the feeling of inferiority, and particularly without this feeling in relation to oneself.

The theory of positive disintegration, which engaged in the explication of the dynamisms of the global development of man, through the forms of psychic loosening, and even the periodic disintegration of a structure, introduces the concept of the feeling of inferiority in relation to oneself; it is one of the signs of the process of disintegration.

It should be noted here that in order to understand this conception we must distinguish, in the individual's internal psychic milieu, such elements as "lower" impulsive dynamisms, which furnish the individual with proof of the feeling of inferiority in relation to himself, and higher dynamisms, which provide a basis for comparison with the first dynamisms and are a source of hierarchical estimation.

The development of the internal milieu is connected with the working of consciousness, which distinguishes in this environment the levels of value, that is, a scale of values and the awareness that one possesses developmental dynamisms. The feeling of inferiority in relation to oneself reflects on estimation and internal experience of the relation one has with one's own personality ideal, and the feeling of "infidelity" in relating to this ideal, arising from the tendency toward, and the fact of, the deterioration of higher values.

The ideal of personality, the feeling of its place in the individual's structure, is, therefore, very often a source of the feeling of inferiority in the developing personality, and particularly in the periods of the slackening of one's moral behavior and dissatisfaction with oneself, in the periods of "descendance" to a lower level in relation to already attained achievements. An individual moving on the road to development feels in a sense a betrayal of himself in contradicting a value which has

---

[1]C. M. Campbell. *Towards Mental Health: The Schizophrenic Problem.* Cambridge, Mass.: Harvard University Press, 1933.

already been acquired.

A developing individual cannot always remain at the "peak" of development. Tiredness, nervous exhaustion, some states of anxiety and fear often bring about the "descent" to a lower, more primitive, level of one's personality. However, an individual clearly moving along the road of development cannot remain for a long time at this level, and the fact of the former and repeated "stay" of his activities and internal experiences at a higher level, incites the states of dissatisfaction with himself and the feelings of guilt and inferiority in relation to his own personality ideal. Kierkegaardean "fear and trembling" accompany the states of affectional memory and are associated with a conviction that one's level has been lowered. The formation of the feeling of inferiority in relation to oneself cannot take place without this dynamism, of which we shall later speak.

What are the chief differences between the feeling of inferiority in relation to the external environment and the feeling of inferiority in relation to oneself? In the first place the fundamental difference is reflected in the very term *relation* to the environment and *relation* to oneself. The feeling of inferiority in relation to the external environment is a phenomenon of constant or transient characteristics with all people – with psychopaths, people with neuroses and psychoneuroses, and those with other mental disturbances. The feeling of inferiority in relation to oneself is manifested, as a rule, by individuals with the capacity for distinct, accelerated development, in neuroses, psychoneuroses, and sometimes in psychoses, but it is never observed in psychopathy and with persons offering no promise for the development of personality.

The feeling of inferiority in relation to other persons is usually connected with conflicts with these persons. The feeling of inferiority in relation to oneself, if it is not a pathological phenomenon, is a prophylactic factor in relation to external conflicts (an anti-conflict factor).

The feeling of inferiority in relation to oneself reflects a process of intensive moral and cultural development; on the other hand, the feeling of inferiority in relation to the external environment is a rather general and primitive phenomenon.

The feeling of inferiority in relation to the external environment does not associate itself with the loosening and disintegration of the internal environment, but is usually connected with the structure's integration at a low level.

As for the feeling of inferiority in relation to oneself and the process of self-education, it should be stressed that self-education is not at all possible without this feeling. In the process of self-education there must exist an awareness of one's own personality ideal, the feeling of the necessity of a closer approach to this ideal, through the assignment of the disposing and directing center to a higher level, through the activation of the third factor with its opposition to lower levels, both in the internal life and in external activity. Directing of the activity "upward" and "downward" and activation of the ideal are connected with an increasingly stronger self-awareness and with an affirmation of oneself, which leads to a very strong experiencing of the feeling of inferiority and to an increasingly more intensive activation in the reshaping of the inner milieu – that is, in the process of self-education. The feeling of distance between realizations, their shortcomings and breakdowns, and the level of the ideal, which is more and more recognizable, becomes a ground for creative tensions, directing one to the development of increasingly intensive self-educational activities.

Self-education presupposes experiencing of the dualistic attitude by an individual, the attitude of incessant divisions of oneself into subject and object, into that which lifts and educates and into that which is lifted and educated. This is the already mentioned "subject-object in oneself" process.

The great majority of creative individuals, prominent persons in moral, artistic, and even scientific worlds, have manifested the feeling of inferiority in relation to themselves in their developmental dynamisms. With such men as Michelangelo, Dostoevsky, Gandhi, St. Augustine, and many, many others, the feeling of inferiority was a fundamental dynamism. Furthermore, with the majority of prominent psychasthenics (Proust, Kafka, Zeromski), the feeling of inferiority constituted one of the basic dynamisms in their psychic life. Beers and Ferguson, who represent the American psychiatry and mental health movement, have themselves passed through mental diseases and have demonstrated the feeling of inferiority and of superiority in relation to themselves.

The above remarks clearly show that without the feeling of inferiority no process of positive disintegration can take place, that there is no possibility for the effective realization of the personality ideal, and that there is no possibility for attaining increasingly higher levels of this ideal.

Subject-Object in Oneself

Disclosure and observation of oneself passes from such primitive forms as seeing one's image in a mirror, to an intense and all-embracing examination of oneself, one's structure, tendencies and aspirations, one's internal life in general. Taking an interest in one's own "internal environment" and observing it sometimes becomes a permanent habit of internal self-observation. From this habit there is but a step to intervention in one's own psychic life – this is, however, a matter belonging to the problems of another order.

We call this taking of interest by an individual in his own psychic life, and the ability for an ever wider and deeper penetration of it, the dynamism of "subject-object in oneself," that is, in the psychic structure of one and the same person. The advent of this dynamism means that interest in the internal environment begins to prevail over interest in the external world. This dynamism is a key that permits the individual to open his own psyche for observation by himself. Thanks to this dynamism the subject "objectifies," as it were, its contents, grasping them almost as external phenomena, which permits a fuller, matter-of-fact, less subjective knowledge and treatment of them. The mechanisms of this dynamism, combined with the progressing development of a personality, become for the person an ever more subtle and ever more universal instrument in self-cognition, in discovering in oneself and becoming aware of the subliminal contents thus far unknown to oneself.

Progressive self-cognizance, realized by means of the "subject-object in oneself" dynamism, permits one to utilize this cognizance in a more purposeful, more effective, and accelerated shaping of personality in oneself and facilitates the work of other developmental dynamisms.

This dynamism should not be identified with the conception of introspection accepted in psychology. Psychological introspection is used by us, in the observation of our own psychological processes, exclusively to determine the form of their course, their correctness, associations, and so on. The significance and the tasks of the "subject-object in the psyche of one and the same individual" dynamisms are considerably further-reaching: with its help the individual knows himself in the sense of knowing the motives and aims of his own actions, his own moral, social, and cultural self. In other words, this dynamism serves the aims that are connected primarily with one's higher development, with the development of one's own personality, and not only those connected with cognition as such, or cognition for purposes of scientific research. The character and the very genesis of this dynamism, therefore, show that there are essential differences between it and the introspective method in psychology.

The advent of the "subject-object" dynamism is determined by the developmental instinct in its higher phase, in the phase of breaking away from the mediocre life cycle of a man. This dynamism is, therefore, a dynamism of the period of disintegration, which is an instrument, as it were, of this instinct. An individual developing toward personality is subject to positive disintegration which, by way of conflicts, contradictions, and collisions, leads to an internal loosening or even disintegration of the thus far more or less uniform structure of the individual. This disintegration causes the internal life of an individual, his inner psychic milieu, to develop and enrich itself and, at the same time, to lose its tenacity. This loss of tenacity, this disintegration of the internal structure, is reflected by just this "subject-object in oneself" dynamism, this division into a cognizing subject and the object of the cognizance, which lies at the root of self-knowledge in general.

The already emphasized internal difficulties, conflicts, and contradictions experienced by a man developing into a personality generate, among others, such dynamisms and processes as the already discussed anxiety over oneself and dissatisfaction with oneself, the feeling of guilt and the feeling of inferiority in relation to oneself. In just these processes is outlined, though in a vague way, the "subject-object in oneself" dynamism.

As the psychic development of an individual in the process of positive disintegration deepens, the dynamism in question begins to take shape and mature gradually and increasingly. However, besides such gradual nascency and maturation, it may manifest itself suddenly, unprepared, or rather prepared unconsciously, in the form of a synthetic act, succinctly expressed in French: *prise de conscience de soi-même.* It is an act of illumination, as it were, an act of a sudden understanding of the sense, causes, and purposes of one's own behavior. As a consequence of repeated acts of *prise de conscience de soi-même* arises the "subject-object" dynamism. It is, therefore, a permanent continuation of these acts and as a consequence of this continuation the division into subject and object becomes something stabilized, something enabling the individual to possess a permanent insight into himself, not by way of unforeseen, surprising flashes on the mind, but by conscious insight into himself.

The "Third Factor"

The direction, quality, and intensity of a man's development depends, not only on the influences of the environment and inherited or innate properties, but also on the "third factor." This dynamism approves or disapproves of the tendencies of the inner milieu and the reaction to the external environment, and cooperates in the shaping of an ever higher level of the developing personality. As a result of this dynamism the individual begins to realize what is essential, lasting, and advantageous for his development, and what is secondary and temporary or incidental in his own development and behavior and also in his reaction to the external environment; he tries to cooperate with those forces which favor the development of his personality, and to eliminate all that hinders this development.

The conception of the "third factor" is, therefore, a new and fundamental element in the chain of factors that decide the development of a man (besides heredity and environmental influences), and is a reflection of a new force, which determines a new direction of development than that followed thus far.

The chief periods in which the third factor comes forward are the periods of pubescence and mature age. During the period of maturation the attitude of affirmation and negation, which was vaguely present in childhood, becomes dynamic. This process is favored by enhanced affectional, psychomotor, imaginational, sensual, and mental excitability. In this connection the phenomenon of evaluation, as one of the fundamental characters of pubescence, becomes distinctly marked. A young man, experiencing a loosening in his own internal and external environments, observes both these environments more or less attentively and manifests the mental and emotional attitude of "subject-object in oneself." He then assumes a critical attitude toward himself and the environment, attempts to check his opinion with reality and to transpose his own moral experiences to other persons, and his observations of the external environment to his own experiences, and places on himself and on the environment clear-cut demands of a moral character. The awareness of ambivalence calls forth in him, by turns, the feelings of superiority and inferiority, and also the feeling of guilt, dissatisfaction with himself, and a more or less strong foresight into the unknown future or reflection into the experienced past. During the period of pubescence there arises and develops in young people the need for a realization of the meaning of life and often of the purpose of education and of the educational ideal. Posing these problems, philosophizing in this respect, with the participation of a strong experimental component, is a characteristic sign of the intensification of the developmental instinct and of the passing of a given individual to a higher level of development.

The third factor assumes, therefore, in the period of maturation, a more conscious form than in the period of childhood, made more dynamic through the uncertain attitude of affirmation and negation, in the service of the new disposing and directing center at a higher level, which emerges in a shadowy and unsteady form.

The period of maturation slowly passes into the period of psychic harmony within oneself, in which there ensues a greater internal equilibrium and greater rapport with the environment, and gradually there forms a structure, integrated at a level higher than the former. At this stage the need for being noted by people, the need for possession, and consequently the need for winning a position, for establishing a family and so on, become the disposing and directing center. As the integration of the psychic structure advances, the activity of the third factor weakens and even dies away.

This factor usually continues to exist, and even develops, however, with people showing enhanced psychic excitability and sometimes the weaker forms of neuroses and psychoneuroses. With such individuals the process of disintegration extends, the developmental and moral ideals continue to play a considerable role, there is manifested a psychic lability, and undue sensibility, a "freshness" of feeling, and that which one might call a continuance of certain infantile traits. The disposing and directing center is, furthermore, in a vacillating, uncertain, "ascending" and "descending" position. This psychic unbalance and certain tendencies to nonmorbid disintegration, a lack of quick approach to the determination of psychic structure, usually is evidence of the freshness and strength of the third factor, and of the capacity for the development of the personality along the lines of the realization of its ideal.

It must be said, therefore, that with adults the continuance and intensification of the third factor occurs parallel to the process of the extension in them of the period of maturation, with all its positive and some negative aspects. One may add, here, that this extension of the period of maturation is clearly connected with the developmental instinct, with greater creative abilities, with the tendencies to perfect oneself, with the advent and development of the tendencies that point to the most profound self-awareness, self-affirmation, and self-education.

The third factor, in its germinal state, has appeared already in unilevel disintegration, but its main domain is multilevel disintegration. The disintegrative activities are correlated with the activity of the third factor, which judges, denies, selects, and affirms certain external and internal values. It is, therefore, an internal and fundamental part of multilevel disintegration. It is an active conscience, as it were, of the nascent personality in its process of development, which judges what is more and what is less valuable in self-education, what is "higher" and what is "lower," and what is or is not in accord with the personality ideal, what points to internal development and perfection, and what leads to a diminution of internal value.

A human being at the level of a developing personality controls his instinctive life. This process consists in separating that which, in every instinct or group of instincts, may be considered distinctly human from that which is distinctly animalistic. With respect, for example, to the self-preservation instinct, this will consist in the separation and a negative estimation of that which is egocentric, in the sense of aspiring for the realization of one's own egoistic aims, regardless of the interests of, and wrong done to other people. In the sexual drive, what will be negated will be only its somatic, uncontrolled, nonindividualized level, possessing no tendencies to exclusive affectional bonds.

The role of the third factor in controlling sexual life by personality is not limited to the activities of selecting and denying. This factor, through its above-mentioned qualifying actions, actively assists the de-

velopment of higher drives, the creative drive and the drive for self-perfection.

During the period of the advent and development of the third factor,
the individual changes slowly, but fundamentally, his attitude toward
the social environment. He passes, increasingly more distinctly, from
the attitude of "dodging about," of apparent subordination of himself,
of a partially conscious but affirmed compulsion, to distinct and decided
attitudes toward the social group, attitudes of which one becomes conscious and which one affirms during a long process of development –
that is, in accordance with the developing personality. In his external
activity, therefore, different forms of inadaptability and conflicts may
occur. These conflicts and inadaptability reflect external disapproval
of the direction and level of the group's demands, which do not correlate with the personality ideal. In many cases such an individual is
estimated as being hardly sociable, not adapted, quaint, and difficult.
This estimation is unjust, because a man in the period of intensive action of the third factor manifests, besides the attitude of disapproval,
opposition, and negation – which concerns only the temporary "constellatory" conditions and the pressure calling for absolute subordination
of oneself to the group, or for adaptation to instinctive tendencies of a
lower level – syntony and cooperation with the needs of social life. Such
an individual is usually characterized by alterocentric introversion, or
as Rorschach puts it, by contact introversion.[2]

The beginning of self-education coincides in general with the beginning of the process of positive disintegration, and this is also the time
at which the third factor appears. At this time the activities of developmental autodetermination begin to oust the thus far existing het-
erodetermination, and the adaptational difficulties and developmental
disturbances are removed by means of autopsychotherapy. From this
moment the moral evaluation and attitude of a given individual toward
the environment begins anew, as it were, and the past is in a sense
isolated from the present and the future. This process is represented by
the following opinion, expressed by Brzozowski in *The Legend of Young
Poland*: "Man is not a continuation of evolution but a rupture in its

---

[2]H. Rorschach. *Psychodiagnostics: A Diagnostic Test Based on Perception.* Translated by P. Lemkau and B. Kronberg. New York: Grune & Stratton, 1951.

thread; when he [man] comes to being, all that preceded him becomes his enemy."[3]

A person in the primary phase of self-education is suspended, as it were, between the reflection of distinctly lower instinctive tendencies, which gradually lose their strength, and the reaction of personality dynamisms, such as the personality ideal. and the disposing and directing center at a higher level, which only gradually form and confirm themselves. This phase is the period of the Kierkegaardean "fear and trembling," in which the individual cannot find support in the thus far existing primitive instinctive dynamisms and the "normal" forces of the social environment, nor in the personality dynamisms. One might call this phase a period of moral or personality maturation.

The period of true and essential moral maturation is often a period of psychic vacuum, isolation, solitude, and misunderstanding. This is the period of the "night of the soul" in which the former meaning of life and the forms of bonds with this life lose their former value and attractive force. This period ends, however, in the elaboration of an ideal and in the advent of a new disposing and directing center, as well as in the appearance of negating forces, which close off the way back to the original level. In this way personality arises, and at the same time the primary phase of self-education comes to the end. The third factor, which is clearly heard, does not permit one's withdrawal from the road to the personality ideal.

The Disposing and Directing Center

We may call the disposing and directing center the dynamism which, taken most generally, decides on the kind and direction of a given individual's activities. At its roots would thus be found different driving forces, from lower to higher, unconscious and conscious, morbid and nonmorbid tendencies, which arise and develop in a tenacious or disintegrated structure. In a narrower sense, which interests us here, we denote by this term a tenacious dynamism, existing both at a lower as well as at a higher level of the individual's development and embracing either only a certain "psychic area" or the whole psyche of a given

[3]S. Brzozowski. *Legenda Mlodej Polski.* (*Legend of Young Poland.*) Lwów: Makl. Ksieg. Poskiej, B. Polonieckiego, 1910.

individual.

This center is a governing, volitional, and realizing factor, which takes up and executes decisions based on the direction determined by the fundamental instincts or on the developmental process which steers toward personality development. In the latter case the disposing and directing center strictly cooperates with other dynamisms of the developing personality.

With primarily integrated people the disposing and directing center usually embraces all functions. A newborn child may serve here as an example, in that with such a child all activities are subordinated to the fundamental biological instinct, or a psychopath with whom the disposing and directing center is represented by twisted primitive instincts.

In the phase of positive disintegration the disposing and directing centers are represented by various tendencies which, not rarely, contrast with each other and differ in intensity. This plurality of centers and variability of their domination results in ambivalences and ambitendencies, alternate feelings of inferiority and superiority, often aversion to oneself and maladjustment to the external world, criticism and self-criticism, prospection and retrospection.

If the disintegration is positive in character, there gradually comes to the fore a new and stronger disposing and directing center at a higher level than that of the former one.

The period of maturation presents particularly favorable circumstances for, and at the same time a good example of, disintegration. This period is for a young man, as E. Croner[4] expresses it, exactly what a revolution is for the body politic of a state. "It shakes the foundations of the body and soul; demolishes, with elemental force, all that which thus far was considered as orthodox; new thoughts and ideals violently push their way and point to new objectives; old values collapse; the childish dream is over; after a period of naiveté there comes an awakening to a 'conscious' life and to self-determination." This particular revolution ends with the birth of a new man. This, in our words, would be a man integrated anew, with a new and clearly dominating disposing and directing center.

---

[4]E. Croner. *Psychika Mlodziezy Zenskiej.* (*The Psychical Structure of Female Youth.*) Lwów: Ksiaznica Atlas, 1932.

The material of which is formed the disposing and directing center at a higher level marking the developing personality consists of, initially, only vaguely realized positive disintegrative contents and tendencies for transcending present moral standards and habits, the actual level of instincts, and actual environmental influences, moral judgments, and feelings.

The Personality Ideal

The aim pursued by an individual through positive disintegration is, generally speaking, the fullness of manhood. This aim is common to many men, but its realization runs in a different way with particular men. For every individual is a different, unique type with a specific psychic structure, with different inherited, innate, and acquired dispositions, with different, with respect to kind and degree, "weak" and "strong" sides, with different courses of developmental crises. With respect to autogenesis, therefore, every developing individual has to accomplish tasks which are peculiar only to him. If he perceives them more or less adequately for his needs and developmental possibilities, and experiences them correspondingly, they become his personality ideal.[5]

This ideal embraces, synthetizes in itself, as it were, all the most essential positive, more or less general, and also individual traits. It is usually embodied in reality in an idealized character (father, mother, tutor, prominent contemporary or historical personality), but it may also be only a conceptual "sum" of character and type traits, made more or less particular. In both cases the personality ideal plays the role of a model, or pattern, it is strongly experienced and made particular by the individual's needs to complement and modify his own properties. It is, therefore, an internal dynamism and a source of energy for the

---

[5]S. Szuman states: "The ideal seems ... to be, not only the highest intensity of some property or function, but also the harmonic conjunction of many positive traits, so that each of them complements others and thus raises the values of the whole to a maximum." (Quoted in J. Pieter and H. Werynski. *Psychologia Swiatopogladu Mlodziezy.* Warsaw: Ksiaznica Atlas, 1933.) F. Znaniecki characterized the personality ideal as "projected into the future an excellent complex of activities as an object of human aspirations." (*Wstep do Socjologii.* Warsaw: Ksiaznica Atlas, 1926.) In other words as "an idea of some new form of life, evoking and organizing these activities that are required for its realization."

development of all the actual and potential psychic qualities of the individual and for the inhibition of his primitive instinctive dynamisms.

The ideal of personality is thus a distant pattern, which we realize, and at the same time it is a reservoir of organizing active forces which is formed in the phase of multilevel positive disintegration and secondary integration. We ascertain the existence of the personality ideal, and its continuously increasing role in the formation of personality, by way of intuition and a simple judgment by every individual realizing self-education, but we cannot seize it other than in a "global" outline.

Two periods may be distinguished in the shaping of the personality ideal. In the first it has a completely distinct form and is a hierarchically changeable value, which depends on age, the developmental period, work upon oneself, cultural level, and on other factors. In the second period it becomes an ever more distinct and ever more stable structure. The line of demarcation between both periods is the "birth of personality." The forming personality not only becomes ever more clearly aware of and experiences the contents of his ideal, but he also takes part in its building and development. The dynamization of the personality ideal is also achieved through profound reflection upon this ideal in moments of detachment from everyday life activities and moments of internal calm.

Interdependence between the Main Dynamisms

After this very summary discussion of the main dynamisms which form themselves and are active in the internal environment, or psychic inner milieu, of an individual in positive disintegration, let us now give some thought to relations and dependencies between these dynamisms, in order that these dynamisms may be more precisely understood.

Let us reflect first on the so-called third factor, which is the estimating, active self-awareness, as it were, of the developing personality, an active qualifier of this personality's actions. This dynamism in order to be able to appraise, accept, correct, or reject certain values and tendencies which are manifested and collide in the inner milieu of the forming personality, must avail itself of the cognitive material supplied to it by the subject-object dynamism acting in this environment. In other words, only an individual who is aware of his own self, and fairly familiar with the motives and aims of his own behavior, is capable of correcting himself, of selective action which corresponds best to the actual phase and direction of his development.

On the other hand, the ability to qualify one's own examined and known tendencies and behavior must be based on some criteria – the individual must have foundations, criteria, or patterns to go by in his estimates. These kinds of foundations are supplied to the developing individual by another dynamism, namely his personality ideal. It is this idea, this force, this pattern, according to which the individual, using the third-factor dynamism, qualifies, accepts, or rejects certain contents, tendencies, and mechanisms of his actual internal environment.

Cognizing and qualifying the motives of his behavior, his tendencies, and actions does not necessarily mark the individual as developing in the direction of personality. This is because one may acquire the knowledge of oneself to a greater or smaller degree, know how to qualify one's actions and their motives, mentally see the ideal to which one would like to come closer, and ... not budge. This is the state of the individuals who stay, impotently, in permanent disintegration and who are unable to do more than make short-lived attempts to extricate themselves from it.

The factor which coordinates the results of the action of other dynamisms, which links them together, organizes them, and, based on them, realizes the personality ideal, is the dynamism, which we have called the disposing and directing center. The disposing and directing center at a higher level is, therefore, a central dynamism of the forming personality, other dynamisms being its tools (with the exception of the inspirational dynamism – the personality ideal).

Of course, the action of all more important dynamisms of the forming personality here discussed is conjugational, responsive, mutually penetrative, and complementary in character. All these factors together form, strictly speaking, an organic set, whose various characteristic functions have been in fact abstracted from the whole, in the form of particular dynamisms, in order to acquire an easy orientation, an easy approach to the complex inner milieu of the forming personality. This we should keep in mind when approaching a study of personality.

Aftereffects of Positive Disintegration

The Influence of Positive Disintegration on Particular Instincts

In this section we shall deal with the developmental dynamisms of particular instincts.

The Self-Preservation Instinct. This passes in its rudimentary development through phases of rather automatically acting dynamisms, namely through the phase of the biological behavior of an individual, through the phase of retaining certain structures and the weakening and waning of others (period of maturation), through the phase of preserving oneself by propagation, with consequent preservation of memory about oneself. Finally, through the self-preservation instinct, a man aims to preserve his psychic individuality or personality, in this or that form. The higher phases of the development of the self-preservation instinct are connected with a more or less conscious resignation, sacrifice, usually after the struggle between the "lower" and "higher" structures and with a tendency to divorce oneself from the former. At this point a negation drive, as it were, arises in the primitive dynamism and reflects itself in an attitude diametrically opposed to the instinct of life; this drive becomes especially marked during intensive development.

In these circumstances the instinct of life passes through an imaginary or real attenuation, or even suppression, of one structure to preserve another. We recall the saying that it is necessary to lose one's life in order to gain it. This is a truth expressed symbolically. The sacrificing of oneself in work for others, developing in oneself the faculty of looking at oneself as an object, leads to the transformation of one's egocentrism into alterocentric individualism, a factor of great importance in the structure of personality.

As an aftereffect of the development of the self-preservation instinct (through a weakening or destruction of its original lower structure) there arises an instinct of a higher form, namely the individuality instinct or, in other words, the personality instinct.

The Possessive Instinct. In its most primitive forms, the possessive instinct reveals itself in the tendency to possess those objects needed to satisfy the self-preservation instinct. In the lower, animal world, this instinct aims at obtaining food, shelter, warmth, and, so on. In the human world, the possessive instinct, distinctly coupled with the self-preservation instinct, reveals itself in the need to accumulate reserves, to obtain for oneself suitable lodging, clothing, and the like. In this world one may also observe a transformation toward seeking goods which are of less direct import for the preservation of life. The possessive instinct begins to express itself in the need for the possession of estates, or other material goods and servants or subordinated employees. The tendency to possess also reveals itself in the paternal and sexual instinct. At the higher developmental stages the possessive instinct reveals itself in the need for authority, superiority in this or that respect, in impressing and in "shining" due to the possession of various objects or virtues. The possession of something as one's own is closely related with the possession of certain properties of social value.

At yet a higher level we come into contact with the tendency to gain fame, renown, moral authority, to be remembered by posterity, and even with such sublimated needs as the possession of a hidden subtle moral and intellectual influence, without renown, without deriving any personal profit from it, and without recognition on the part of one's contemporaries (Lao-Tze).

In the process of the elevation of the possessive instinct, from a lower to a higher level, one may sometimes observe automatic, and also conscious, resignation from the need for lower forms of the possessive instinct in favor of higher forms. Lao-tse, Kierkegaard, Dawid, and other personalities distinctly passed through the process of the loosening and then the dissolution of tendencies to primitive possession, for the sake of winning higher forms. Resignation from more material goods, and the annihilation of needs connected with them is a sublimating process, without which no real spiritual development is possible.

The Fighting Instinct. Like all other instincts, the fighting instinct passes through many developmental phases. Among animals we deal principally with the physical fighting instinct. This form of instinct is encountered most often with the culturally primitive and "average man"; it is revealed in physical fighting, in wars, in forcing others to meet one's demands if one is stronger, and so on. However, in addition to fighting in all its stages, man uses such primitive means as strategy, cunning, blackmail, deceit, and the like. All these means of fighting lead to such aims as conquering the weaker, or the weakening of an equal in force, all this in order to win material success or a higher standard of living for an individual, social group, or nation.

The conflict of the material interests of individuals and groups in the world of organized communities leads in general to the use of more or less camouflaged threats, various systems of propaganda, and different forms of ideological fighting. At a considerably higher level there occurs a clash of opinions, convictions, and views. However, we usually also contact at this stage subjective arguments of the opponents, which are based on material and personal interests involving prestige. The fighting individuals or parties look for the weak points of their adversaries, direct the "spears" of their arguments, not to the essence of the matter, but to points which are in fact secondary, and whose importance for the problem is only apparent. Socratic irony used in such cases does not aim at bringing to light essential truth, but only such "truth" as a fighting individual or party wants to prove.

At a higher level of cultural development we find tendencies to fight objectively against an adversary; here one's own interest, ambitions, and prestige are put aside. This is fighting for ideas, by way of proving them objectively, fighting for social welfare and for unselfish truth. At the highest point of this level, one may find an attitude such as was assumed by President Lincoln who, in his debating, endeavored to represent the attitude of his adversary, considerably more clearly and better than the adversary himself could do it, and then, in an objective and a matter-of-fact way, assailed his erroneous view.

Fighting is most often conducted with a view to the realization of actual tasks. However, it also happens that the fighting parties have in view matters which extend in time far beyond their personal life, such as moral or ethical reforms or fundamental changes in a nation or state. In such cases the realization of aims is always given high priority over personal material, the mental or moral needs of a fighting individual.

In the transformation processes of the self-preservation instinct, as well as of the possessive and fighting instincts conjugated with it, there appears a mechanism for the disintegration of lower levels, for a loosening of the link between the higher disposing and directing center and the lower structure. A particular role is played here by such factors as a high sensibility to the internal and external environments of the individual, a weariness brought on by monotony, by the automatic and stereotypic character of instinctive activities, the capability of prospection, and a sensitivity to the "new." These factors cause a gradual loosening of affectional and mental attitudes to instinctive activities. One finds oneself in opposition to them and disintegrates, and as a result the individual with developing sensitivity to stimuli of the higher order and an increased indifference to stimuli of the lower order, begins to reshape himself and steer toward the new ideal.

Here, fundamental mechanisms of multilevel disintegration are active, just as in the case of every other instinct – the already often-mentioned feeling of dissatisfaction, the desire to free oneself from that which is now considered as worse and lower, the tendencies to prospection and to changes in one's own internal milieu.

Sexual Instinct. Disintegration of this instinct, with particular individuals, may be manifested by abstinence for a long time from all kinds of sexual intercourse, by some disturbances in the sexual drive, or by the weakness of this drive with infantile types. It appears that the infantilism of the disintegrative stage would signal the development of a human being in which the somatic sexual bond would lose its strength in favor of the "spiritualistic" form. On the other hand, and in our opinion, which differs from that of Von Monakow, the integration of individual sexual experiences (idealistic, Platonic experiences in relation to the object of affection, and a brutal venting of the sexual drive in relation to other persons) would not be a reflection of development. Sexual exclusiveness marks a certain "nonspecies orientation" of the sexual drive.

Control over the sexual instinct, emphasis on nonsexual bonds, and partial advancement in the process toward a nonspecies-oriented sexual instinct, with respect to the self-preservation instinct, reflects itself in the personality instinct.

Social Instinct. The development of the social instinct proceeds from the receptive phase, the phase of the need for contact in order to gain food, care, the tenderness a child needs, through the phase of various forms of living together in a family, the maternal and paternal phase, in which parents are the givers. As Von Monakow rightly states, the social instinct is linked in its advent and development with the self-preservation and sexual instincts. A proper development of the social instinct does not impair the development of an individual or his drive toward the perfection of his personality. A reasonable devotion to a child, on the part of a mother or father, connected with respect for him and the ideal of his development, should not interfere with the realization of one's own development. Even the greatest sacrifice and renunciation allows for the preservation of the right of one's own development.

While rising to increasingly higher levels, the social instinct passes from the phase of vital social interest, from the phase of sociability, of social adaptability, to the phase of consonance with the various different environments, without an accentuation of social needs. This consonance is always realized through disintegration. This is because one cannot learn to know, understand, and "feel" other people in their individual types, in the scale of their development, in the variety of their affectional attitudes, without the ability to observe one's own reactions, experiences, affectional states, tensions, and conflicts. Only the appraisal and structuring of one's own inner milieu and one's behavior, connected therewith, gives the necessary empirical measure of feeling and understanding of others. The love of one's neighbor is based on the ability to "equorize" the whole history of one's experiences, the whole vast area of introspection; it is the ability for consonance, with a continuously increasing participation of consciousness.

The Religious Instinct. This instinct reflects various phases of its development which accompany, as it were, levels of the self-preservation and social instincts. We have here egocentrism, religious egoism (quietism, narcissistic mysticism), an enhanced feeling of exclusiveness and jealousy in relation to the Deity, an attitude of conviction that one is granted by the Deity exclusive rights over a more or less wide area, the bigoted, external, ceremonious attitude, the attitude of losing oneself in the church, as an exterior organization, with a simultaneous absence of the need for contact with the transcendental world. We observe eventually the Kierkegaardean attitude of "fear and trembling," longing and hopelessness, awe and love, humility and supplication, growing objectivism and consonance, a losing of oneself in love and a "building" of good, with a simultaneous weakening of compassion for oneself and a continually animated compassion for others. We observe harmony between the feelings of our own dignity and smallness, between humility and pride, which is often connected with the phase of development of the intuitive, meditative, and contemplative faculties, which introduce the feeling of the reality of our bond with the transcendental world, of a psychic bond with the Absolute Being.

Consequently the development of the religious instinct must also overcome, in itself, the attitude of appearance, the external attitude, and reach the attitude of conflict, of dissociation, of the subject-object process in itself, of the feeling of inferiority in relation to oneself and others, of the feeling of guilt and sin, and of the feeling that one has to go a long way to reach one's ideal. In this way the road to secondary integration is paved.

Disintegration in the Development of Feelings

According to Mazurkiewicz,[6] the cerebral cortex stores, by way of its selective functions, only those sets of sensations which awaken interest solely because they are pleasant or unpleasant. The emotions participate in the development of function, from the initial protopathic forms, which are localized in the thalamus and hypothalamus, to the higher forms, which have their center in the cerebral cortex.

The observations of the affectional behavior of persons subjected to lobotomy are interesting. It has been confirmed that in instances of pains of a central type and of obsessions connected with them the operation does not abolish pain and does not even appease it, but destroys the emotional reactions to pain stimuli.

What light is cast by these two kinds of observations on the development of feelings? They seem to point primarily to the fact that the narrower the development of the animal hierarchy, the more enhanced are reactions to the pleasant and the unpleasant, to the painful and the pleasurable.

However, our observations also show that the level and quality of these reactions vary at different levels of culture. We may state, with certain reservations, that an individual with a highly developed personality is more sensitive to moral than to physical pain. We know that in torturing people this point of view was accepted, and two kinds of tortures were applied, depending on the cultural level of the tortured

---

[6]J. Mazurkiewicz. Dwoista funkcja ukadn nerwowege. (Dual function of the nervous system.) *Rocznik Psychiatryczny*, 1949.

individual. There occurs, so to speak, a diminution of physiological sensitivity, and rather a transference of sensitivity and of the affective attitude associated with it, from a union with physical pain to a union with moral pain. At a higher level of development the role of the volitional factor in the endurance of pain increases.

What phenomena occur in the disintegrative processes in the area of fundamental feelings? We know that the processes of unilevel and multilevel disintegration coincide and cannot be distinctly separated in their temporal development. In the case of the disintegration of feelings, these two fundamental mechanisms act almost simultaneously. As for integration in cases of hysteria, we deal with anesthetic areas; it is, therefore, easy to suggest the nonexistence of pain in cases where it is felt, and vice versa. There occurs here, therefore, a narrowing or widening of the pain-feeling area, and there is present a "changeability" – a transference of the pain-feeling area, depending on the suggestion.

There appears, furthermore, a phenomenon of another kind. Both in psychoneurotics and in many normal individuals we see in disintegrative phenomena an experiencing of fundamentally opposite feelings, of pleasantness and unpleasantness, as mixed feelings, experienced at the same time.

In the case of multilevel disintegration, which is usually a long-lasting process, we are concerned with the passage of the affectional tone from one level to another, with a temporary linking together of disposing and directing centers of various levels. This passage may take place in the attitudes of mixed feelings, in the nearly simultaneous experiencing of unpleasantness and satisfaction, connected with one's awareness of stronger or weaker association with a given area or level. The resistance of "lower" stages, their strength – despite certain links they have with the center of a higher level – may result in states of aversion to and abomination for oneself, and thus in the experiencing of the feeling of pleasure or moral satisfaction, because, for example, of one's material misery and difficult situation, or in states of ecstasy in physical suffering. Ascetism, self-abomination, or suicide often reflect a lack of equilibrium in multilevel development. This process is seized by Swoboda in his writing about Weininger: "One likes the resistances which one overcomes, and dislikes those to which one succumbs." Aversion, abomination, and negation in relation to one's "first self" and affirmation in relation to one's "second self" are the foundations for a variety of mixed emotions at various levels.[7]

Consequently, the concepts and experience of job satisfaction and happiness are, so to speak, multilevel, and they cannot be the only goals of life. They must be combined with other goals which taken together and considered on a high level of development can be expressed in personality and its ideal. In other words, satisfaction and happiness as goals of life must be viewed within the framework of a whole set of developmental goals, whose empirically accessible ideal is personality.

Therefore, the experiences of satisfaction of a multilevel nature must be the outcome of the process of disintegration. The necessity of accepting and experiencing the fact that often the factors which supply us with the most intensive feelings of satisfaction and joy become the source of most painful experiences transfers our expectations of "pure," ultimate joy to the sphere of ideals. In reality, we assume complex emotional experiences, which are partly pleasant and partly unpleasant as something real and decisive for our development.

Therefore, a confusion of the unpleasant with the pleasant, an easy transmutation of the unpleasant into the pleasant, and vice versa, a simultaneous experiencing of unpleasantness and pleasantness in various areas of one's own disintegrated structure, introduces confusion and affectional tension. The primitive feelings lose their sharpness, undergo disintegration, pass into other, higher, structures, and this leads to their losing their self-dependence and character. We are dealing here, not only with the isolation of various levels of pleasantness and unpleas-

---

[7]The way in which the process occurs, and it occurs even with small children, may be illustrated by the example of a 3-year-old girl, P—. The child, who was emotionally very strongly attached to her father, from time to time screamed, and her screaming was detested by her father. When castigated by her father, she responded by saying, "Mommy is good" – this was because her mother did not react in the same way to her screaming. However, she immediately added, "Daddy is good." This second remark was an obvious result of a confrontation of the deeply rooted feelings she had for her father with her temporarily hurt feelings and astonishment due to the unexpected severity of her father. A clear separation followed into two "selves," one that was loved by her father and the one whose screaming he detested. When she wanted to cry she covered her mouth with her hand or she attempted, in her imagination, to "send" her screams to the sea, so as not to violate her feelings toward her father.

antness, but also with a gradual arising of other "subliminated" feelings, connected with the advent of new guiding values.

These guiding factors are represented by a sense of the proper path of development, by one's ever greater participation in one's fate, by the feeling of a widening and deepening of one's consciousness and learning to know, increasingly more broadly, the internal and external reality. As we have already pointed out, this is the experiencing of a personal drama, of a tragedy, in which the elevated dominates the desperate, and the developmental dominates that which is being annihilated.

Disintegration in the Sphere of the Will

We come into contact with volition in all cases where two or more contradictory tendencies or acts come into collision. In the preparatory process of the act of volition imaginative acts, hesitations, resistances, the presentation of pros and cons of varying appeal, and finally the decision to perform a given act play a part. The acts of will are stronger, exertion when making the decision is greater as the contradictory tendencies become more equal in strength. The intelligence then organizes, on both sides, its pros and cons, which are the instruments of emotional sets, arranged in various combinations in the changing, fluctuating current of the increasing struggle between tendencies. Where there is no struggle between tendencies, there is no act of volition. The purely intellectual choice, with the lack of a strong experiential component, not associated with the struggle and exertion to overcome the resistances, does not in fact concern the act of volition.

What is the actually arising act of volition? Does it only reflect the actually arisen set of incompatible intentions, without the background of many conflicts and struggles? Are the struggling tendencies just the actual reflection of the history of one's experiences engraved upon the memory of the human species, and before all of the history of experiences in a man's life cycle? We think that, as a rule, the act of volition is a serial, chain operation, connected with many conflicts, many resistances, many overcomings on the road to phylogenetic and ontogenetic development, with affectional memory accompanying this operation. This act reflects the emotional attitude connected with the psychophysical type of a given individual.

The act of volition arises, therefore, in the area in which other various acts of volition preceded it. It implies the division, loosening, and disintegration of two or more tendencies, some of which, with their anticipations, weaken or even vanish, and others consolidate, grow, and gather strength. The volitional act is, thus, one of the advanced hierarchical acts in a given area and in a given sphere, possessing a rich history in a smaller or larger sector of a given individual's life cycle.

The volitional act may concern external acts and internal resistances; its essence, however, is internal conflict. As we have already pointed out, the exertion of will increases when contradictory tendencies are almost equal in strength. In the pursuit of personality this exertion of will is a result of a struggle between the lower and the higher dynamisms. The exertion of volition may also reflect a very high tension, even when the lower levels are indeed clearly controlled, but the endeavor for the ideal, the need for binding oneself to and for unification with the higher hierarchy of values, is so great that the tension does not abate; instead the individual is "consumed" by the need for a "full" and complete denial of the lower levels of his personality. This tendency, which at its highly developed level could be called an instinct of death, aims periodically at the destruction of the individual's biological life, or at evoking sufferings in him, which would intensify his aspiration for the union with higher values. Such a state is characteristic of individuals who aim at perfection (St. Teresa). Such a state is described by Kierkegaard in *Fear and Trembling*[8] as obligatory for the man who would be "fearless amidst terror, passions and temptations of life, who should move forward along the path of faith, which, though steep and dangerous, will lead him to the goal. The faith must be calm, humble ready for sacrifices, sufferings and hardships. Silence, fear and trembling – this is how it is reflected. However, to attain such faith one must go through the wild and ghastly forest full of thistles and thorns, in which one must struggle along, after the fashion of Dürer's knight, who is self-confident and trusting in God, whom he serves and whom he loves." Such a state was experienced by St. Paul when he said that he was no more acting himself but was an instrument of God.

---

[8]S. Kierkegaard. *Fear and Trembling and The Sickness Unto Death.* Translated by W. Lowrie. Garden City, N.J.: Doubleday, 1954.

On the road to personality, volition will identify itself with an increasingly higher-rising disposing and directing center, just as it identified itself, at a lower level, with the self-preservation, fighting, power, and other instincts. The volitional acts in everyday life are particular reflections of these great forces.

At the lower levels of human life volition is not free, but it forms a whole with a drive which manifests itself as such with greater or lesser intensity in a wider or narrower area of individual or group life. Nietzsche sees this problem as follows:

> One man is dominated by a need in the form of a passion, another by the habit of obedience, a third by his logical conscience, and a fourth by a whim and licentious satisfaction, because of his deflection from the way. All of them, however, will seek freedom of their volition just where each of them is most strongly tied: this is as if the silkworm sought the freedom of its volition in the spinning of silk. Where does it come from? Obviously from the fact that everyone of us considers himself most free just where his feeling of life is the greatest, that is, as has been said, in passion, or in duty, or in cognition, or in licentiousness.[9]

At a higher level of development it is not the volition, but the personality that is free. In the first case "volition" reflects an integrated instinct or instincts. When these instincts lose their integrality, they begin to demonstrate clearly the action of volition. In the second case it reflects a psyche integrated at a higher level. In the period of disintegration it manifests itself in distractions and collisions and it is a function of disintegrated dynamisms, which tend to secondary integration, to personality; volition then becomes a function which ever more identifies itself with the very personality, and thereby becomes increasingly less "free."

Disintegration in the Sphere of Intellectual Activities

Experiences, observations, and self-observations lead us to a better consonance with various points of view, with various attitudes, methods of

---

[9]F. Nietzsche. *Bd. Der Wanderer and sein Schatten.* (*Wanderer and His Shadow.*) Stuttgart: Kroner, 1921.

work, and with various types of mentality. We begin to develop, in ourselves, new receptivities, new attitudes, and new structures of mental activities. We begin to look retrospectively and prospectively on our own mental structure, on the history of our development, on our "black periods" which are not sensitive to certain mental stimuli, on our excessively developed unilateral structures. Through emotional tensions and analysis we begin to disintegrate solidified structures, and to make them sensitive multilaterally. We no more place confidence in our own judgments, in our own opinions. As Nietzsche puts it: "Never conceal from yourself and never pass over in silence in yourself that which could be thought against your thoughts. Swear it to yourself. This is the primal honesty in thinking. Every day you must struggle with yourself. Every victory and every rampart captured no longer concerns you, but the truth concerns you, and also all your setbacks no longer concern you."[10]

Then we have a certain hierarchy of needs which we expand, increase, analyze, disintegrate, subordinating anew one to the others, while we ever more surely seize the principal lines of our development. We may, therefore, say that our needs change with the development of personality. The needs connected with our aspirational and affectional structure, integrated at a low level, begin to weaken in favor of broader, more universal needs based on retrospection and prospection.

New needs reshape the former ones and dissolve their tenacity. The needs for biological preservation are transformed into self-preservation needs in the suprabiological sense; sexual needs succumb to the domination of factors of friendship and exclusive bond; and the social needs pass from the phase of distinguishing oneself and dominating in the social group into needs of adapting oneself to the group. The needs of societal life are transformed into a deep syntony with an ability to sacrifice oneself. It results in the development of the attitude of understanding and love.

In connection with these processes the intelligence ceases to be coupled with protopathic emotionality, with primitive subcortical emotionality but, after the dissolution of conjugations with the forms mentioned and after the phase of disintegration, it conjugates gradually with higher

---

[10]F. Nietzsche. *Morgenrothe.* (*The Morning Star.*) Stuttgart: Kroner, 1921.

forms of the aspirational and affectional structures and remains at their services. This is a transition from the phase of intelligence at the service of instincts to the phase of intelligence at the service of personality. This new conjugation of intelligence weakens the tendency to commit errors arising from reasoning corrupted by instincts, weakens the subjective attitude in judgments, removes egocentrism and the tendency to bring forth those arguments in polemics which, through an unskillful grouping, give the appearances of truth, throwing light only on part of it.

The intelligence, when acting in the service of personality, and when coupled with understanding and love, provides a basis for objectivity, broadens one's horizons of thought, increases the capacity for knowing people, and removes obscurity caused by the instincts. This approach is in conformity with the content of the chapter on love from the first letter of St. Paul to the Corinthians: "Love does not do anything indecent, does not look for its own gain, is not quick-tempered, does not think evil, does not enjoy seeing injustice but enjoys seeking truth." In contradistinction to the conjugations of intelligence with instincts, where, as a rule, one does not seek the objective right but one's "own" right, the new conjugation of intelligence consequently leads to objectivity in thinking.

This frequency of conjugations of the instinctive attitude with intelligence, or the personality attitude with intelligence, and the effects of the conjugations, are responsible for the opinion of many persons that logic is of little value, either in research or in practical matters – logic which is, as it were, cut off, abstracted from the multilevel aspirational and affectional factors.

On the basis of the above considerations we may say that, on the way from a primitive structure to the cultural personality, we pass, in the domain of thinking, through the manifestations of a loosening and disintegration of mental structures. We pass from thinking entirely united with the primitive forms of instinctive activities, to thinking fluctuating in gnostic forms, such as magic, to prelogical thinking, to logically conjugated thinking, and then to the loosening of each of these forms of thinking. As the higher structure develops, these loosened forms combine into a whole, into a higher synthesis, into a uniform creative resultant of particular forms of thinking at their highest level.

The very "operation of thinking," as defined by Dewey, "begins from a situation, which we may call a crossroad, from a vague position which presents a dilemma and shows different alternatives"[11] – that is, it represents certain processes of disintegration.

We have already pointed out that the activities of intelligence, the activities of thinking, are instrumental activities of the aspirational and affectional dynamisms. Disintegration of these dynamisms disintegrates also the thinking activities connected with them. Love, unselfishness, conscious ability to sacrifice oneself, contemplative ability, all purify, elevate, and broaden our thinking, introducing it to a more objective area; they widen our horizons of thinking, weaken the factor of the lower passions and cunning, which are associated with the basic instinctive dynamisms.

Should one infer from these considerations that an individual who does not pass through disintegration and is at the level of primitive integration cannot be a good mathematician, physicist, technician, and so forth? Such a statement would not be sufficiently justified. We may say that he will be a scholar with a narrow mind, that he will possess much more restricted creative possibilities than a person who has passed through the phase of disintegration, that his conceptions, his general assumptions will be insufficient, built too closely into his life's interests, without the possibility of separating them from their primitive structure, the level which will be reflected in the area of his scientific work.

Let us now stop to think for a moment about the problem of creative intelligence. Let us pose a question: what is creative, the intelligence or the whole personality of the creator? What is the process of development of creativity, at what moments is it evoked, and what are the conditions accompanying the advent of ideas? Of course, here we can make only some sketchy remarks. To the first question we can answer that, in general, the share of the creator's whole personality is proportional to the depth and extent of the creative processes. The advent of a creative idea, the development of a creative process, contains in itself several fundamental elements: an intensification of attention, the workings of thought within the scope of a given problem, the unrest

---

[11] J. Dewey. *How We Think*. Boston: D. C. Heath & Co., 1933.

that accompanies the advent of ideas and the lack of sufficient elements for their development, states of general mental and psychic disequilibrium, and states of irritation and enhanced excitability.[12] Very often after this period there ensues a phase, as it were, of separation from the spontaneity of the creative process; there comes a period of calming down, of "rest," not infrequently of meditation and contemplation, sometimes a period of turning one's back, for a certain time, on a given area of one's interests. The creative idea usually arises in the first period, and develops in the second, though this is not always the case. There are creators with such wide interest, with such creative passion, that the above-outlined process goes on almost permanently. In many other cases we come into contact with longer or shorter intervals, with "nights of the soul" in creativity, analogous to such intervals in general psychic development.[13] We often observe the ebb and tide of creativity. A great flow of creativity, changing direction, reach, subject, and level of the creativity, often follows after great defeats in life. Freshness of creativity, frequency and originality of ideas are often found in the essence of such psychic structures as certain types of infantile structure, with an enhanced excitability of various kinds, with fluctuating feelings of inferiority and superiority, excitement and depression, and internal conflicts (Slowacki). In any case, the process of disintegration seems to be at the root of great "inflorescences" of creativity, in which the struggle of contradictory sets of tendencies, an inadaptability to reality, a disposition to prospection and retrospection, dynamisms of one's ideal, all play a fundamental role, particularly when it comes to poetic, literary, plastic, and philosophical creativity, to say nothing of reformatory creativity in the realm of religion and education.

It appears that the developmentally positive process of disintegration entails rather essential changes in mental structure and operations, which are reflected in (1) a more creative character of mental operations; (2) a weakening of exclusively formal thinking, and a weakening of tendencies to coarctation; (3) a stronger conjunction of mental operations with the whole personality of an individual; and (4) the equilibrium of

---

[12]Dewey, *op. cit.*, p. 201.

[13]"When a mind is penetrated by the feeling of a real anxiety (no matter how this feeling is produced), such a mind livens up and becomes penetrating, for it is excited internally." Dewey, *op. cit.*, p. 201.

analytical and synthetic attitudes in thinking.

Disintegration in Religious Life

Within the process of religious perfection take place such disintegrative manifestations as asceticism, meditation, contemplation, religious syntony, and other metaphysical and religious experiences (the problem of good and evil, sin, conscience, free will, reward and punishment, and grace).

Asceticism in the present meaning of the term consists in the dampening of natural instincts with a view to attaining a higher goal, usually of a religious and moral character. We see in ascetic practices a clearly conscious introduction of multilevel disintegration into the process of self-perfection, through a multilevel struggle between soul and body, between instincts and higher aspirations. In the Eleusinian mysteries the role of ecstasy was to purify a man of lower elements. Greek asceticism was connected with philosophical inquiry and a conviction that two elements exist in man (changeable matter and unchangeable form). Christian asceticism was a resultant of Jewish practices in abstinence, Eastern and Greek influences, and chiefly, of the principles taught by Christ, supported by His life and death. Individuals practicing ascetism manifested, on one side, enormous sensitivity to the ideal and its realization, and on the other, very strong sensual experiences, and affectional and sensual excitability. The ability to reshape oneself through positive disintegration was characterized by developmental "compulsion," by the necessity of overpassing the thus far attained level, and by the insufficiency of "real" experiences. Ascetic exercises and struggles with the instincts made one capable of separating oneself from one's lower level.

Meditation and contemplation are forms often preparing an individual for secondary integration. Meditation makes one learn internal observation, to reflect on the essence of one's spirit, on the complexity of one's psychic structure, and on the transcendental world. Contemplation is a process of bringing oneself in touch with the transcendental values, of separating from the instinctive structure, of gathering psychic and moral strength for one's internal reshaping. In contemplation a process of knowing the higher reality, through love, sets in.

Through the growth in strength of various forms of sensitivity to the effects of one's own instinctive acts which injure others, through the overcoming of interest in oneself, and through the development of keenness in relation to the needs of others, an attitude of syntony which fundamentally differs from the attitude of adaptability is born and developed. Adaptability is an "as if" attitude, an attitude falsifying the resistances of instinctive structures in the name of "interest." Syntony is a capacity for coexistence and reflects an easy and liberal dispensing of love.

Finally, let us investigate the participation of developmental disintegration in the shaping of such metaphysical and religious concepts and attitudes as the concept of good and evil, sin, conscience, free will, reward and punishment, and grace.

In the concept of good and evil we distinguish that which is actually good or evil, temporarily, from that which is apparently evil or good at a higher level. Denial of actual "goods" and "evils" leads to confusion in the protopathic feelings of pleasures and unpleasantness. Under these circumstances one is convinced, not that this is good because it is pleasant, but that what is evolutional and what one approves in his structure is good. Evil is that which is involutional, what we do not want in us, though it is pleasant.

The appearance of the feeling that one is committing a sin ("sin phase") foreshadows the turning point in the moral development of man. This is a period during which one passes from a full instinctive integration to a gradual multilevel disintegration (feeling of guilt, shame, responsibility). Hesitations, decisions to retire, and inhibition of pressure on the part of instincts develop one's self-awareness and are accompanied by the feeling of internal collision, by the feeling that one descends to a level lower than that which one thinks most proper for himself – that is, with the experiencing of sin. We may say that at the level of primitive instinctive integration there is no sin, but only offenses and evil. At the level of positive disintegration we experience the feeling of sin and misdemeanor. On the other hand, at the level of secondary integration there is no evil or misdemeanor, but a strong feeling of sin.

Conscience reflects the disintegration of "pro" and "con" tendencies. This is Socrates's daimonion, considerably modified by Freud's censure, reflecting the conflict between "I" and "not I," between "more I" and "less I"; this is the voice of appreciation of what is evil and what is good, what is sin and what is not sin, and what is evolutional and what is involutional. This is a developing dynamism of negation, confirmation, and anticipation of development.

In the psychophysiological structure of man, the problem of "free will" arises only at the level of disintegrative, introspective activities. One can hardly speak of free will in almost automatic instinctive attitudes. In man's cycle of development we may speak rather of the process of "growing richer" in freedom. The development of man proceeds from biological determination to psychological indeterminacy (the phase of developmental disintegration) and then to secondary moral "determination" (the secondary phase). We may, therefore, say that in the middle phase we have an unsteady will, and in both extreme phases free will experientially does not exist.

As the personality develops, punishment and reward become increasingly more introverted, internal, and become ever more independent of external sanctions. More and more often, punishment takes the form of "pangs of conscience," a coupling of volition with low aspirations, a feeling of going away from the ideal. On the contrary, reward takes the form of the feeling of leaving the instinctive couplings, of an ever better anticipation of the effects of one's action, and ever stronger unity with the ideal.

In the drama of development, in the phase of disintegration, in the phase of struggle and internal conflicts, in descents and ascents, in negations and confirmations, the glimmer of calm, of harmony, of a union with the higher disposing and directing center, are described as the action of grace. This may reveal itself in a sudden understanding of a certain truth by way of illumination or intuitive insight, by an impulse to such a deed, behavior, or saying as would not be effected when one exerts consciously his intellect or volition, or retrospective action when the coincidence of events actually not understood, difficult, or painful, is positively estimated from the perspective of time.

Secondary Integration

The Concept of Integration

As we know from previous chapters the term *integration* denotes an integrated structure and activities more or less well organized and subordinated to the disposing and directing center.

We may be dealing with global integrations, embracing the whole psychic structure of an individual, or with partial integrations, concerning structures and activities in a narrower area, embracing a certain sphere of instinctive dynamisms. In the psychic structure we may have one or more integrating sets performing integrative activities in a given man. Such partial integrations, within a sphere of a given set of qualities and dynamisms, usually points to a simultaneous disintegration of a wider area, sometimes embracing almost the whole structure of a given individual.

From the temporal point of view we may come into contact with integrating stabilization, global or partial, or with periodic integration, which, after some time, undergoes anew a loosening or dissolution. This form of integration takes place, in most cases, with the fundamental, wider process of disintegration, embracing usually the structural and experiential area in which take place prospective projections, partial and global reshaping actions of the personality ideal, longer or shorter "pauses" of the disposing and directing center in a higher or lower area, or a temporary return to the level of primary integration, during which the organization or shaping of the attained phase takes place. When the "pauses" at the primitive level are too long, there occurs a strong affectional shock, which compensates for this "stopping" by the feeling of guilt, sin, dissatisfaction with oneself, shame. Such temporary integration is, therefore, unsteady and usually reflects a more or less short-lived process in the wider area of the positive disintegration process.

Pathological integration concerns structures in which the disposing and directing center is formed by a strong and usually narrow set of instincts, the action of which makes an individual "deaf" and "blind" to other impulses, other forms of reaction, and to dynamisms other than the narrow and usually strong disposing and directing center just mentioned. Such integrations may be exemplified, in the first place, by psychopathic integration, which represents an integrated aspirational and affectional structure, within which a given individual does not possess sufficient impulses for inhibiting his own strong instinctive dynamisms, and, secondly, by integration of paranoidal or similar dynamisms, in which the disposing and directing center is formed a by a set of delusions of superiority and persecution, with a strongly enhanced feeling of one's own value, which does not permit one to control his own behavior because of nonadmittance of the controlling influence of the external environment.

Secondary Integration and Its Types

Let us consider so-called secondary integration. Such integration, in its fundamental form, is a new, tenacious system of structures and activities, which arises after a long or short, more or less global loosening or disintegration of a former structure in a given individual.

Secondary integration as a recurrence to primary integration in perfected forms

As we have already repeatedly mentioned, individuals with a narrow scope of interests, with a narrow and a rather simple sensitivity, individuals with "narrow horizons" in thinking and in aspirational and affectional activities may undergo disintegrative processes of a rather special character. An individual of a similar type may realize a clearly laid out line of life in a consequent, continuous, and strong way; he may advance in the direction of the attainment of this or that hierarchy of aims, such as attaining a position, a professional, social, material, or personal rank, which would give him satisfaction, would enhance his self-esteem and would satisfy the tension of the fundamental instinctive needs. In view of weak plasticity or its total absence, in view of the weakness or absence of sublimating nuclei and mechanisms, in view of the absence of sufficient capabilities for internal reshapings, serious injuries, disappointments, a loss of fundamental possibilities of development in a fairly clearly determined direction may bring about a breakdown of a given individual's line of life, a breakdown in the possibilities of realizing his aims. There may then arise a serious reactive state which sometimes leads to suicide or to mental disease (due to a lack of other psychic possibilities for getting out of the situation).

In rare cases, an individual of the type just mentioned can experience and reflect upon the developed situation and, after much effort, he may effect certain, usually not too far-reaching modifications of his own line of life, as, for example, a completion of studies, a move to a profession closely resembling the one in which he was engaged, a change of environment, and so forth. These will be, as we have said, rather superficial modifications, or reshapings which in fact will not change the fundamental form of his line of life. We are dealing here with a process of secondary integration in more or less perfected forms, but without a substantial reshaping of the fundamental instinctive and intellectual structure or of the main directions and aims of activity. This is to a large extent an apparent secondary integration, and, strictly speaking, a recurrence to primary integration with not very essential modifications.

Secondary integration in the form of a new, but not a higher hierarchy of aims

We come into contact with this type of secondary integration in a great majority of cases of psychophysical reshapings, connected with developmental periods, and primarily with the maturation and climacteric periods.

A considerable majority of changes in the period of maturation consist of psychophysical changes in which a fundamental component, a "new thing" in the psychic life, becomes important, namely the sexual instinct. These new forces reorganize the whole psyche of an individual and form new disposing and directing centers. They organize new needs, a new hierarchy of aims, new sensitivities. However, in the majority of cases, the psychic richness, after the maturation period, decreases considerably as compared with the richness of that period. The nuclear inclinations to self-criticism, to dissatisfaction with oneself, very often vanish, and the sensitivity to values and needs of other people weakens. It results in a gradual stiffening of psychic structures and dynamisms around the new disposing and directing centers. The individual engaged in social and professional life finds his place, so to speak, brings into play "ripe" forms of the self-preservation instinct, of the fighting and aggression instincts, and similar ones, and realizes them, more or less strongly, in participation with the newly arisen and developing driving forces. With respect to moral value, value of ideals, internal refashioning, and the extent of sensitivity in relation to the external and internal environments, there are, in fact, no essential changes. The new instincts which arise and act are really new, but their level, their capacity for reshaping, and their richness does not differ greatly from the former genotypic driving forces.

The changes of dominants in the climacteric period has a somewhat different character. This is usually an unpleasant period of adaptation to new demands made on a man by society and family. A gradually increasing handicapping of the strength of professional, social, and intellectual capacities, a weakening of the sexual instinct, are often compensated for by an increase in tutelary tendencies. The self-preservation instinct adopts, in fact, the attitude of *ekklisis*, of retreat, of subordination, and of soliciting favors from stronger people. Components of the weakening of the psychophysical forces, in the form of regression to the period lived through, arise or are accentuated; rumination appears, new self-indulgencies arise or gain strength, and a stereotyped pattern reveals itself. One's vigor weakens, and the awareness of the necessity of one's retreat from dominating positions may bring about a psychic and psychophysical breakdown which causes or deepens the inclination to general sickness. Psychic disturbances are often the result, and sometimes, though not as frequently as in the maturation period, this process may result in suicide.

A frequently observed solution to the difficulties under such circumstances is secondary integration, effected to some extent in the form of usually primitive compensations, virtually pressed upon one, necessarily new, but not higher in the hierarchy of aims. Also a frequently observed solution is psychophysiological retreating and withdrawing, with or without the participation of morbid disintegration.

The way out of the situation that is least often observed is secondary integration following a full, conscious reshaping of one's aspirational and affectional structure, of one's thus far existing hierarchy of aims, and of one's attitude toward the environment. The latter form of solving the difficulties is, however, not brought about simply by a reaction to changes, which are characteristic of the climacteric period, but is based on distinct developmental nuclei, distinct personality nuclei, which existed and made themselves dynamic before that period, and for which the climacteric period comprised only one of the determinants.

Secondary integration in the form of a new structure with a new hierarchy of values

This kind of secondary integration belongs to processes which are usually the effects of a more or less strong, or of a more or less long-lasting, all-embracing multilevel disintegration. We have repeatedly shown that this integration consists in fundamental changes in one's own internal milieu, in one's own attitude toward the environment, and in the working of one's consciousness. This form of secondary integration is based, on the one hand, on the attainment of independence by the psyche, which oscillates around a clearly realized and dynamic personality ideal, and on the other hand, on experiential conquests obtained in the process of multilevel disintegration.

In factual changes and in the experiential processes accompanying them, one level of reality is distinctly disapproved, denied, and abandoned, while the other becomes strong, essential, and cardinal. The "new" arises partly by way of distinguishing in the "old" that which is essential, permanent, and valuable from that which is apparent, impermanent, and possessing no value. Eventually, that which is of little value is gradually repudiated, and that which is new and valuable is gradually brought from the background to the foreground.

In its global form, the process of secondary integration occurs rather rarely. It takes place with persons who are "prepared" for it, universally sensitive, and who possess a distinct developmental readiness. This process is often shaped by poignant experiences, suffering, and failures in life. It is shaped from the personality nuclei, by way of the realization of a program of internal perfection set by oneself which is continually made dynamic by one's feeling of the multilevel character of reality, and by the feeling of reality of a higher dimension. This process is most often observed with outstanding persons, the moral leaders of societies.

The Beginnings of the Process of Full Secondary Integration

Reshaping of the unordered disintegrative process into an ordered and ever more consciously controlled process

The development of a man proceeds from instincts in their primitive forms to the globally conceived instinct of development, through a more or less partial, more or less strong disintegration of the preceding structural form. Unpleasant experiences which one has while realizing primitive instinctive needs cause a loosening of this primitive structure, the advent of inhibition, fear, reflection, deliberation; of course, this is so when the nuclei of development in the direction of secondary integration also exist. The gnostic structure gradually liberates itself from the primary whole; the feelings often diverge from the instincts; there arise and develop new instincts, new dynamisms, superstructures of the former, opposing their mother dynamisms.

New experiences are accompanied by the attitude of caution by fully examining new situations to prevent reacting on a lower level as one might have in a similar past experience. Other, usually disagreeable experiences felt on one's way to the realization of the primitive instinct enhance this state and lead to a kind of "emergency corps" being brought into play, in the service of new experiences; on the other hand, the experiences cause the advent and development of a prospective attitude, an attitude that anticipates difficulties, an attitude of considering the situation, and of checking under what circumstances one could realize his tendencies at a later time, without now going through unpleasant experiences. But, one's realization that there are unpleasant things which cannot be omitted, that experiencing them is necessary for the realization of one's aims, reflects the appearance of the factor of awareness in the process of disintegration. This conscious factor causes, therefore, the creation of a certain hierarchy in the process of those experiences which occur in the realization of instinctive needs. It also leads an instinct to a further disintegration through a strengthening of the gnostic factor and through the introduction of an ambivalent factor into the scope of affectional reactions – that is, through the introduction of complications into the structure and dynamisms of feelings (namely, the factor of mixed feelings). Important here is the participation of increasingly more distinct dynamisms of the personality ideal, which accentuates the developmental interest of an individual to the detriment of his actual and usually narrow aims. The person in times of unanticipated difficulty or stress will utilize dynamisms such as self-sufficiency, introspection, memory of similar difficulties that were surmounted, and the like in order to handle new threatening developments.

The factors of unrest, fighting, and conflict are no longer regarded as negative, but are accepted in many cases as positive; often they are even deepened in order to beset and reject more fully the primitive structure. The feelings of guilt, sin, inferiority are often deepened; one does not look for the causes of feelings of inferiority and injury in others, but primarily in oneself. In relation to suffering one does not adopt an exclusively negative attitude, but begins to accept it as something that has meaning, as essential for cultural development, and as a necessary element of one's psychic enrichment. There arises a conviction that it is better to have had difficult biosocial conditions than to resign, by way of improper compromise, from moral and world-outlook values. The venting of one's instincts in the form of affectional outbursts, or the strong, conscious stifling of these instincts, is now considered permissible and necessary. The feeling of void and "otherness" is not considered simply a symptom of a sickness, but each set of symptoms is differentiated by virtue of its meaning, causes, and aims, and one comes to the conclusion that the set is often positive.

In states of depression a man does not always aim at removing the conditions that brought it about, but at a deeper association with them (in contrast to the stereotyped advice that one should change his conditions of living immediately after the death of a close relative). In relation to phantasy, dream, exorbitant prospections, there is a tendency, not to diminish their strength and scope, but to mentally elaborate and deepen them. In relation to dreams during sleep one does not come to a belief that they reflect suppressed wishes or are manifestations of an archaic structure, but one asks the question whether they are not a reflection of a widened consciousness, beyond the actual sphere, and of the moral reshapings of personality. This is an attitude of frequent seizure by the consciousness of the developmental inner life, which overruns the framework of actual reality, a reality consisting of a narrow system of stimuli and receptors, and of the framework of biological causality.

The appearance of the integrating factor and conditions for its consolidation

The phase of the entry of a conscious factor into the process of disintegration characterized above is not limited to the strengthening of disintegrative processes taking place thus far by the conscious work of an individual. Simultaneously, there arises and develops an integration process, which might be called the process of secondary integration, and this because it is integrative and not reparative; its work is not restitutory, but one which reshapes and integrates one at a higher level. This integrating factor is represented by the developmental instinct which, in its fundamental reshaping positions, manifests the strength of an instinct, in the sense of a force that increasingly overcomes the personality. We have already pointed out that the primitive instincts, when possessing a proper disposition, and after the periods of disintegration, reshape into higher instincts, or superinstincts; the reshaping, of course, takes place through the primitive instincts' being complicated by the impact of gnostic, affectional factors, self-awareness, and the self-affirmed and self-educating unity of fundamental psychic properties – that is, by the impact of personality.

In the opinion of Mazurkiewicz[14] the factors that perform this work of reshaping a man, leading him from the primitive instincts to higher levels of development, are the feelings that lead to the shaping of character. As Mazurkiewicz puts it: "The longest developmental stage (lasting about 2 decades) of the 'upward' wandering of the cortical processes of a man is this last stage of the cortical engraphia of the individual in the process of shaping his character. The exceptionally long duration of the process is understood when we consider the hard work which must be done at this stage and which consists in a loosening of those immensely strong ties found in the instinctive subcortical mechanisms."

This loosening and breaking of strong instinctive ties is, of course, considerably stronger, more thorough, and firm with persons developing their character, and later their personality, through disintegration.

In what does the process of the secondary integration of tendencies which are in disintegration consist? This secondary integration consists

---

[14]J. Mazurkiewicz. Zarys fizjologiczny terorii uczuc. (Physiological outline of the theory of feelings.) *Rocznik Psychiatryczny*, 1927.

of a reshaping, the primitive instincts being elevated to a higher hierarchical level through the multidimensional process of disintegration, through the self-preservation instinct receptors' being made sensitive to supraspecies stimuli, through the complication of the affectional structures and activities (mixed feelings), and through the participation and extension of the cognitive elements in inhibitory actions.

The nuclei of secondary integration may have already been manifested during the entire process of disintegration and may have taken part in it by a preparation of the future form, integrated at a higher level. These nuclei are the feeling of dissatisfaction, discouragement, of protest in connection with external and internal conditions, which comes as a "surprise" to a given individual in his mental work and affectional experiences. On the other hand, these nuclei are formed by the need for and the feeling of something "new" which comes from the higher hierarchy of values and which becomes a part of the gradually created personality ideal, and is anticipated and seized by the individual. These nuclear structures and states create or enhance the sensitivity of a man to his external and internal environments, cause changes in the structure of the primitive instincts and slowly accentuate their higher levels. The attitude of negation arises in relation to the lower levels of the external and internal environments; frequent selective acts appear and the attitude of the confirmation of values forming new tenacious structures arises. States of high tension in life and development crises which take place in the process mentioned usually cause a strong need for removing oneself from this situation by the remolding of one's structure.

With the intensification of secondary integration, the inner psychic tensions, the process of the "ascent" and "descent" of the disposing and directing center in one's own inner milieu, the conflicts, all weaken, but there develops in one, on the other hand, an alertness to dangers based on a strong engraphia, a strong affective memory, connected with dramatic moments in the history of the individual's development or experiences.

An example of secondary integration in the full meaning of this term is the psychic integrative process in the developmental drama of Wladislaw Dawid, an outstanding Polish psychologist, who, after a personal tragedy, after a period of disintegrative confusion, developed in himself a new structure with a new disposing and directing center regrouping his principal interests, his methods of work, his world outlook, in what he himself and his closest friends estimated to be a reflection of a higher form of development. The process entailed the mobilization of considerably greater moral forces, a strengthened and developed alterocentrism, and it tied his personal life and his new world outlook into an inseparable whole.

Michelangelo, genius that he was, is an example of an unfinished process of disintegration and secondary integration which reflect the process of negation in relation to actual reality, and the gradual formation of the attitude of affirmation in relation to the arising reality of a higher dimension, with participation of the negation and death instincts, as well as the self-affirmation and perfection instincts.

What then, in conclusion, is the process of secondary integration? As we have already shown, the nuclei of secondary integration transform themselves into a fully developed new structure, into a new function of reality, drawing its strength from an increasingly more distinct personality ideal and from a realized personality. In the further phase of the disintegration process, an increasingly more conscious factor takes part and orders the thus far automatic and chaotic course of the phenomena. Ambivalences, struggles, conflicts, states of depression and elevation, feelings of inferiority and superiority expand and deepen one's psyche, remold the nuclei of a half-conscious personality, which is still dependent upon the "owner" of the processes taking place in it, upon the directing force. A sublimated affectional structure, superinstincts, a growing self-awareness bind the precedent attitude with the succeeding one through the actual attitude, form a new structure with a new hierarchy of aims, and allow a new multidimensional method of enriching the personality – self-education.

The process of secondary integration, therefore, leads the psyche to the level of a secondary, superinstinctive structure, the feelings, intelligence, and volition of which act in unison, with a large degree of instinct like infallibility but at a considerably higher hierarchical level.

Chapter 4

Methods of Shaping Personality

The Meaning of Personality

It may be seen from our former considerations that personality, conceived dynamically and teleologically, is an aim and, at the same time, an effect of the process of positive disintegration. In other words, positive disintegration, when developing correctly, leads to the building of personality and to the realization of its ideal.

The main task in the shaping of a concrete personality is understanding, by proper persons, in the environment, of the individual's "personality" by its indicators (e.g., tendencies for introversion, creativity, sensitivity, etc.), that is, in its not yet shaped characteristics which are, however, susceptible to development, and in its disintegrative dynamisms revealed in the initial phase (e.g., feelings of inferiority, guilt, disquietude). At the same time both the person desiring to shape a different personality and, to a lesser extent, the object of his educational efforts must, though not in the same measure, set individual programs of personality-shaping.

For this purpose it is necessary to distinguish with the individual possessing personality indicators:

1. The characteristics which are to be shaped

2. The nuclei of disintegrative dynamisms, that is, the fundamental instruments of the shaping process

3. The internal and external conditions for this shaping, such as age, sex, developmental period, type, the level of intelligence and its individual structure, family, school, and other factors which may distinctly influence the development of personality

We have already pointed out above that in the elementary period of the development of personality the brunt of its shaping is borne by the educator, but always with the participation of the individual, at least in the beginning of self-educational work, the scope and level of which should be rather strictly measured by the educator.

Seizure of the above-mentioned personality indicators by the individual, by an educational team, in their peculiar form, in their mutual arrangement in connection with the individual's period of development, is fundamental, not only for the development of the individual himself, but also for the whole society, since the possession of the greatest possible number of matured personalities by a society is decisive for its proper development, for its place in the family of societies, for its future.

Every individual with personality indicators should be shaped accordingly. An opinion, frequently expressed, is that individuals possessing personality indicators "discover" themselves after some time and, possessing as a rule creative capacities, can cope with their own development. We have, however, observed very many cases of vitiated development, one-sided development, and serious mental diseases which arose when an individual with personality indicators was not given proper help in his development. Therefore, although self-education is the main method of the development of personality, aid in this development by a competent person is advisable, and often necessary.

Self-Education – The Main Method of Development

Argumentation

The fundamental method for the development of personality is self-education. This is so because it is only when an individual attempts to understand and experience, even in a way that is incomplete and intuitional, the main problems of individual and social life, that he reveals a deepened attitude toward more important realities in his environment. Only then may he actively assume an attitude toward himself and his environment.

Of course, the process of self-education may be more one-sided or more full, more or less conscious, more or less deepened. It is clear that with children and young people, and even with persons possessing a distinct disposition for self-education, the self-educational process is weak and fluctuates in intensity and depth, in various periods, and is clearly a partial process. As the personality develops this process becomes increasingly more stable and more conscious and it is deepened. Nevertheless, during the whole development of the personality, unconscious, changing factors which depend on various compositions of the internal and external environments take part in this process.

Slowly, as the process of positive disintegration correctly develops, the individual attempts, on the one hand through deliberation, and on the other through the participation of strong emotional and volitional dynamisms, to introduce a more or less changeful progress and plans for his own development; he tries to grasp the importance of the need for becoming conscious of the hierarchy in his own inner milieu, of making it dynamic, and of starting work on his development.

Self-education must, therefore, be based on the seizure of multilevel values in oneself and on the previously described dynamisms of multilevel disintegration. The diagnosis of the internal hierarchy of values in oneself and of the hierarchical dynamization of one's own structure is, therefore, the basis for self-education. It is based on an ever fuller, an ever broader, and consequently on an increasingly more conscious seizure of that which is "lower" and "higher" in us, of that which is more valuable and less valuable, of that which should be eliminated and of that which should be retained and developed. Consequently, self-education implies a certain structural and dynamic dualism – that is, it entails the dynamism of the feeling of inferiority in relation to oneself, the "subject-object in oneself" dynamism, many other dynamisms being brought into play.

These precise dynamisms decide the question of one's passage from the state of "being educated" to the state of self-education.

The development of personality, as we see it, is usually a slow process (although there are exceptional cases of sudden "jumps" in development, and "revelation," as it were, of the personality), in which it comes to self-awareness, self-affirmation, and self-education, slowly and partially.

This ripe phase, as it were, is preceded, as we have said, by innumerable experiences, seemingly of little importance, which disappear into the subconscious, wait for new experiences and a new summation of them, and then, in moments most suitable for the development of personality, appear in a more mature form, "consolidate," and are consciously included in a more or less distinct program of self-education.

Beginning from the unconscious dynamic attitudes of a small child, expressed by the attitude "I by myself," through the more conscious but poorly calculated attitudes of a young man, expressed by the saying, "Although this is very difficult, I shall get through it myself," we pass to a clearly developing personality, in which the main dynamisms are realized and affirmed, difficulties better calculated, and one incessantly makes determined efforts to develop oneself. The process of self-education is a trying process of humanizing oneself through positive disintegration.

Conditions or "Aids" Facilitating the Development of Personality

We will present here, in a very concise form, the conditions for self-education, placing great stress on some of the necessary internal conditions. As for the question of age, we must bear in mind that, with very few exceptions, we cannot speak of a distinct process of the shaping of personality in the period before maturation.

Nevertheless it is of paramount importance to seize even faint traces of personality indicators with a small child or with a child of preschool or school age. We have already pointed to the period of contradictoriness.

The period of maturation is most suitable for the shaping of personality, but it also presents a great danger of the weakening or destruction of disintegrative processes.

With respect to the problem of which psychological types are most prone to development, our observations point to a more frequent appearance of personality indicators with schizothymic, introverted types than with the opposite types.[1] Among the types of increased psychic excitability, the most susceptible to positive disintegration processes and

---

[1] *Schizothymic* is Kretschmer's term. It refers to an asthenic bodily type having such psychic characteristics as theoretical rather than practical abilities, difficulties in contact with people, and some tendency for internal conflict.

consequently to the development of personality are types with increased affectional and imaginative excitability.

One cannot think about the proper shaping of personality without considering the above-mentioned typological structure and without watching the positive possibilities of acting upon it. It should be stressed here that for the development of personality psychic "plasticity," within the framework of a given type, is of a greater importance than the concrete typological traits. In any event the determination of the type of an individual (and acting upon reshaping of a type) constitutes a very important condition for educational work.

Internal conditions of the development of personality would include certain intellectual equipment, namely, various kinds of qualities and intellectual difficulties, connected functionally with the oscillation of the disposing and directing center "upward," that is, to a higher level. Our most recent extensive investigations of the correlation between outstanding capabilities and psychoneurotic symptoms show that a higher level of intellectual and artistic interests and capabilities correlate positively to about 80 per cent of subjects with light psychoneurotic sets. We shall not consider more intensely at this point the matter of sex; according to our observations sex is not an essential problem in the development of personality, although the direction, rate, and scope of the development are in some measure dependent on this factor.

In the first part of this work we have pointed to the importance of external factors, "constellatory" factors and environmental influences, which facilitate or hamper the development of personality. We shall not further discuss these problems at this point. We shall only recall the fact that excessively bad material conditions of living or, on the other hand, too good material conditions, weaken the possibilities of the development of personality in its early phase. Furthermore, in a child's life too rigid educational conditions or those not liberal enough, in the surrounding reality, are considered negative phenomena in the development of personality. They constitute a great obstacle in the initial period of development, and cease to present an obstacle when this development is well advanced.

The fundamental conditions for the shaping of an individual's personality are what fate brings to him, what injuries befall him, what errors are made in his education, the presence and influence of somebody from the environment who is qualified to help him in the development of personality. Various kinds of frustrations, separations, complexes, and "lost complexes" usually constitute very important elements in the development of psychoneuroses in children and adults, and particularly neuroses characterized by anxiety or obsession. On the other hand, in the presence of reactions that help in the "correct" experiencing of such injuries, they may constitute a positive element in the development of personality.

We will speak in the next section of the importance of an adviser who can, in proper moments, help one in the elaboration of injuries and difficulties.

Let us now pass to a short discussion of aids facilitating the development of personality. These will include, among others, access to libraries, museums, theaters, and scientific institutions. All these institutions, when properly used, decide the richness of the stimuli, the application of which may constitute, in this or that system, the selective and specific factors assisting in the development of personality. At times a book presenting a story of a hero which, in its psychological and ideological aspects, makes the nuclear dynamism sensitive to the development of personality may be an important factor in stimulating this development. The same is true of theater plays and many works of plastic art. A proper scientific, social, or artistic environment which stimulates one to creative work, presence at a discussion, taking part in an excursion in the company of proper people may constitute a positive factor and consequently an auxiliary medium stimulating the personality.

How many of us continue under the impression of a feeling of the greatness of creative "flights" when contemplating the works of Michelangelo, how many of us experience entanglement and depth as a result of the diseased creative genius of Van Gogh, and how many of us experience ineffaceable moments when we recall reading the works of Camus or Faulkner? How deeply one is influenced by reading Gandhi's autobiography! We recall a conversation with one of our acquaintances who told us that he often reverts in these experiences to the epigraph on the monument of A. de Musset in Paris,[2] the words of which concern the

---

[2]A. de Musset. "La nuit de mai." ("The May Night.") In *Les nuits.* (*The Nights.*)

indissoluble link of greatness with suffering: "Great poetry is often the product of weeping, depression, distress and even agony."

If the candidate for personality is in the period of great creative tension, if he is advanced in development, and consequently if he reveals the sharp tenseness of multilevel disintegrative dynamisms, then of great help at this stage may be an isolation in peaceful conditions, which helps one to order one's sensations by an interruption of actual sensations and by a deepening of certain elements of the inner milieu. The conditions of "satiating oneself" in such an internal "constellation" with plastic sensations, music, and primarily with calmness would be compatible with the impressions and opinions of Aldous Huxley as to the importance of these sensations for the spiritual life of man.

The Adviser and His Role

The Adviser in Various Phases of the Development of Personality

We shall not return at this point to the problem of phases in the development of personality. We must, however, lay stress on the fact that in every phase, and particularly in the initial and following phases – that is, in the period of great conflictive and creative tensions, the period of a very real possibility of a breakdown – the adviser plays a fundamental role in the development of personality.

Whereas in the first phase the main role rests with the adviser – that is, with the tutor, teacher, parent, or physician – in the second phase of development the main role passes to the developing individual himself. Nevertheless, this does not mean that help in the development of personality is more difficult to give in the first phase or that it is easier or superfluous in the second phase. On the contrary, the passage from a rather passive sensitization to the phase of the mobilization of one's own forces, to the phase of a strong actuation of one's internal milieu, to the period of disintegration, requires greater responsibility and vigilance on the part of the adviser. The help of an adviser must be increasingly more imperceptible, ever more subtle, ever more "helpful," so as not to

---

Paris: L. Conard, 1905.

interfere finally, injudiciously, and too distinctly in the developmental process of an individual.

This help is also needed in the last phase, in instances where the development of personality goes on automatically, as it were, and is determined by the individual's own psychic forces. This help is usually based on the developing personality "requisitioning" it, on unlimited confidence in the adviser, and on a tradition of cooperation. Under these circumstances there arises a bond of cooperation aimed at the mutual development of personalities, of whom one is more, and the other less, experienced and mature.

Characteristics of the Adviser

The qualities of an adviser would include two groups: the extent and traits of the development of the adviser's own personality, and special qualities and capabilities permitting him to fulfill his role.

Regarding the first group of properties it is, of course, obvious that the fundamental characteristic trait of the adviser is that he himself should be a "rounded" personality or a personality-in-the-making, with a high level of achievement. Of course, one should not expect an adviser to be, as a rule, a full or nearly full personality. However, he would have to have behind him, more or less complete, at least two of the above-mentioned phases in the development of personality. He would have to have behind him the passage, in its fundamental lines, through the process of positive multilevel disintegration in its sharp phase; he would have to have a developed and conscious internal milieu, a developed third factor, a distinct hierarchy of aims, and a clear ideal of his development as a personality.

Moreover, he should realize sufficiently his shortcomings in the area of some of the structures and dynamisms of the development of his own personality and should also fully understand the necessity for asking the cooperation of others.

Besides the qualities most closely connected with the structure and level of development of the adviser's personality he should also possess the inborn and acquired capabilities needed for very difficult work in the realm of education and psychotherapy. Before we pass, however, to a short characterization of these capabilities, we must mention one

important quality which is at the border of the qualities arising natu-
rally from the development of personality and the qualities which are
acquired and improved through studies and experience. This is good
will (coupled with psychological intuition), without which the work of
an adviser is unthinkable. This trait is connected with an "openness"
to the specific character of the individual's structure, a devotion to it,
and, based on studies and attainments in one's own development, an
adaptation of the methods of proceeding to the needs of a given individual (to his personality development phase, psychological type, period of
development, special capabilities, and soon).

The adviser must also be well prepared, in the areas of psychology,
psychopathology, and pedagogy, and must know how to use the most
modern methods of these branches of science. One should not, of course,
expect the adviser to have completed graduate studies in all these disciplines. The adviser should, however, have completed graduate study
in one of these disciplines and he should possess a good theoretical and
practical knowledge of the realms bordering his discipline. He should
have, primarily, a deep knowledge of developmental psychology, psychopathology, individual education, self-education, psychotherapy, and
autopsychotherapy.

We still have to mention one more fundamental quality of an adviser.
This quality is philosophical development and preparation – that is,
a knowledge of the fundamental directions and achievements of philo-
sophic thought which link themselves to the essential needs and experiences of a man moving along on the road to the development of his
personality.

Who May Be an Adviser?

Advisers in the above-mentioned sense may be parents, tutors, teachers, physicians, and others, provided they are thoroughly acquainted
with the laws and processes of the development of personality, with the
main dynamisms of this development, and provided they themselves are
advanced in the development of their own personality.

We stress once more that one cannot expect to find a sufficient number of ideal advisers who themselves represent a matured personality or
are near such maturity. Such advisers can be found only rarely. We

are talking of individuals who, as we have indicated, realize personality in themselves, possess a knowledge of its development, and understand the need for help in the development of personality. They would be exceedingly useful in all cases where there arises, with children and young people, a concrete hint of a problem of personality, although present in an embryonic form.

An adviser with high inner qualifications is necessary in those cases where we are concerned with essential and deep changes in the structure of an individual moving along the road to personality, with intensified internal conflicts, or with difficulties in overcoming them. In a family, in a school, in an educational institution, problems arise that require counsel from various special advisers, and require not only the mastery of knowledge from the borders of psychology, education, teaching, self-education, autopsychotherapy, and vocational guidance, but also greater knowledge and experience in order to help in solving certain special, individual problems in the development of personality. There also comes into play, therefore, one of the most fundamental requisites for mental health, the "team" requisite, or, more precisely, the group work of many specialists, every one of whom, besides his own specialty, the knowledge of which he has in hand as a starting point, would have a knowledge of, and achievements in, the development of personality (the child, young people, adults, the level and scope of the development of personality). This would be a personality development team adviser.

It is a matter of course that the postulate of the possession by a society of matured, "all-round" advisers in the development of personality, and even the postulate of advisers with partial preparation for the fulfillment of their duties, has little possibility of being realized at present. Therefore, in the present phase of the development of societies it may be realized in some families, in some educational and mental health centers, or in some special experimental centers. Nevertheless the positing of this postulate clearly and in a good form, and realizing it, even within a narrow scope, may have great educational influence, through the suggestive influence of the results obtained in the development of personality, this most difficult and most important social and moral field of human development.

With these assumptions the role of an adviser in the development of personality, and consequently the role of at least some parents, tutors, teachers, and physicians, becomes fundamental. This role should not be forced into the background by the seemingly "realistic" policy of superficial education of society, without the participation in the policy of those tendencies and methods which serve the recognition of personality indicators and their intense and proper development.

The Adviser's Intervention in the Process of Self-Education

The educational process concerns in the first place children and young people as unshaped beings – that is, those with whom it is possible to modify both the positive and negative traits qualitatively and quantitatively or, in other words, those with whom it is possible, in the majority of cases, to bring about a smaller or greater predominance of positive developmental traits in their structure.

The process of self-education usually does not express itself with children and young people in steady self-educational needs, but in more or less distinct emotional and intellectual projections in this direction. The proper seizure of these projections, therefore, requires help from an adviser, requires his keenness and vigilance with respect to the indicators of personality development demonstrated in these projections.

Such intervention is not easy. It requires clear apprehension of the psychic structure with which development of personality is concerned, of the phase in which the development occurs, of how the educational process appears here – what its intensity is, to what degree the individual is conscious of it, in what area this intensity is weak and in what area it is strong, what shortcomings and what positive sides in disintegrative activity this process represents, and, finally, what critical states are revealed in the development, that is, states which on the one side show its acceleration and, on the other, are often almost pathological.

This interference of an adviser in the self-educational process calls sometimes for haste and sometimes for expectation, for temporary, improvised help, or for preparation of a long-term program.

An adviser who intervenes in the self-educational process must have the best possible, all-embracing diagnosis of the individual with whom he is to deal; he must be fully aware of the type that the individual in question represents, of what qualities are present and what advancements have been made in the process of positive disintegration, of its dangers, of what the state and degree of development of the particular dynamisms of the developmental process are, of what the actual needs for intervention in the self-educational process are, in order to accelerate it in certain sections, to deepen, diminish, intensify it, and even to bring about a strengthening of integration at a lower level, for some time, with the aim of counteracting a too feverish and too tense disintegration "projection," which takes place frequently, as indicated above, on the border of pathological manifestations.

Positive Disintegration as a Personality-Shaping Method

Groups of Dynamisms

In previous chapters of the present work we have discussed in detail the main dynamisms of multilevel disintegration and of secondary integration. We shall now consider some methods of developing these dynamisms. We will deal here with the following dynamisms: shame, anxiety over oneself, the feeling of guilt, the "subject-object in oneself" process, the development of the third factor, making the personality ideal concrete and dynamic, the ascension of the disposing and directing center – all within the framework of the general development of the inner milieu and its relation to the external environment.

It must be emphasized here that the discussion of the methods of development with respect to particular dynamisms of multilevel disintegration is greatly artificial, since the method of developing any one of the dynamisms automatically becomes the method of developing several or a whole series of other dynamisms of multilevel disintegration. For example, the development of the feeling of anxiety over oneself represents, at the same time, a method of development for the feeling of dissatisfaction with oneself, the feeling of guilt, the feeling of inferiority in relation to oneself, the development of the third factor, and so on. Similarly, the development of the "subject-object in oneself" dynamism constitutes a more or less distinct method for the development of the third factor and the development and ascension of the disposing and directing center.

In order to partly remove ourselves from these difficulties we shall try to distinguish, roughly and for methodological purposes, certain groups of these dynamisms and briefly discuss the methods of their development. This division is as follows:

1. Disintegrative dynamisms: anxiety over oneself, dissatisfaction with oneself, the feelings of shame and guilt, and the feeling of inferiority in relation to oneself.

2. Dynamisms consciously organizing the disintegrative process: the "subject-object in oneself" dynamism, and the third factor dynamism.

3. Secondary integration dynamisms: the personality ideal, and the disposing and directing center at a higher level.

Development of Particular Kinds of Dynamisms

Disintegrative dynamisms

The disintegrative dynamisms usually arise, along with the proper rudiments of personality, in a man's early life. These rudiments of personality and beginnings of disintegrative dynamisms may be brought to light and effectively shaped by a competent guardian or adviser. Because these matters are of importance we shall give, though in a general and schematic way, the adviser's procedure in discovering the beginnings of these dynamisms and in their shaping.

1. To be able to help in the development of personality the adviser must, in the first place, try to get acquainted with a given individual most thoroughly and in all respects, and orient himself to the specific character of his psychological structure, his tendencies, interests, and so forth.

We have already referred to the methods of getting acquainted with an individual. The commonly known methods are observation of behavior, the creation of proper situations, a conversation with a young man, hearing the opinions of people from his environment, properly selected and differentiated tests, analysis of night dreams, and medical examination.

2. Having acquired general orientation within the structure of the individual and within its specific properties, the adviser endeavors to determine and isolate those traits of the structure, those tendencies and interests, which may constitute conditions for the development of personality, in which "personality indicators" inhere potentially, as it were. Eventually, the adviser ascertains that those germs of personality have left the potential stage and begin to be outlined sufficiently clearly.

The interpretation and synthesizing by the adviser of the results of his investigation and observation, completed as the need arises, should go, speaking most generally, in the following directions:

a. The determination of the positive and strong sides of the given individual's structure

b. The determination of his natural egoistic, pleasure-seeking tendencies, his desire to dominate, and so on

c. The clearly negative sides of his character

d. The strong tenacity of the structure which is revealed in more or less impulsive behavior, the contradictory character of which the individual himself does not note

e. The individual's sensitivity, its kinds and degree of intensity

f. Difficulties, conflicts, nervousness, neuroses, and psychoneuroses

g. Plastic structure, susceptibility to loosening

h. The shadowy outlines of disintegrative dynamisms (anxiety over oneself, dissatisfaction with oneself, sense of guilt, shame, and inferiority), or the lack of same, the possibility of "waking up" the same

3. Having ascertained the personality nuclei (positive qualities such as the desire "to be better," sensitivity, susceptibility to "loosening," and so on), the adviser proceeds to a gradual awakening or proper shaping of already faintly outlined disintegrative dynamisms, trying at the same time to work out methods and ways of adapting them to the structure of the individual.

In this connection the adviser should proceed along the following lines:

a. On one hand, he should do all he can to make the individual conscious of the fact that his tendencies and behavior often contradict each other, that he sometimes departs from the principal positive tendencies and does so without perceiving this himself. These contradictions are caused by the primitive egoism of the individual, by the difficulty of projecting oneself into someone else's situation, by a too impulsive yielding to pleasure stimuli, by the desire to distinguish oneself, and so forth.

This awakening of the individual to the contradictions existing in himself, based on examples and situations from his life, leads at the same time to a loosening of his primitive, tenacious structure. Self-insight facilitates the increasingly clearer division of one's often masked qualities into positive and negative. It also helps to "purify" and strengthen the positive qualities, and to trace the proper line of the individual's behavior.

In the period of the more distinct crystallization of this process even a temporary departure from the line of one's behavior will cause the disintegrative dynamisms to be brought into play: anxiety over oneself, dissatisfaction with oneself, shame and guilt, and the feeling of inferiority in relation to oneself.

b. On the other hand, when the adviser comes across already faintly outlined or active disintegrative dynamisms in an individual, he should familiarize himself with their genesis, structure, and intensity, mold them, and properly inhibit, strengthen, and change them, and set them on the right course. There are various ways in which an adviser may help, usually indirectly, to build the germs of disintegrative dynamisms and to shape the faintly outlined dynamisms. At this point we will note some of the ways in which the adviser should act upon an individual.

One is to observe more thoroughly the phenomena taking place in the individual's environment and in his life. Another is the attempt to interpret these phenomena both from the psychological and moral points of view (by way of discussion of important events, of theater and film shows, of books read, as well as of the experiences and behavior of the individual).

He may also help develop sensitivity and aversion to automatic approaches, attitudes, and acts, to the attitudes of external authority, to ritualistic ceremony, and to routine and superficial judgment. He may also teach criticism and self-criticism, independence in thinking and behaving. He may help the individual to fight egocentrism, to attempt to disintegrate it, through training him in the "art" of entering into the situations and experiences of other persons, "taking to heart" their concerns and experiencing their experiences.

Cooperation with the individual in the disintegration of his theoretical attitudes and opinions which do not agree with his own behavior, the developing and deepening (in judgments and experiences) of the sense of responsibility for one's own attitudes and deeds (growth of the sense of guilt for not discharging one's duties, for not being true to one's conviction) are other ways in which the adviser may aid. He may also help the individual to become increasingly more aware of the reasons for his behavior, his conscious or half-conscious aspirations and mental processes – reasons lying at the roots of the disintegrative dynamisms (anxiety, the feeling of shame, and so on).

Dynamisms which organize the process of positive disintegration

In this group of dynamisms belong the "subject-object in oneself" dynamism and the third factor. The first dynamism, as is known, facilitates insight into oneself and into the motives of one's behavior, the second, using this acquired capacity, aims, within the perspective of an increasingly more clearly outlined personality ideal, at clearing the individual's way to this ideal through the condemnation and rejection of those of its traits and primitive tendencies which hinder the approach to it and through the affirmation and strengthening of those which promote this approach. The adviser helps the individual in the development of these dynamisms of conscious organization of positive disintegration by acting upon him and cooperating with him in the following respects:

1. By developing in the individual the capacity to observe himself, to discover his "true" self, and by training him to look at himself objectively (experiencing himself as an object)

2. By training the individual to fight with the tendencies to affirm and justify, rashly, his own interests, to develop a mistrust of "certainties" in his own behavior, to fight back the tendencies to

subordinate intelligence to instincts, treating the former as a tool of the latter

3. By developing the individual's capacity for the conscious organization of his own internal milieu, for localizing and placing into a hierarchy the values of this environment, and for checking and controlling its level of development

Secondary integration dynamisms

In the development of the personality of an individual, the dynamism of the personality ideal and the dynamism of the disposing and directing center at a higher level play the main, though at first poorly defined and only partially conscious, role. Both dynamisms have already begun to appear at the time of the advent of the rudiments of personality, and the personality ideal appears to be at the root of personality. It constitutes an "idea-force," as it were, which may dynamize the whole inner life of the individual and enlist him in its service. These dynamisms are nothing less than the fundamental and integrating forces which give their stamp to the process of disintegration and constitute the essence of secondary integration.

The role of the adviser in the birth of both these dynamisms and in their development may be great; however, as the personality matures and when these dynamisms begin to dominate and fix their position in the entire inner environment of the individual, this role decreases and fades. As a result of the "drawing" force emanating from them (the nearness of the realization of the ideal, the actualized high level of the disposing and directing center, which one does not want to lower), these dynamisms begin to act automatically, as it were – that is, they no longer need great help from the outside.

These dynamisms cause the advent and the bringing into play of all the disintegrative dynamisms, freeing the indicators of personality from the encumbering, primitive, and negative traits of the individual. The disintegrative dynamisms are a kind of separating tool, that helps to "clean" and develop the individual's personality ideal and the disposing and directing center. The adviser, therefore, who helps the individual in the development and shaping of his disintegrative dynamisms helps at the same time in the shaping of integrative dynamisms. Methods used by him in forming both kinds of dynamisms do not differ greatly.

As for the direct development and formation of integrative dynamisms, the adviser should seek to gain familiarity with and then to act upon and cooperate with the individual in, among others, the areas discussed below.

He must learn to know the individual's structure, his psychological type, temperament, and the essential traits of his character. With that aim in view, the adviser should use the results of the investigations mentioned in the earlier section on "Disintegrative Dynamisms" (p. 148) and should try to familiarize himself with the persons distinguished by the individual from the environment, history, literature, films, and the like, and with the extent to which he identifies himself with these persons.

He must watch the psychic process, the affectional maturation of the individual, his evolution which reveals itself, in one way, in a change of interest in particular persons, and in a simultaneous faithfulness to some qualities which they have in common. He must aim at a clear understanding of and cooperation with the individual in his striving for a complete image of his own ideal, and in his endeavors to actualize it in everyday life.

He must be orientated to the shortcomings, gaps, and dangers of repression encountered by the individual's disposing and directing center in its rising to an ever higher level of development; he must intervene in difficult, complicated situations, and help in maintaining the center at the already attained level.

The following is an example illustrating the majority of positive disintegrative dynamisms taken from the autobiography of a 36-year-old patient, N—, suffering from psychasthenia, and at the same time clearly developing his personality (the author considers autobiography and biography as one of the important research methods):

> Much is said about knowledge of oneself. However, these words are understood only by great men or by those who feel an inner compulsion for seeking the answer to the most important questions of being. I think that in order to win knowledge of oneself one should aim at reshaping himself, for the state of stabilization hinders the acquisition of knowledge, makes all automatic, and

makes self-cognizing a mental game. Are there many people who experience the fact that they have teeth if not using them for chewing and crunching, that they have sexual organs and glands which periodically demand their activity and that, therefore, so-called sexual love is only the way of facilitating the activity of these glands? Does one know much about entire systems devised to mask the brutal interest of individuals or groups, in order that they may be more easily realized? How many Germans have taken, or now take, to heart the fact and methods of mass exter-mination of people in death camps? Do we differ much from cats which, while jumping charmingly, murder singing birds, or do we differ much from birds, wonderfully colorful birds, which murder insects with lightning speed? Do many of us think, while chewing savory meat, about the methods of murdering animals in great municipal slaughterhouses? Do many of us know and experience the fact that ideological declarations, opinions, and treatises are in most cases tools for placing oneself in more convenient circum-stances, of getting the upper hand in a fight with the interest of others? Do many people feel ashamed of their primitive instincts and their manifestations; do many people feel sorrow because of having caught themselves nourishing low, egoistic tendencies, and how many of us would accept and realize the conviction that "yes" is "yes" and "no" is "no"? The battle with others is easy, but the battle with oneself is much more difficult. There is no courage without courage in relation to one's lower "I"; there is no justice without justice in relation to oneself.

There is no realization of perfection without pain, experienced in disappointments about oneself, about one's own littleness, about the frailty of one's own moral attitude ...

Such thought and experiences tormented me for years – no, I have become sensitive to others and to myself; this paralyzes, at least for the time being, my activity, and inhibits me in my judgments. Sometimes, however, it seems to me that something is being born of these distractions and inner struggles, something that will give me more light, a greater possibility of knowing, and deeper awareness of who I am and how I should behave.

Shaping of the Universal and Individual Qualities of Personality

We have repeatedly mentioned the "indicators of personality," which are a condition, as it were, for a good development and shaping of personality. As we have also pointed out, these indicators reveal themselves, on the one hand, fully equipped with elementary, though fairly distinct, positive qualities, about which we wrote in the first part of this work, and on the other, as the indicators of positive disintegration dynamisms.

We may say that, as a rule, the initial and the latter indicators develop simultaneously and cooperate with each other, and that the development of the first entails development of the second and vice versa.

For example, the ability to know oneself and others is not possible without the development of the dynamism of dissatisfaction with oneself, of the feeling of inferiority in relation to oneself, without the development of the subject-object dynamism, and of the third factor. This is because these dynamisms incessantly develop capabilities for objective acts in one's own inner milieu. Moreover, they develop this milieu, as knowledge of oneself always implies the division into subject and object in oneself, implies the ability to place into a hierarchy the values in oneself, and, finally, implies inner differentiation. Development of these dynamisms considerably facilitates one's understanding of others, and facilitates the transposition of the experiences of others to one's own and vice versa by freeing the intelligence from dependence on the instincts and by coupling it with the dynamisms of personality, which puts an end to the "blinker attitude" which brings about narrowness of attitudes, stiffness and egotism, and egoism in judgment and behavior.

When proper indicators exist, the acquisition of "all-round" knowledge by means of one's studies is deepened by these dynamisms. General psychic sensitivity and the "holding off" of the instinctive egocentric attitude ensure that nothing that is human is strange to a man.

Independence of feelings, appraisals, and behavior is based again on the development of twofold indicators (positive qualities and dynamisms of the internal environment). Independence from the functions of the lower instincts and from the suggestions of the external environment which favor these instinctive needs, the dissolution of these tenacious structures, and the structuring in the internal milieu make this environment sensitive to the higher dynamisms, increase the suggestive force of the personality ideal and the disposing and directing center. Objectivity in relation to oneself and others increases, therefore, and also the independence of the feelings, appraisals, and behavior from the lower instinctive structures and primitive reactions.

Moral and social qualities, courage, and truthfulness increase under the influence of an example, by communion with positive heroes in art and in everyday life. Conscious courage and conscious truthfulness shape themselves only when we become independent of our primitive instincts, of the judgments of the environment and of cliques. It is shaped with the cooperation of many dynamisms of positive disintegration and secondary integration.

The capacity for unselfish love and friendship, for exclusiveness and faithfulness, for taking responsibility for persons closely and remotely associated with us is shaped on the one hand by the elaboration of experiences of everyday life, by trial and error, by an example, and on the other by the shaping of the hierarchy of values in one's own internal milieu, by reaching for the ideal of personality, by the development of the higher dynamisms of the internal milieu and by their transposition to the external environment, to other people.

We will speak briefly about one of the qualities of personality which is connected with one's attitude toward the world of existential needs and tendencies, namely, the adaptation of oneself to suffering and death. The development in oneself of retrospective and prospective attitudes, a "running ahead" of the present moment, experiencing the transiency of our life, with a simultaneous development of the main dynamisms of disintegration, weakens the primitive traits in relation to suffering and death and leads not only to acceptance, but also to experiencing the universality of this phenomenon. On the other hand, it increases the need for finding the answer to the chief enigma of being, consequently also to the sense of suffering and death, to the sense of separation from one's near relations and friends with whom the bond has become deeper as a result of the development of the dynamism of multilevel disintegration.

We therefore have the need to transfer these experiences to a higher level, feel the pressure of tendencies to approach transcendental problems, and experience the need for meditation. One thus increases one's sensitivity to the suffering of others, and resistance to one's own sufferings; there increases the awareness of death, "familiarization" with it, although simultaneously transcendental unrest increases.

The process of positive disintegration also shapes the "dramatic attitude toward life." Life becomes "thought," experienced and not instinctive. On the stage, in art, and in one's own life, the problems of life, death, love, creativity, and development come to the foreground. As expressed by Wyspianski, the individual is conscious of the entire drama of life. He is actor and stage manager in the internal and external play of changes, disappointments, and development.

The fundamental quality shaped by the everyday effort of the individual aiming at personality is the ability to meditate. We have referred to it repeatedly. It has its origin in a form of reflection, a predisposition for deep meditation, the ability to interrupt one's daily activity, and the need for frank "philosophizing." The individual may avail himself of the many works of various schools dealing with spiritual life in order to deepen this capacity for meditation. Retrospection and prospection and periodic isolation of oneself give definite results here. They clearly promote all those activities which develop the inner environment and its hierarchy of values – that is, they promote all the dynamisms of multilevel disintegration.

We will now briefly comment on the shaping of individual qualities of personality such as chief interests and capabilities, the ability to form exclusive bonds, and the feeling of one's "oneness" and identity. They develop from the indicators of personality and are shaped by many factors, such as the propagation of these qualities in the family and at school, the example of close relatives and friends, and vital experiences. The deepening, through positive disintegration, of self-awareness, the development of knowledge in all directions, the raising of the level of affectional experiences, the shaping of adaptability to suffering and death, and meditation, exert a fundamental influence.

Through these phenomena, taking place in the individual and shaped by him, there results the "denudation" of many thus far accepted values and the development and shaping of those general and individual qualities which become, for the individual, the condition absolutely essential for his unique being.

Methods of Positive Disintegration as Applied to Children and Young People

Children and Young People – The Main Area for Application of the Method

Children and young people are the most proper group in which to seize the indicators of personality and to act upon them. This is due to the plasticity of a child's psyche – that is, its susceptibility to the reception of positive stimuli to act upon those indicators – and to the psychical freshness of children and young people, the richness of their imagination and prospection.

During his whole development the child is susceptible to developmental stimuli. However, these stimuli must be adapted to his phenotypic and genotypic aspect and to his particular period of development. These periods of development, however, should not be considered as too distinctly separated from the complex development of children's and young people's psyches.

Through diagnosis of the childish forms of attitudes to one's own internal environment, through help in the proper shaping of the main dynamisms of this environment, through an awakening of the initial tendencies towards autopsychotherapy, one introduces a certain order into the perturbed internal environment characteristic of the process of positive disintegration and particularly of its elementary forms, and one excites a certain directional disposition.

It is clear from the above that the most advantageous area in which to gain knowledge of the personality nuclei, together with the manifestations of disintegration connected with them, are the periods of childhood and adolescence. In these periods one may observe not only the more distinct, but also even the weakest personality nuclei, which later, in mature age, grow weak and vanish, submitting themselves to the integrating functions of the fundamental instinctive dynamisms in a man's life cycle.

The seizure, therefore, not only of distinct personality manifestations, but also of their very weak manifestations is always of value for education, and an increasingly deeper understanding of these matters should constitute one of the basic tasks of educational circles. As already stated above, this is the main task of different specialists who are united by common features, namely, the understanding of what the personality is, what its indicators are, and how important correct guidance is in the development of personality.

How to Apply the Method with Respect to Children and Young People

It is a fact, known from everyday life, that making man's psychic structure sensitive is connected with a certain loosening, and even with a disintegration of his primitive instinctive dynamisms, with the halting and reshaping of many primitive attitudes. The Freudian mechanism of the libido's collision with reality and pronounced resignation from the principle of pleasure in favor of the principle of reality represents, in certain respects and on a certain level, a reshaping dynamism.

The disintegration of primitive structures raises us from the egocentric sphere, permits us to free ourselves from the sphere of stimuli and reactions allotted us by the regular experiences connected with man's life cycle.

Education consists in developing the possibility of resignation from primitive needs; it consists in partial frustration, in experiencing the feeling of dissatisfaction with oneself, in developing self-control, inhibition, retrospection, and prospection. These phenomena display certain mild forms of disintegration without which the education process would be unthinkable. The pain and suffering of a child, his failures, his experiences of shame, and his feelings of inferiority or guilt are the fundamental dynamisms that reshape his primitive structure. They are positive dynamisms if, at the same time, they are offset by pleasant experiences – joy, satisfaction, ambitions, the feeling of superiority, the feeling of having fulfilled one's duty well, the experience of praise, and the like. This alternate action of unpleasant and pleasant stimuli is indispensable for the gradual "awakening of the inner milieu," for its structuring, for differentiation, and for elevation of the level of sensations, for moral estimates and deeds; it is an indispensable factor for the proper arrangement of one's relations to the social environment; it is necessary for the advent and development of positive conflicts both in the internal and external environments.

If one possesses the appropriate dispositions to direct these dynamisms, then their proper weakening or strengthening, their grouping in certain most advantageous sets become, in the hands of a good educator, fundamental tools for the development of a child's personality.

The passage from the egocentric to alterocentric structure, from the introverted attitude to the complex extravertive attitude, and vice versa, from excessive sociability to an adequate social attitude, from undue excitation to the complicated inhibition of lower dynamisms and awakening of higher dynamisms, is not possible without the positive disintegration process.

At a level proper for the level of the child's sensitivity, for his type, and for his period of development, one may activate all the fundamental dynamisms of multilevel disintegration. The point here is to observe two principles: the principle already mentioned, of the adaptation of the method of disintegration to the requirements of the concrete psychic structure of the child, and the application of this method, not in verbal, explicative, interpretive, or persuasive form, but in association with concrete situations, experienced by the child and causing the advent of a concrete set of problems, problems that are a matter of keen concern to the child.

The explicative method may, in a plastic way, be applied only when the child, irrespective of the concrete situation of experiencing his own difficulties, may accept and fix certain disintegrative stimuli as a consequence of further experiences connected with his having read a book, with his presence at a theatrical spectacle, cinema show, concert, or in situations in which he observes interesting, delightful, or shocking phenomena.

All the situations in which the child perceives the suffering of an animal or a man, someone's injury, lameness, or sickness, someone's humiliation or aggressiveness, someone's injustice or exceptional goodness, may be used for the application of the method of the disintegration of primitive attitudes, because such situations, when one is interested in them or experiences them, produce natural sensitivity to given stimuli – that is, they produce a state of susceptibility to loosening, and consequently to disintegration also.

We have already drawn the reader's attention to the problems of individual adaptation, by prepared parents, teachers, and tutors, of positive disintegrative techniques for particular periods and developmental difficulties. The main requirement, thus, in applying the positive disintegrative technique would be a thorough acquaintance with child psychopathology.

When applying the disintegrative method one should not, as a rule, intensify tensions, unrest, fear, and the feeling of guilt with an individual possessing indicators of personality. On the other hand, it is advisable that certain forms of loosening or even disintegration of tenacious instinctive structures should ensue in a positive way – that is, through the strengthening of the individual's positive traits, his interests, and capabilities, by falling back upon his closest patterns. On the basis of these patterns and through unification with them, the egocentric tendencies become weaker and the too tenacious instinctive structure loosens.

Sometimes a discreet and subtle application of the method may give satisfactory results.

The world of children's ideals is most accessible to the child through fairy tales and fables, by way of phantastic content, through introducing him to the world of nature invigorated by phantasy. This is but only natural, for on the one hand, this world expresses the imaginative and phantastic needs of the child, his magical and animistic needs, and on the other the child seeks compensation, in this world, for his feeling of weakness and for his need of care, which is more enhanced by the presence of the narrator who combines protectiveness, nearness, and the strength that revives the child's phantasy. By linking the child with the world of heroes and magicians who readily bring help to the weak and injured, one develops in the child the tendency to transfer to himself the characteristic qualities of these heroes.

One should always take into account that a child, as a developing being, usually possesses a sensitive imagination and capacity for phantasy and that he "completes" the stimuli acting on him, with his own creative contents.

If in their relations with children the parents combine warmth with authority, and make proper demands on the children, they have the best possible chance for loosening, and even disintegrating, the tenacious instinctive drives of the children. Skillfully controlled exposure of the child to the difficulties in the environment of his peers is one of the important sources of refashioning the child's attitude, for his equals are considerably more direct in behavior, and often considerably more objective, than older people, even parents. The environment of peers becomes, therefore, an environment creating conditions for reshaping the egocentric, egoistic, imperious, and other attitudes.

The Positive Disintegrative Method as Applied to Particular Developmental Periods

Early manifestations of personality indicators

An early grasping of personality indicators by educators (a parent, teacher, physician, educational therapist) depends, of course, on the structure and level of the educator, on his ability to discern psychological factors, on his understanding of what the personality is, and on his ability to seize the various manifestations of the early phases of the development of personality. These "indicators" may, as we have said above, be manifested in various degrees and in varying strength. They may be certain positive qualities which become marked, such as courage, ambition, truthfulness, sensitivity to the injury of others, and so on. They may be the early manifestations of contradictoriness and stubbornness in a more or less hidden sense. They may be more or less marked, already present in the first years of the child's life, in attitudes of being dissatisfied with himself, masked by excitement and depression.

A 6-year-old girl, L——, gifted, greatly egocentric, and introverted, revealed a strong irritability or childish depression, lasting sometimes for several hours. Although she had great confidence in her father and mother, it usually took many hours for her to confess, during a sincere evening talk, often accompanied by sobbing, that she was impossible, for she knew that she behaved badly with respect to one of her parents, but she could not come out and say it. When she was asked to explain why she could not speak about it, she answered that something kept her from doing so, that she had to wait until she felt "easier in her mind."

In the period of maturation, and even before that period, there may appear strong tendencies to evaluate within one's own internal environment and in relation to the external environment. These may be weak or strong signs of anxiety over oneself, dissatisfaction with oneself, the feeling of inferiority in relation to oneself, the sense of guilt; these may be strong tendencies to idealize the outer environment, to place moral cases in a clear light based on principles, and with the tendency to harmonize moral principles and one's behavior.

These "indicators" may reveal themselves in the form of philosophizing "seriously," in the form of a too inconsiderate, too straightforward, and even aggressive fight against meanness, in the form of an undue adaptation of oneself, and so on, which may cover the states of dissatisfaction with oneself, states of inferiority, and also other states. Finally, they may reveal themselves in the form of difficulties in adapting to the environment, in too individualistic attitudes, and the like.

Twelve-year-old M—, of outstanding intelligence, schizothymic in character, very early experienced the difference between what is "true" and what is "appearance." One day she had a long, emotionally hot conversation with her father about lasting affectional "serious" bonds, which to her were the only worthy bonds and the only ones having meaning. This conversation took place after the girl had for many months experienced these problems. She could not accept and explain to herself the ease with which her so-called friendly relations with her girl friends changed. It was difficult for her to make such contacts because she realized their changeability and temporariness. She did not know that with the "demands" she was making, it was not easy to have good friends.

Manifestations of personality "indicators" may also consist in excessive psychic sensitivity in relation to the environment and to one's own behavior, as well as in remarkably vivid, creative, and broad interests in various realms, and finally in various forms of increased psychic excitability and in various forms of psychic disequilibrium and light psychoneurotic symptoms (for example, obsession connected with moral problems in relation to people and to oneself, unrest, depression, and a feeling of strangeness in relation to the environment, the feeling of one's "otherness," that one is being difficult, that one is not as good in making contact with people as others are, and so on).

If the child experiences and is conscious, even if only vaguely, of these states, we may see in the child the possibility of personality nuclei. We observe, again and again, in children and young people in the period of maturation, and not so rarely even with six- to seven-year-old children, plans for work upon oneself in order to overcome the phenomena which appear as negative to the child.

Seven-year-old S—, who was gifted, inhibited, timid, had worked out for herself a plan for fighting back uncertainty and inhibitions, through exercises in overcoming the difficulties she had when dealing with new problems. She knew that she too greatly exaggerated the difficulty of the problem when she encountered it for the first time. In this connection she had worked out a "table of mistakes" made during a given month, judging certain exercises as difficult. In this childish way she had worked out the percentage of negative estimates; on this basis she could increase her certainty in new trials and improve the objectivity of her own estimates.

All these phenomena, normal in a child's life, or all the above-mentioned sets of symptoms from the border of the norm to psychoneurosis, should draw the attention of those from the environment who are prepared to help the given individual. Both the above-mentioned phenomena, those within the norm as well as those bordering the norm, may constitute indicators of personality development and may also be the sign of more serious psychoneurotic disorders if not observed in time and, still worse, if not treated properly and in all aspects.

These various forms of increased psychic excitability and psychic unbalance, these various forms of "inadaptability" to oneself and to the environment, these various forms of accentuation of "otherness" and the individuality of a person's structure should be observed with the utmost alertness, "disclosed" with equal alertness, and properly diagnosed.

One final point – we have pointed out above that an individual possessing personality indicators often takes part in this process of "disclosure." This participation should be realized, controlled, shaped, and directed, very subtly, by those entitled to work on the development of personality indicators.

The periods of contradictoriness and maturation

We will now deal in greater detail with the application of the method of positive disintegration in particular periods.

The specific feature of developmental periods is that they constitute more or less automatic, more or less temporary, more or less creative natural signs of disintegrative processes. They constitute, therefore, the natural biopsychic ground for applying, in cases where the individual is susceptible, a worked-out, conscious, and individual method.

Among the periods most favorable for the application of disintegrative methods are the period of contradictoriness and the period of maturation. Somewhat less susceptible are the boyhood and maidenhood periods and the climacteric period.

With many individuals we observe "permanent maturation," as it were. This phenomenon is observed in individuals possessing increased psychic excitability, and in many psychoneurotic individuals who show some signs of psychic infantilism.

Let us briefly characterize these periods and give some methodological hints as to the shaping of the personality indicators.

The Period of Contradictoriness. In this period an attitude of independence from the environment awakens in the child. This is a period in which the child does not agree with the environment in this or that respect, opposes its injunctions, and protests against the power imposed by elders. This is a period of opposition; moreover, this opposition is manifested many times without apparent reason. It develops, as it were, and may have deeply hidden reasons. It is frequently manifested in the child's exasperation and protest. Depending on the level of development, on the richness of the psychic resources of the child, or on the type of his nervousness, such a period may last from several months to several years; moreover, certain qualities of this period may last for a considerable part of the child's life.

A sensitive child, possessing rich personality indicators and protesting against the environment, may experience at the same time a certain, usually half-conscious, dissatisfaction with himself, the feeling of inferiority, and even the feeling of guilt. In the manifestations of contradictoriness and opposition he is simultaneously accentuating his individuality and independence.

Of course, these nuclear experiences from the region of multilevel disintegration should under no circumstances be deepened; they should be leveled and utilized for the positive development of the child, realizing that in the next period, that of greater harmonization of the child, these dynamisms may be enlivened and developed and added to the developmental forces of the child.

A 6-year-old girl, S—, with whom there was a pronounced continuance of strong symptoms of contradictoriness and obstinacy, displayed a passionate need for seeing, on television and at the cinema, formidable, phantastic pictures, abounding in adventure, ambushes, raids, battles, and so on. For several months the child had strong and alarming nightmares. The parents forbade her to see such films. Most probably in response to this, the nightmares increased and, at the same time, the symptoms of obstinacy increased.

The child was of outstanding intelligence, and of the type displaying affectional and imaginational excitability. She had an early and pronounced attitude of ambition; she accepted no interdictions and she reacted well to persuasion. When her father explained to her, in a way understandable to the child, why her parents had forbidden her to see such films, S— said: "Father, I must know all that and manage to get through it." After several longer talks on the matter, the parents made an agreement with the girl that she would be allowed to see the films as before, provided that she would cover her eyes with her hand or turn her head away when the dreadful scenes she feared were about to take place. With the girl's consent the agreement also provided that in case she failed to perceive such scenes early enough, one of the parents would give her a sign by touching her hand. This agreement took effect and was observed rather strictly. When similar methods were applied in other areas of the girl's sensibility, the nightmares completely disappeared.

The method of weakening this tenseness, not by opposing the resistances and obstinacies but rather by discharging them by way of natural rechanneling and persuasion, as well as by agreements with the child, permitted the child to preserve and increase her ambition, her independence, and introduced elements of psychotherapy and autopsychotherapy into her inner life, thus raising the process of positive disintegration to a higher level.

Prematuration and Maturation Periods. The maturation period is most appropriate for the application of the positive disintegration method. It constitutes the most normal area, as it were, for the application of this method, since it reflects the periodic disintegration in man's life cycle. It is to this phase of natural biopsychic disintegration that one may most easily introduce the shaping, straightening, and sublimating method of disintegration. Ambivalence, symptoms of excitation and depression, the feelings of superiority and inferiority, the feeling of agitation in one's own internal environment, and half-conscious attempts to structure it, should be slowly leveled, while one gradually deepens the nuclei of multilevel disintegration, which exists, in most cases, in the form of the inclination to evaluate oneself and others, the feeling of dissatisfaction with oneself, and the unconscious drive to make oneself "excel." These are good conditions for the sober and individual promotion of the process of making unconscious disintegration more conscious, of making the unordered more ordered, the automatic more voluntary, and they lead from unilevel to multilevel disintegration.

Children or young people seek, at this time, a proper external and internal footing. The external footing may become one of the parents, a tutor, a teacher, or even an elder friend, provided they possess certain more developed traits of personality in relation to those who seek such a footing. Such footing may be found in the positive qualities of young people, such as courage, truthfulness, love of people, creative capabilities, and the birth of new attitudes toward oneself and the environment, which, seized and strengthened in this period, may cause great positive "developmental jumps." This is so because their discovery, affirmation, and strengthening is subjectively most needed by children and young people, and they allow for a more healthy, faster building of a new disposing and directing center.

We now turn to a case of a 17-year-old girl, W—, with a belated maturation period, infantile emotional traits, and high intelligence, and with whom introverted qualities predominated. W— passed with some difficulty through changes in her attitude toward her parents and particularly toward her mother whom she trusted fully and idealized. This process differentiated itself and moved in three directions: (1) periodic aversion and aggressiveness in relation to her parents and particularly to her mother; (2) depression, aversion to life, and the existence of maidenly attitudes; (3) the feeling of guilt in relation to her parents, experienced and interpreted, alternately, in the direction of dissatisfaction with herself, the feeling of her own worthlessness, suicidal thoughts, and so on.

The method of working upon the girl carried out by the wise parents, with the aid of a competent medical adviser, proceeded primarily in three directions: (1) convincing the daughter of the identity of the parents' moral attitudes with stress laid on the disclosure of faults and deficiencies; (2) convincing her of the value of the changes she was undergoing; (3) lifting her experiences to a higher level through her deeper participation in her own reshaping.

The first point was impressed upon and experienced by the girl by means of several serious talks with her mother, which were held at the proper time and in the right atmosphere. As for the second point, the parents, in connection with the adviser, made an attempt, based on examples from life and literature, and on proper emotional stimulation of the daughter, to bring her to see the positive side of the disintegrative process. Treatment in the third area was based, in the first place, on activating, or rather on strengthening, the girl's creative attitudes. After some time the parents were successful in convincing her that the psychic development of a person should not consist in passive subordination of oneself to the automatic developmental cycle, but rather in the increasingly more conscious participation in this process. She was encouraged to think about the problem of whether the knowledge of all the deficiencies of a person, and his efforts in the direction of humanizing himself, was not a much more valuable attitude than idealization based only on imaginative function.

It was suggested to the girl that she should develop the need for the transformation of the passive experiencing of the feeling of guilt into an active attitude of helping others in all cases where it was needed. It was also suggested to her that she should augment her attempt at existential philosophizing by linking it with the elements of good will and helping others, by being more sensitive to the affairs of the "other."

In many other cases it has been possible in educational and psychotherapeutic work to intensify the structuring and evaluating dynamisms to the detriment of symptoms of unilevel disharmonies, and it has often been possible, in the shaping of personality, to accentuate strongly the integrative elements (the formation of a new disposing and directing center).

This was so in the case of a 16-year-old boy, G—, with whom it was possible to sublimate suicidal tendencies and to direct him to the act of negating and eliminating some of his deficiencies and to the creation of distinct nuclei of a positively acting disposing and directing center, the main elements of which were the elimination of certain traits and development of others. This, among other things, increased his courage, psychological keenness, and his work in making his educational ideal concrete.

As is known, the periods of boyhood and maidenhood, in a sense, terminate the period of maturation. In this period the youth stabilizes, increasingly more distinctly, around new disposing and directing centers, which shape themselves under the influence of various tendencies, such as the tendency to make oneself notable in social life, or, with marriage partners, the tendency to realize the sexual, parental, and cognitive instincts.

Depending on whether the young people possessing "indicators of personality" display certain positive traits of the extension of the maturation period, and on whether they are under the care of appropriate advisers, they will be more plastic in development, they will have more or less developed resistance to the "stiffening" of maturation and they will be susceptible to the further development of the internal environment. The main tasks of the educational environment are counteracting the stiffening stabilization and development of the above dynamisms.

Wherever possibly harmoniously developed disintegrative factors exist, it is advisable to use the essential tendencies in this period for an increase of activity, for the organization of personal life, for placing emphasis on "organic" work, in order to increase the tendencies of ambition and attainment, and in order to utilize these tendencies by laying great importance on the development of positive qualities such as courage, veracity in relation to oneself and others, broad interests, and knowledge of oneself. The reading of well-selected biographies, examples from life, and keeping a diary with stress laid on the realization of one's decisions and noting one's achievements within a given sphere may be of considerable help here.

It is also greatly advisable to introduce the realization of certain dynamisms of disintegration and secondary integration in the area of the tendency for affectional bonds of friendship and love, which is strong in this period, by supplying the individual with intellectual and affectional materials in the way of exclusiveness, faithfulness, and responsibility for one's near relatives and friends. These individual qualities of personality, as a complement to general or universal qualities, should be understood and accepted as essential traits of humanization of the individual's aspirations.

Briefly, it seems to us that, in the method of positive disintegration and secondary integration, the following functions should dominate:

1. The counteraction of the tendencies for automatic development in man's life cycle, which are displayed in developmental "stiffening"

2. The utilization of the natural tendencies of this period, as mentioned above, for the development of positive general and individual qualities of the individual

3. The retention and further slow development of the dynamisms which build the psychic inner milieu

4. The building of social and friendly relations in harmony with a moral responsibility for oneself and the environment, based, on the one hand, on the development of social feeling, and, on the other, on the injunctions of the developing inner milieu

We shall quote here several sentences from the diary of S—, in which importance is attached to certain methodological questions of educational work in this respect.

> ... I have difficulties which I cannot solve. I am very sociable; I like to have friends; I like to win as many hearts as I can, and, on the other hand, there are many things in the "friendly" life which shock and repel me. I feel myself responsible for what I see and experience. My classmates like me in general. But my interventions in matters of friendship, responsibility, and moral behavior alienate my classmates, and are the cause of various epithets being directed to my quarter, which cause me sorrow. I often do not know what to do or how to act.

We see from the above that a proper adviser would have a great deal of work here.

The climacteric period is susceptible to positive disintegration of man's life cycle, although to a lesser extent than the maturation period. Because of the character and scope of our work this problem will not be developed here in great detail. We will just mention that the proper adviser in this respect would be a physician specializing in neuroses, psychoneuroses, and psychotherapy, and generally sharp in psychological affairs. Such an adviser could do a great deal here (in the compensation and sublimation of depressive states, of the feeling of inferiority and uselessness) for persons with indicators of the development of personality, with respect to some processes periodically weakened by the pressure of somatopsychic difficulties of the climacteric period.

The method of positive disintegration as applied to difficult and nervous children

When attempting to apply the method of positive disintegration to cases of educational difficulties, nervousness, neuroses, and psychoneuroses, one should be aware of the scheme for shaping these disorders according to the theory of positive disintegration. In general, educational difficulties consist in various forms of social inadaptability which are a result of mistakes made with respect to the child and of the application of improper attitudes and educational methods (sociogenetic causes). Nervousness is characterized by increased psychic excitability (psychomotor, affective, imaginational, sensual, and mental) and intact cognitive powers. Nervousness or increased psychic excitability is based on innate dispositions.

The main causal factors in educational difficulties, therefore, are environmental factors, and in nervousness they are innate factors. In both disorders, however, besides the main causal factor, which dominates, there acts also a secondary factor (in educational difficulties, innate susceptibility, and in nervousness, the influence of the environment). In both groups of disorders there occur, on the one hand, difficulties with proper and correct development (the lack of a sufficiently developed internal environment), and on the other hand, a great susceptibility to development because of the lack of stiffening and the presence of plasticity and increased psychic excitability. Inadaptability in educational difficulties causes opposition, aggression, states of fear, social distortions, and moral depravations; and increased psychic excitability (nervousness) causes, in inadequate educational conditions, an increasingly greater increase of tension, social inadaptability, and eventually a nervous state.

In educational difficulties, as well as in the nervousness of children and young people in the period of maturation and after it, one should develop the internal environment by placing stress on moral sensitivity and responsibility, self-educational and autopsychotherapeutic tendencies. As we have shown, one should apply the following as important additional methods in the developmental periods, and in other periods as chief methods, usually prophylactic in character: the development of interests and capabilities, creating (usually outside the consciousness of the person being educated), from the disposing and directing center, conditions for the affirmation of the individual's positive qualities, with a negation of the negative qualities in conditions of concrete experience.

Of importance here is the method of praise and the method of trial and error, introduced into the area of experiences of the "friendly" life, the suggestion method, and finally the example method. The application of the method of discharging tension in the world of nature and sport is also of marked importance.

The following is an example of the application of these methods in the case of a difficult and nervous child.

M— was a 9-year-old girl, gifted and impulsive, with an inclination to rapid reactions, and with great affective and imaginational excitability. From the time she was 18 months old, M— displayed an inclination to obstinacy. The parents tried to eliminate these symptoms by using the method of not yielding to the child's obstinacy (she was very well liked and rationally educated). This method gave no results, and, at the same time, nightmares were noted. Obstinacy and symptoms of an "affectional wrecking" increased considerably.

After many discussions, the parents decided not to apply, for a long time, any prohibitions or injunctions with respect to any of the symptoms of the child's obstinacy, but displayed (though very slightly) their dissatisfaction by pretending to be careworn or afflicted, and by a discreet withdrawal from the area of the child's psychic tensions. They also became more careful in not letting fear-creating stimuli enter the child's imagination. Simultaneously, a whole system of education for the child was created and her relaxation through play and through contact with nature, animals, and so on, was provided for. After this program was applied carefully for a year, nightmares disappeared, and a childish control of her own behavior, of her impulsiveness, increased, and gradually led to the beginnings of the psychic development of the child's internal environment in the most proper way (the advent of the dynamisms of dissatisfaction with oneself, of "subject-object in oneself," and of the third factor).

As for neuroses and psychoneuroses, particularly with children and young people, we have called attention in other works[3] to their main etiological and pathological factors, and to their developmental dynamisms. Lighter neuroses and psychoneuroses, occurring much more frequently than the more serious ones, reflect various disorders of a different strength and level of the psychic dynamisms, both in the internal and external environments. Symptomatic of neurotic and psychoneurotic individuals are increased psychic excitability, accelerated developmental possibilities, and, most frequently, an "incorrect," discordant development of various dynamisms. In my opinion this discordant development is not rightly appraised when called incorrect in comparison to the control group of "normals," as it should be appraised according to principles worked out for development through psychoneuroses, which points to the peculiar correctness of this way (the way of accelerated development).

We consider fundamental the following elements of positive disintegration as applied to psychoneuroses:

1. Help in the acceleration and crystallization of the maturing dynamisms of the internal environment (for instance, the feeling of guilt, making the ideal concrete, the third factor, the disposing and directing center on a higher level)

2. Help in the multilevel localization of some of the immature, instinctive tendencies and dynamisms of the internal environment

3. Help in the transformation of certain psychoneurotic forms, when expressions of a single neurosis, into more advantageous ones, from the point of view of development

4. When symptoms of several neuroses are observed, help in the accentuation of a psychoneurotic set, the presence of which points to a higher level of development of a given individual (for exam-

---

[3]K. Dabrowski. *Positive Disintegration*. Boston: Little, Brown and Co., 1964; *Inner Psychic Milieu* (in preparation).

ple, the coexistence of psychasthenic as well as neurasthenic and hysterical symptoms, with accentuation placed on the former)

5. Help in the development of partial disintegrations and integrations

6. Help in the development and consolidation of full secondary integration

Because of the exigencies of space, we have to omit detailed description and examples of the application of all these methods. Only a few examples and their interpretation will be given.

L—, a 16-year-old boy of introvertive type with a markedly increased affectional and imaginational excitability, very gifted, experienced a strong and inappropriate dislike of his father (characteristic of the maturation period of such individuals), arising from the weakening of the parent's authority and from his severe criticism of him. Up to that time the father was for him always an authority and a highest example; the boy was simultaneously very much attached to his mother. In this period many features of the father, his movements, gestures, attitudes, ways of doing things, became annoying and even repellent. These states were so strong that there developed a strong feeling of guilt and a state of collision between this feeling of guilt and the boy's growing critical attitude toward the father which was accompanied by a weakening of the father's authority. At that time L— transferred his ideal opinions and feelings from his father to one of his acquaintances, who stood much lower than his father with respect to type, interests, and capabilities.

The father, with the help of an adviser, carried on educational work in the following way:

1. In a confidential talk with the son, held in an appropriate atmosphere, he explained to him certain correct and incorrect aspects of such an attitude and encouraged the son to read, with him, a number of short books on the subject.

2. Knowing his son's capabilities and the somewhat exceptional and original character of the boy's development, he encouraged his son to develop in himself some critical attitudes in relation to the "laws" of man's developmental cycle in the period of maturation, and not to submit himself to these laws uncritically.

3. It was agreed that the son, with the help of the father, would check his attitude of dislike for his father and the attitude of undue enthusiasm with respect to the above-mentioned acquaintance, in whom he saw his new ideal.

4. The father promised the son to discuss with him the positive and negative elements of the feeling of guilt after he (the son) realized the tasks set out for him in the last point.

5. It was agreed that both would return to their first (basic) talk after six months, and until this time the father would try to give technical advice concerning the son's work upon himself – however, only on his request.

This method of working upon the boy gave the desired results – that is, a return to the son's former attitude toward the father, but on a more mature level – the affectional tensions of the boy were weakened generally, as well as in this area, and there occurred a weakening and in fact a reshaping and deepening of the boy's relation to guilt-feeling mechanisms, and an acceleration and strengthening of the "correct" development of the boy. In this way the father helped the boy to deepen some dynamisms of his internal environment (the "subject-object in oneself" dynamism, the feeling of dissatisfaction with oneself, the feeling of guilt); he excited and enhanced self-educational and psychotherapeutic tendencies; he deepened the understanding of developmental dynamisms in the sphere of the partial process of positive disintegration. This influenced the whole psychic development of the boy.

In another case we came into contact with a student from a polytechnical institute, F—, who was characterized by great affectional and imaginational excitability and by considerable originality in literary ideas. F— displayed distinct asthenic and hypochondriacal traits, accompanied by tendencies for conflicts with the environment, phantastic attitudes toward life, a weak function of reality, timidity, fearfulness, and literary existential interests. The method applied here was the sublimation of symptoms, in the sense of "advancing to a higher rank" some of the psychoneurotic symptoms. The development of the boy's creativity was acted upon, the publication of his first works was brought about, and when he was about to finish his Polish-language studies he was urged to enter the faculty of psychology, with the aim of bringing about a deepening of his creative analysis of literary characters and analysis of external observations needed for creativity, and in order to keep the patient's mind off superficial analysis of his own symptoms and excessive, though superficial, philosophizing on existential matters.

An attempt was made to weaken his daily conflictive contacts with the environment and to deepen his creative imagination. The purpose of this effort was to accentuate some symptoms to the detriment of others, to shift to the foreground the psychasthenic symptoms, to develop the beginnings of secondary integration (strengthening of interests and creative work), and to make the imagination extravertive. At the same time Schultz's method of relaxation was applied.

The author ascertained here a distinct accentuation of the process of positive disintegration and a "catching on" of the elements of secondary integration (deepening of the disposing and directing center and the personality ideal becoming concrete).

We will refer to one more case which exemplifies both the methods of helping in the development of, and strengthening of the process of, secondary integration and the methods of the accentuation of certain advantageous psychoneurotic symptoms. The case is that of a 26-year-old seminarian. The patient called on a psychiatrist and asked him for help due to his self-uncertainty, scruples, and difficulty in distinguishing what is sin from what is not sin.

From childhood he had been in general sensitive and nervous. He was drawn to prayer, and he felt the need to understand others and to help them. He entered the seminary because he felt called to be a priest. For years he had doubts as to whether his thoughts and acts were right. He had the feeling of inferiority, was convinced that he was worse than others. He forgot rather easily many experiences, and remembered those which had "even the shadow of sin."

Later, this shadow grew increasingly greater. When he saw somebody who was poor or sick, or witnessed violence and could not remedy the situation, he was gripped by the feeling of guilt and of unfulfilled duty. He was very sensitive to the suffering of people and animals. He experienced very intensely the thought that he might have caused sorrow to somebody, that somebody might have a grudge against him. He always doubted whether he confessed rightly, whether there were no failings in his confession. It seemed to him that God would judge him harshly. He feared professors and examinations. There were no sexual disorders. Heredity was of no particular importance.

He was an individual of high psychic excitability from childhood, brought up in conditions of moral sensitivity and moral injunctions. He was of the reflective, introvertive type, inclined to exaltation, and he possessed a distinctly marked disposing and directing center at a higher level which was headed for development of the personality ideal. He was shy and oversensitive. On the ground of these qualities, through experience, there developed the process of disintegration with the feeling of inferiority, dissatisfaction with himself, guilt, and sin.

This was a case of obsessive psychoneurosis, as can be seen from the following facts: increased excitability, scruples and fears, as well as the feeling of inferiority, the feeling of guilt and sin, which are understandable in the light of increased excitability and educational conditions. The case was further complicated by an excessive conversion of psychic experiences into the vegetative nervous system.

Psychotherapeutic measures applied included attempts to influence a change from the obsessions the patient had about shortcomings in his moral structure to the attitude of elaboration and realization of a hierarchically laid plan of working for the good of others. Care was taken to accentuate and work out the dominant of the synthetic attitude in relation to the analysis of oneself dominant and in relation to experiencing. These psychotherapeutic operations were closely associated with the weakening of the dominant of multilevel disintegration in relation to the dominant of secondary integration (methods of relaxation, meditation, and contemplation).

Based on the author's conceptions of the positive role of nervousness as well as neuroses and psychoneuroses in the development of man, it is evident that, with this conception, the method of psychotherapy composes an integral part of the personality-shaping methods. If we assume that the various forms of inadaptability to the internal environment (educational difficulties), manifestations of psychic hyperexcitability (nervousness), and the numerous forms of neuroses and psychoneuroses constitute indispensable developmental processes, then – extending the thus far accepted meaning of the term *psychotherapy* and treating it as a method of education and self-education in difficult developmental periods, in conditions of great tensions and conflicts in the external environment and in the internal environment – we will be able to understand properly the above-given conception of psychotherapy.

In short, in personality-shaping, psychotherapy and autopsychotherapy are closely connected with the methods of education and self-education in the course of the development of personality. The difference between these two methods of acting upon someone in special developmental periods and in special difficulties resides in the fact that psychotherapy and autopsychotherapy are applied to special difficulties of everyday life and to patients manifesting psychoneuroses.

Therapeutic Methods of Positive Disintegration Applied to Psychoneuroses

Some Principles of Psychotherapy

As a sequel to the discussion pertaining to psychotherapy proper which was brought up in the last section, we would like here to consider the psychotherapy of more specific psychoneurotic sets. It is evident that the shaping of personality under discussion in this volume can be more fully understood if we also include a discussion of the psychotherapy of psychoneuroses, which is, at the same time, one of the principal methods of personality-shaping.

Now what would be the main principles of the psychotherapy of psychoneuroses on the basis of our theory of positive disintegration?

Before answering that question, let us recall the fundamental general principle which must be considered in diagnosis, namely, whether a given psychoneurotic process is connected to unilevel or to multilevel disintegration. During the entire duration of psychotherapy we have to keep that in mind and adapt therapeutic techniques accordingly.

In this section we shall briefly discuss the principles and methods of psychotherapy in psychasthenia, obsessive psychoneurosis, psychoneurotic depression, anxiety, and infantile psychoneurosis. In psychotherapy of psychasthenia we are concerned with stimulation at a higher level, stimulation and development of creative forces, increase of prospective tendencies, awakening or increasing the patient's faith in his own powers and worth, with some emphasis, from time to time, on an increase of the reality function at the lower level in order to counteract the tendency for separation in these two functional complexes (at higher and at lower levels) and excessive underdevelopment of the latter.

In obsessive psychoneurosis, or in obsessional factors in psychasthenia, we have to endeavor in the first place to increase the interests and creative capacities of the patient, to divide into two channels, as it were, his obsession and the activities of his daily life so that the latter may be exercised with the utmost honesty and responsibility, in spite of the coexistent and coactive obsessions. We should go as far as to introduce certain obsessive elements which may have a positive developmental effect into the patient's daily life, such that the totality of obsessions (lower level) is reduced and the introduced "positive" obsession loses its pathological influence and plays instead a more positive role in daily life.

It is important to introduce elements of joy and satisfaction into the patient's life (reinforcement of creative tendencies, conviction of their worthy results, reinforcement of family position as well as social position of the patient) so that they may remove and channel obsessions. Finally – as has been emphasized – it is necessary to raise the level of obsessions to a higher plane, reinforce their developmental character and their positive coupling with daily life, in order to organize in their structure new forces in the service of personality. An attempt at regulation of daily life, in its private and social aspects, has a decisive importance here for loosening and disintegration of those negative elements which are the main factors in the growth of obsessional forces.

Concerning psychoneurotic depression, our basic psychotherapeutic indications are to bring to the patient's attention and make him aware of the positive possibilities of his depressive conditions in the sense of convincing him that a creative role may be hidden behind his periods of alternating excitement and depression, namely, the development of creative inspiration, tension for work, ease of synthesis, awakening of new ideas and their realization during periods of excitement. Behind the facade of depression there may be hidden a psychological withdrawal and recession wherein self-criticism, self-analysis, self-control, a justified dissatisfaction with oneself, feelings of inferiority with respect to one's own possibilities for achievement, all indicate potential for positive growth.

The development of self-control and inner psychic transformation can be effected through the binding of symptoms of depressive psychoneuroses with the entire process of multilevel disintegration and secondary integration, that is to say, through participation of both phases of depression in cooperation with the main dynamisms of development, with the general processes of multilevel disintegration and secondary integration, and with their main representative dynamisms, such as the third factor, the disposing and directing center at a higher level, dynamization of personality ideal.

With respect to anxiety psychoneurosis, it is important, whenever applicable at all, to recover the connection between the anxiety conditions of individual experience and those of a universal character, characteristic of a cultured society, and having a general existential nature. It is important to bring the patient to the realization that some of his conditions of anxiety, decreased activity, fear, tendency for monakowian *ekklisis* are commonly indicative of positive human developmental possibilities. The recovery of the connection between the "pathological dynamisms" and the most important dynamisms of secondary integration on the one hand, and on the other with the release of tensions according to the principles described elsewhere (forms of normal energy release, of psychic rotation of stimuli, interests, etc., regulation of family relations, development of clear elements of personality development such as positive interests and abilities, and relaxation therapy) are here the most fundamental requirements. The last statement emphasizes the importance of administering proper psychotherapy while definite elements of unilevel disintegration are being observed.

With respect to the therapy of infantile psychoneurosis, our directives are as follows: (1) to assist in appropriate recession into an individual phase of positive regression; (2) to help in the orderly development of creative elements; (3) to foster insight into some positive values recoverable from depressive conditions and from some other dynamisms of positive disintegration (this may be done by direct psychotherapy among adults, youths, or even some children, as well as by indicating helpful literature, such as biographies of outstanding people, and by proper encouragement in becoming acquainted with it); (4) to organize a most warm and hearty milieu, especially in the case of children; (5) to encourage involvement with nature and organization of healthy energy release in that area (sport, continual contact with flora and fauna, and so on); and (6) to encourage gradual development of control and strengthening of affects.

Two Individual Cases and Treatment

Even though we have considered many cases, particularly concerning children, in a preceding section, we would like to review here, in greater detail, two further cases.

The first case concerns a man of 33, a scientific worker possessing literary ability with a light obsessional tendency, with increased emotional and imaginational excitability, with preponderance of unilevel disintegration over the multilevel type, but with some definite elements of the latter recognizable. In what follows we produce an excerpt from a discussion with the patient.

> *Psychologist*: You say that you are sick, that you have a psychoneurosis and that you are afraid of falling into a psychic illness, is that correct?
>
> *Patient*: Yes, I am increasingly more concerned about my condition.
>
> *Psychologist*: Do you understand what is the cause of those fears in you? Are you afraid of that which is called "becoming mad"?
>
> *Patient*: Yes, this is what I fear, I am afraid to fall into a low level of self-awareness, of losing my human dignity.
>
> *Psychologist*: Can you say that you are presently losing that "human dignity," that your moral and intellectual forces are weakened, that your refinement is decreased, that you are becoming much less creative?
>
> *Patient* (following reflection): No, I could not say that as yet, I do not notice such deterioration, but I see an increase in my fears, depression and obsession, weakness, and chaos in my human contacts.
>
> *Psychologist*: Let us stop for a while to consider the latter. Does it mean that your understanding of people has deteriorated, along with your capacity for sympathy and ability to help?
>
> *Patient*: No it's not that. What has been increased is the feeling of helplessness, feeling that my attitude of help for others meets

with a vacuum, that I am incapable to help them. However, I do feel their troubles, sadness, helplessness, and often hopeless situation.

Psychologist: And your efficiency in work – is it being decreased, say during the last months, in both quality and quantity?

Patient: Yes, I thought so, but my colleagues say that I think and talk of issues in a more interesting manner during recent months, but that I work unevenly.

Psychologist: Now, do you have some complaints physically, such as headaches, indigestion, sleeplessness?

Patient: Yes, I sleep with difficulty, have strange and depressing dreams. I often wake up with symptoms of anxiety and headache. I often dream of animals, wildly and obsessionally looking at me, terrible and yet unknown to me. I dream of gray walls, ditches; I flee before the unknown, become lost in unknown cities. I am becoming dependent on some strange and unconnected situations. I feel deprived of will, condemned to unexplained activities directed by fate.

Psychologist: Tell me please, what are your most common experiences in real life, what actually causes your anxiety at work, in your social life, in your family?

Patient: I often have psychic tension when dwelling on the objective valuelessness of all that which has for me, and my friends, a great subjective value. It seems like captured in a poetic vision of that which is objective, expressed by a deadly machine, animosity and brutal force against subjectivity, which is for us all the highest type of reality, being however destroyed by the first one. It seems to me that reality is a tragic misunderstanding. I wake up at night to see all things in cruel realism. I notice the shamelessness and limitations in thought and feeling, and the super power of the so-called realists. I see the damage, injustice, and humiliation of people who are spiritually strong but weak from the point of view of ability for adjustment to everyday life. I see around me death, waiting for me as it were. I see the cowardly and nonsensical omittance by people of essential issues. You must understand and observe I am sure, doctor, that in all of which I am speaking there is much existential content. Yes, I have been fascinated for years with existential philosophy. But this is not for me an expression of a passing vogue or snobbery, or of my literary bent. It flows rather from my experiences and interests, which, as it were, went out to meet existential philosophy. I feel very strangely that our subjective reality is something very essential for us, most essential indeed; that one must go through a rebellion of subjectivity against objectivity or reality, even if that rebellion is a priori condemned to failure.

I feel I must form a hierarchy of moral values, based on inner axiomatic tenets, even if all those axioms and philosophy should be extinguished completely by death. There is something in those tenets of subjective aspiration which checks itself, which indicates its own way, which aspires at objectivity with conservation of individual values, which represents the need for continued being and development because otherwise man becomes dehumanized.

That is why I am sick, doctor. Do you really think that there is a medicine for that?

Psychologist: Now, did you not stop to think at times that you are not actually sick, but rather have something like a sixth sense, in your increased sensitivity, psychic activity, alterocentrism, and creative attitude toward reality? Do you not think that one must pay considerably for personal development or growth, especially if it be accelerated? Do you recall the expression of Korzecki in *Homeless People* when, speaking of himself, he says: "I have too much educated consciousness"? Do you not feel your own high responsibility for all that which happens among the people of your environment, closer and further, in your own milieu? That is normal, very normal, as it manifests the realization, to a high degree, of a "standard model norm." No, you are not sick, you are very healthy psychically and you should not think that conditions of anxiety, of your excessive responsibility, protests, emotional attitude, and actions against the so-called "normal life conditions," feelings of dissatisfaction with yourself, are any pathological symptoms. On the contrary, it would be more pathological to adjust yourself excessively to a reality of a lower order. I don't know if you would agree, but I believe that excessive adjustment to reality of a low level, excessive saturation with that reality, prohibits the cognition of reality of a higher type. One who is adjusted to all that which "is," irrespective of its values, has no possibilities nor creative power and will to adjust himself to that which "ought to be."

Patient: You are right – perhaps I should say I would think you are right – but that is hardly a normal psychiatric treatment, doctor. It seems that psychiatrists do not think as you do. On the basis of my experience I must say that to most of them my case is just like so many other cases – subject to pharmacological treatment, "treatment," while ignoring the real problems and prescribing rest, sexual indulgence, et cetera. Furthermore, I feel lonely with my "pathological" experiences. I am very often alone because I do not want to burden my relatives with my own "fancies." And so my life is passed in ambivalent attitudes between that which is close, worthy, really close, creative, between that which one should live through and digest and the need for fleeing from pain, misunderstanding, and human injustice. It seems that we have to build on ourselves, on our own deep humanistic criteria, and fulfill our obligations "to the end." It may be that out of that "fear and trembling" – as Kierkegaard says – there will finally come real knowledge, discovery of the grain of truth, at present quite inaccessible to us, unexpected, and yet somehow foreseen in our very fight with adverse fate.

Interpretation of Therapy from the Point of View of Positive Disintegration. Of course, according to our theory we don't deal here with a psychoneurosis as an illness, but rather with the symptoms of the process of positive disintegration in its multilevel phase, with basic dynamisms of that phase, such as disquietude, feelings of inferiority toward oneself, sense of guilt, feverish seeking of a disposing and directing center at a higher level and a personality ideal which would express the ability to feel the most universal needs of man, to have empathy toward those needs and aims. The normal clinical diagnosis of anxiety psychoneurosis with existential traits gives us little to go on. The patient is in a condition of very strong emotional tension with depressional and anxiety symptoms. A fundamental help for him is the confirmation of the conviction that his symptoms have all the elements of creative, positive psychic development.

It is very important to secure the sympathy and cooperation of a psychiatrist with the same point of view. Formation within the family milieu of conditions conducive to contact with nature, quiet, an artistic milieu, help in a proper attitude toward his work, and appreciation of his efforts, remain our fundamental directives.

The second case we wish to consider is that of Ella, 7½ years old. She was admitted directly to second grade in a public school on the basis of her admission examination. During the first days of school she had many difficulties. She was emotionally overexcitable, had trouble eating and sleeping, and cried at night. There was a weight loss of five pounds, and she showed some signs of anxiety and transient depression. She asked her parents to transfer her to the first grade of the school.

The patient was the older of two children. Her sister, 5 years and 10 months old, was more of an extrovert and more independent than the patient. The mother was harmonious, rather introverted, and systematic in her work. She was concerned about the long-range implications of the patient's difficulties. The father was of mixed type with some cyclic and schizothymic traits. He was dynamic, self-conscious, and self-controlled. The development of both children had presented no special problems. During the preschool period Ella had been an obedient girl but from time to time emotionally overexcitable, ambitious, independent in her activities, and sensitive toward the external environment, though in a subtle, private way. She had always had a great deal of inhibition. At 4½ she had begun to discuss with her parents the problems of loss, of death, and of life after death.

Medical and psychological examinations were both negative. Ella's I.Q. was 128. Her Rorschach indicated an ambiequal type with some predominance of kinesthetic perceptions. Aptitude toward mathematics, decorative arts, and, in general, manual dexterity was evident. There was a tendency for introversion and systematization of work. The first steps in her work and in a new situation were the most difficult for her. Once they had been taken, she did much better. She was very clearly inhibited, although ambitious, and had feelings of inferiority and superiority.

Interpretation. Ella was an introvert with rather schizothymic traits. She was intelligent, self-conscious, and inclined to be emotionally overexcitable, and her excitability was easily transferable to the vegetative nervous system. She was ambitious and tended to be a perfectionist but was somewhat timid and likely to resign in the face of external difficulties. She had symptoms of transient depression, anxiety, and inhibition. However, her aims and ideals were clear, and she leaned toward moral and social concerns. She presented the type of emotional tension very closely related to psychic development.

We see in this case a fairly early stage of positive disintegration with emotional overexcitability, ambivalences, and the initial formation of the psychic internal environment. There is the gradual construction of the disposing and directing center, hindered by the child's inhibition but supported by her determination to handle new situations despite anxiety, her strong feeling of obligation, and her ambitions. This conflict, increased by her need to meet a new situation, presents a crisis in development.

Treatment. This child must be treated with an awareness of the positive function of her symptoms. In our evaluation we see her as an intelligent and ambitious child with many assets who at present is in a developmental crisis. The wisest course would be to help her surmount this crisis. Her successful handling of the school situation will decrease her inhibition, strengthen her disposing and directing center, and contribute to her further development.

Ella can, and preferably should, be treated at a distance and not through direct psychotherapy. Originally, her teacher had intended to transfer the patient to the first grade. The child knew of the decision, and it increased her ambivalence; she was depressed and she herself asked to be transferred. However, after a conversation with the psychiatrist, the teacher changed her mind. Understanding the situation better, she helped the child by not asking her to participate in class but allowing her to come forward whenever she felt prepared to answer. In six months she was one of the best pupils in the class and received an award for her work. Emotional tension diminished and the dystonia of the vegetative nervous system disappeared.

There are further means of help. One could see the child from time to time at long intervals, following her normal lines of development and her normal internal and external conflicts. We must know the conditions of her family and school life and perhaps help her parents to be aware of her developmental needs and, on the basis of this understanding, of the ways in which they can help her to more permanent adaptation both to herself and to social life.

Discussion. We have viewed this case as that of a normal child with a high potential for development and have seen this development through a necessary crisis precipitated by a new, difficult external situation.

We have not recommended any psychiatric treatment. What might be the effect if these symptoms were seen as psychopathological and treated by intense psychotherapy? The emotional, introverted, and self-conscious child could be deeply injured. The labeling of the symptoms as pathological in itself would have a negative effect. In addition, the social milieu would be likely to view the child as disturbed if she were seen in intensive psychotherapy, as, indeed, would the child herself. The apprehensions of the parents might increase, and the teacher might treat the child in a more artificial manner than she would otherwise. All this would increase the emotional tension of the child, especially her tendency toward an introverted attitude and timidity. These conditions could create new problems and an increasing need for psychotherapy.

Directing Ella's attention to the products of her phantasies could result in excessive attention to them and artificially increase their effect (although knowledge of them would give increased understanding to the therapist). Regarding the symptoms as psychopathological would imply the desirability of their elimination. However, they perform a positive function for this child, and to deprive her of them would be a serious matter. Focusing on pathology might accentuate anxiety, inhibition, and flight into sickness. Viewing and treating these symptoms as psychopathological would itself create conditions that would appear to confirm the correctness of that approach.

Let us conclude this section by pointing out once again that the methods of psychotherapy we have discussed are the basis for multidimensional assistance, especially during the difficult period when the patient is overcoming developmental phases and there occurs the awakening and growth of his creative forces and powers of self-perfection. Thus, in every group of symptoms, and in every syndrome, we try to find the so-called "pathological," but positive, elements; we promote their development through their combination with the principal developmental dynamisms. By this elevation of positive "pathological" elements to higher levels and by the strengthening of the creative elements which they contain, we prevent them from becoming isolated from the totality of personality structure and from developing in a negative direction – that is, from degeneration.

This transition from positive "pathological" elements to negative ones, this degeneration, is also prevented by encircling them with healthy elements (elements of a more conscious and higher level of development), by grafting weak but positive "pathological" elements from a lower level onto stronger elements localized at higher levels, and which are more conscious, better controlled, manifesting greater potential for development. Attempts are continually made to increase the patient's self-consciousness, to thus lead him to an understanding of himself as normal – even more, as having the possibility of creative and accelerated development – and to promote his capabilities for autopsychotherapy.

In the light of the theory of positive disintegration, the patient is assisted in the development of his theoretical and practical philosophy of life by acknowledging the necessity of understanding and of admitting difficulties in his everyday life, the necessity of suffering, the necessity of developmental psychic disturbances as elements in accelerated psychic development. He is thus assisted in the development of a conscious, autonomic, authentic personality which is responsible for its own development, for its own "creation."

Chapter 5

Examples of Historical Personalities

Preliminary Approach

In the first part of this work we discussed the importance of the study of historical personalities, namely, in order to become acquainted with the problems of personality in general. To understand the basic shaping processes of personality it is necessary to investigate – knowing, of course, how imperfect such an investigation may be – the development of historical personalities, including prominent scholars, artists, and civic leaders of the past, known to the ordinary man for their contributions to the development of particular realms of life. They owe the fame, memory, recognition, and love, which they have enjoyed for many years, to their eminent qualities of personality.

The study of historical personalities brings into full view elements of man's development in general and of personality development in particular. Moreover, it throws light on the differences between a personality and a genius, between a personality and an outstanding criminal individual; and, finally, it permits us to demonstrate the need for a multilevel understanding of personality.

In our consideration of historical personalities we will try to point out, among others, the following three problems:

1. The main differences in the structure of qualities in the development of personalities and geniuses

2. Differences in the structure of qualities in the development of personalities and in the development of outstanding criminal individuals

3. The necessity for understanding the personality both as an empirical and as a normative conception

Let us briefly treat the first point, paying attention to the essential differences between the process of positive disintegration in the development of personality and in the development of outstanding individuals and individuals of genius. One cannot here draw a very clear demarcation line; nonetheless, it seems that our former considerations will permit us to highlight the differences between the two groups.

The dynamisms that have their source in the structure of the personality ideal play the fundamental role in the process of disintegration in the development of personality. The functions of disintegration, as well as the functions of denial, of secondary integration, and of affirmation, will also find their main source of potency and dynamism in the personality ideal. The "developmental drama" of personality unfolds itself in the area of the self-perfection instinct.

As regards the process of disintegration among individuals of genius, their "developmental drama" takes place in the area of the creative instinct. Although the aspiration for the personality ideal exists, it is not continuous and the source of its main forces is not the structure of the personality ideal but the changeable structure of the internal milieu and the stimuli issuing from the external world.

While the process of disintegration in the development of personality usually has a total character, since it embraces the whole structure of the individual, the process of disintegration among geniuses may not embrace the entire personality but only some fundamental traits of its structure. The process of disintegration in the development of personality shows predominance of multilevel disintegration, but the process of disintegration of geniuses may display an unsteady balance between unilevel and multilevel disintegration. On account of the fundamentally distinct direction of development and the totalization and canalization of ways between the personality ideal and the different layers of the internal environment, the process of disintegration in the development of personality in general moves along the way of progress, and apart from rare cases, does not deflect toward suicide or involutional mental disease or antisocial forms of protest. In outstanding individuals and individuals of genius, the process of disintegration however, may reveal this danger in its development.

Of course, we have also observed instances of conjunction between the process of development of personality and the development of genius. Such conjunction is most advantageous for the individual and the society.

As for the second point, it must be stressed that there have been many individuals who, in contrast to personalities, have left the worst memory with posterity because of their antisocial behavior (Hitler, Stalin). With every one of these individuals we may point out a discordant development of positive qualities which are possessed even by the greatest of criminals. Instead of harmonious development there occurs the overgrowth of some qualities only, sometimes even positive ones (for example, Hitler's original desire to ensure prosperity for the German nation). With time, some qualities of a personality that are aggrandized, not subjected to the active self-control of personality, thus subjugating the remaining tendencies and even intellectual qualities, become a destructive factor in the further development of an individual. Whoever is acquainted with Goebbels' biography will easily recall that the famous propaganda minister of the Third Reich, who placed his intelligence at the service of humanity's greatest criminals, revealed unheard-of will power, ability to renounce, ability for self-discipline, prodigious industriousness, family instinct, and perseverance. Finally, we may recall that he was the only one among Hitler's close collaborators who remained faithful, and who finished his life with a consequent suicidal death.

The study of historical personalities therefore gives us, by contrast, insight into the structure and dynamisms of outstanding criminal individuals and shows us the following fundamental differences: the criminal individual reveals intelligence functions closely linked with primitive instincts; this is an intelligence in the service of instincts; the outstanding criminal individuals are "deaf and dumb" to aims and values other than their own, to the realization of which they often fanatically subordinate themselves; at the root of the activity of such individuals there is sometimes a morbid ambitional or imaginational nucleus.

As for point three, the study of historical personalities points to the necessity of a many-sided approach to personality and consequently we must treat it both from the empirical and the normative points of view. On the one side, if the elaboration is thorough enough, the biographies of the historical figures represent the outline of the developmental process, with its initial, advanced, and final periods, with its main dynamisms and objective motivation, and on the other, they represent a more or less changing (in the course of development) program and ideal for one's own development and the course of its realization.

In this way both aspects of the study, the empirical and the normative, are combined. Every historical personality has its empirical aspect, including an entire, more or less verifiable, sequence of facts. On the other hand, there is the normative aspect, which finds its expression in their plans for developing their personalities. This clearly visible normative aspect does not eliminate the fact that they are still real personalities, accessible by empirical study.

By watching the development of historical personalities we obtain the pattern of this development through disintegration, and we may observe the direction in which a given individual finally develops. Of course, in each of these personalities particular dispositions develop in a different way; they have various intensities, different scopes of activity, and they are realized in different conditions.

We present at this point five examples of the development of individuals, every one of whom rendered services to mankind in a different respect and lived in a different country and under a different system of government. They are: Michelangelo, the 16th-century artistic genius; St. Augustine, religious leader and the cofounder of Christian philosophy; Jan Wladislaw Dawid, prominent Polish psychologist; Clifford W. Beers, originator of the mental-hygiene movement; J. Ferguson, 20th-century physician and civic leader.

With each of these men the process of personality development took a different course, each of them possessed different qualities and capabilities, the disintegration concerned different periods of life, and in mature age each of them remained at a different stage and level of personality development. Nevertheless, they all may be grasped in the scheme of personality development, through the disintegration process presented heretofore. Furthermore, their individual lives are perfect illustrations of the course of the disintegration process.

Michaelangelo

Introductory Remarks

Michelangelo was both a genius and an individual aiming, with all the richness of his psyche, at realization of moral personality. He exemplifies such a fullness of psychic experiences, such a strong development of dynamisms, such great creative tension, and such a vast scale of interests and capabilities that he was unable to complete his development along fundamental lines. He did not arrive at inner peace, that state which we call secondary integration. As we have shown, his process of positive disintegration, with tension and extent almost unequaled, had no time to crystallize fully, although Michelangelo lived a relatively long life. Despite very strong tension in the developmental process and despite great achievements in this development, his genius and personality were too rich to attain within the span of his life secondary tenacity and the new hierarchy of values with a new disposing and directing center, and to remove himself from creative and instinctive-affectional unrest.

Indicators of Personality and Its Manifestations

Michelangelo is an example of the coexistence of enhanced psychic excitability in various areas, chiefly imaginational, affective, and psychomotor, with exceptionally strong dynamisms of volition and with genius and many-sided capabilities. From his early youth these qualities were outlined very clearly. The hard childhood of the boy only served to deepen his prospective attitude, showed him the brutality of life, and made the sensitive boy withdraw within himself. The hard conditions of growth in his youth cast a shadow over Michelangelo's later life. He lost his mother when he was only 6 years old and he remained under the severe control of his stepmother. His father was a difficult, narrow-minded man who scorned his son's interest in "stonecutting." For any neglect in his studies he was severely and brutally punished by his father and uncles. His brothers, who were unbalanced, narrow-minded, and greedy, were a burden to him all his life. The sight of a hanged man (who attempted to kill Lorenzo de Medici) and the recollection of a scuffle in which a fellow painter mutilated Michelangelo's nose, increasing his congenital facial ugliness, remained in his memory for life.

From childhood he displayed a marked sensitivity of the vegetative system together with the sickliness which annoyed him during his later years. Enhanced sensual excitability and a remarkable sensitivity to colors allowed a frequent and strong conversion of psychic experiences into the vegetative system. He suffered from headaches, neuralgia, toothaches, eye aches, fever, gallstones, and urinary stones.

These disharmonies in bodily and spiritual development were already noticeable in childhood. However, we should keep in mind that, despite the above-mentioned pathological disturbances, Michelangelo was physically resistant and indefatigable in work which required great bodily endurance.

This bipolarity of somatic development caused even in his childhood the disintegration of the structure of Michelangelo's personality into experiences not harmoniously connected with, but growing up in, the physical system. Already he displayed fears, was afraid of being infected with plague, feared persecution and death, was constantly anxious about the health of his family and suffered from vague, objectless anxieties. Henceforth strong and general nervousness dominated Michelangelo's entire life.

The source of the rapid, uneven development of the boy was his undoubtedly eminent innate capabilities which, on account of absorbing the greater part of his energy, weakened the nervous system, in consequence of which there began, among other things, the disintegration of harmonious physical development, of which we wrote above. This innate contrast between a strong bodily constitution and vigorous organism and the instability of the vegetative system also caused psychic experiences connected with the realization of interests and capabilities to bring unbalance to the nervous system. In addition, from the time of early childhood certain very strong developmental dynamisms and a number of personality qualities could not find for themselves the possibility of development. The direct causes of the difficulties were unfavorable conditions of development, lack of guidance, lack of appreciation, stultification, orphanhood, and jealousy. He owed the development of his interests only to his own perseverance and his certainty as to his aim.

The sensitive boy had to make do with an unbalanced development and to give up cultivation of a number of personality traits and qualities with which he was liberally endowed. We find them only in later years, during the long formative period of Michelangelo's personality. We may observe how exuberant they are, how they outrun one another in development, some of them declining, but all – of very great tension – illustrate perfectly Michelangelo's struggle with himself. Reducing the above to a few points, we may say that the indicators of Michelangelo's personality were enhanced psychic sensitivity in relation to himself and his environment, his outstanding capabilities in all directions, his conjugation of the feeling of inferiority, of dissatisfaction with himself, with these outstanding capabilities, as well as the remarkable tenseness of the developmental instinct, and psychic disintegrative nuclei (ugliness and outstanding capabilities, physical endurance and susceptibility to diseases, pride and ambitional drives, and affectional attitudes of a lower type).

The Period of the Formation of Personality

Michelangelo's capacity for genius extended in many directions, beginning with sculpture, through painting and poetry, architecture, defense strategy, and ending with a capability for intuitional mathematical analysis and synthesis. Today the design of St. Peter's great dome would require a knowledge of differential calculus, a knowledge which had not been formulated in the 16th century, but which Michelangelo foresaw by such a brilliant design that it gave the maximum strength to the church's architectural composition. He was enthusiastic about philosophy, was on friendly terms with philologists, willingly talked with men of letters and with scholars, was passionately fond of anatomy, and desired to write a work on the shape of the human body He possessed immense capabilities for representing other people's experiences plastically in carving, painting, and in words, and he had a tendency to aggrandize the psychic and physical aspects of observed reality. He was completely independent in his judgments concerning creativity. He executed innumerable sculptures, statues, paintings, all of great artistic value. Ascanio Condivi, Michelangelo's best pupil and later companion and collaborator, when writing about his creation stated the following opinion: "He was up until now the only creator who so worthily applied his hand both to chisel and brush that today no memory is left of ancient painting; and in sculpture he was second to none."[1]

In the area of Michelangelo's uncommon capabilities positive disintegration revealed itself particularly strongly. His dream of life was to achieve the utmost in his works and to reach the supreme artistic ideal. At the same time he was always uncertain as to the value of his sculptures and paintings. He smashed "The Deposition" with a hammer because he thought it artistically unsatisfactory. It would have been lost to posterity had not his servant gathered the pieces together. He did a similar thing with "Leda and the Swan," ordered by Alfonso, prince of Ferrara. When one of the prince's courtiers, receiving the painting, said, "Oh, this is not of much worth," Michelangelo became so furious that he ousted the messenger and gave the picture to a journeyman (Ascanio Condivi). A work executed with the greatest interest caused his flight into solitude and also resulted in a misunderstanding of the artist by his closest friends. This happened when he executed the frescoes of the Sistine Chapel within 20 months, not permitting anybody to help him, even in triturating the paints. He worked alone, on bread and water, in an inconvenient recumbent position, straining his eyesight. He could not bear any advice in his work, and was hated by many. At the court of Pope Julius II he fought with Bramante who, while erecting edifices at the Vatican, so bungled the work that Michelangelo had to teach him how to erect the scaffolding, strengthen the buttresses and barbicans. This made Bramante his greatest enemy. Another interesting feature of the uneven development of Michelangelo's art is the fact that for 15 years "he did not touch the chisel."[2] He returned to Rome only when Pope Clement VII bade him to come. Within several months he executed all the statues now in the Sacristy of St. Lawrence. The themes of his works are by turns classical and Christian. After the "San Antonello" he created "Faun"; after "The Battle of the Centaurs," "Madonna of the Stairs"; after the "Bacchus," the "Pietà"; after the "San Giovanni," the "Amor"; after "The Last Judgment, the "Venera."

---

[1]A. Condivi. *Vita di Michelangelo Buonarroti, raccolta per Ascanio Condivi de la Ripa Transone.* (*The Life of Michelangelo Buonarroti, As Narrated By Ascanio Condivi of La Ripa Transone.*) Rome: A. Blado Stampatore, 1553.

[2]Condivi, *op. cit.*

The greatest of his works, the "Pietà," he finished two days before his death, living in misery, discomfort, and suffering.

Work in the direction of his own interests became the center of the development of Michelangelo's personality. Around his work settled, on various levels and with varying tension, moral, social, and religious traits. This determination and dissociation of the development, as it were, were the cause of the artist's permanent unrest and of his ambivalent feelings and tendencies. Great vigilance with respect to the hierarchy of values, enhanced by the innate genius of his mind and deepened by prospection and the state of ungratified aspirations, are the characteristic traits of Michelangelo. They expressed themselves in nervousness, so often emphasized by his biographers. The artist set his own ugliness against the beauty of the works he created. Filled with introverted sentimentality, he met with resistances in conveying his rich experiences to his environment. Unable to express his need for love and friendship to other people's hearts, the artist worked the raw, hard stone, conveying to it his most lofty dreams and the ideals of his own personality. Excessive activity, the immensity of his projects and interests, his losing himself in his work, his plans for creation (he intended to carve a mountain into a statue to be seen from afar by sailors), all these were the marks of a man who was always in a state of unrest, fear, dissatisfaction with himself. From these sources originated his changeability of mood, his outbursts of anger, his lack of decision, his vehemence and impetuosity.

One of the most important traits of Michelangelo was his immense and never satiated capacity for love. "The whole life of Michelangelo, whether that spent for writing, carving or painting, reveals to us that he was a lover of love ... was in love sensually and spiritually."[3] Buonarroti was continually in love with everything. Primarily he loved his mother with a melancholy orphan's love. This love finds expression in the "Madonna with Child" and the Roman "Pietà." He loved his family, his servants, pupils, paupers, unfortunates, he loved his fatherland, and the whole of humanity. He loved beauty in all its aspects: freedom and truth, nobleness and strength, poetry and song, wit and straight-

---

[3]C. Papini. *Michelangelo, His Life and His Era.* Translated from the Italian by Loretta Murnone. New York: E. P. Dutton & Co., 1952.

forwardness, beauty of the face and harmony of the human body, "all the marvels and beauties of heaven and earth." He loved art, which for many years was the only meaning of life for him. Finally, he loved God, with a love that, with the passage of years, became the only love. He searched for God in his life as an artist. He created religious works, heard the fiery preachings of Savonarola, read the Gospel, attended Mass almost daily, went on pilgrimages, prayed, and spent 17 years of his life gratuitously building St. Peter's Basilica and Gesu Basilica. Toward the end of his life God became the supreme value for him; he denied even his art. Describing his death Daniele da Volterra writes: "Nobody has ever passed away with better feeling and greater devotion." In the deepened love of God there increased a strongly peculiar attitude of worship, of humbleness, of guilt, of inferiority, and of sin, which grows from yearning and the awareness that one's ideals have not been attained. Buonarroti isolates in himself a better and a worse part, as it were. He writes:

> The more I run away from myself in disgust,
> The more my hungry yearning flies to You,
> And fear torments my soul
> About myself in your nearness;
> In your face I seek
> What the luring Heaven
> Promised us faithfully[4]

The consequence of guilt and sin is the need for expiation. For many years Buonarroti endeavored in various ways (by prayer, almsgiving, work, pilgrimages) to satisfy this need.

Biographers emphasize that to the end of his life Michelangelo remained more faithful in his love and friendship toward his closest relatives and friends than they were to their love to him. He presented his servants with paintings, assisted his brothers financially, provided dowries for poor girls. He gave his servant a large sum of 2000 scudi to make him independent after his death.

Characteristic of Michelangelo is his attitude toward women, expressed in many years of friendship with Vittoria Colonna. About this bond Papini wrote that "on the part of Buonarroti it is based above all on the

---

[4]Papini thinks that this is one of the verses directed to the Madonna.

intellectual esteem for Vittoria's virtues, and on the part of the marchioness a high admiration for the artist. The friendship was also based on mutual fervent faith in Christ."[5] Biographers also make mention of Michelangelo's fatherly approach to Laura Battiferro, wife of a deceased friend, and the master's attitude to his pupil Sophonosba Anguissola, to whom he showed "hearty and honorable affection."

Michelangelo was possessed of a deep sense of social responsibility. He fought against people's dishonesty and thievery. When, at the age of 72, he took on gratuitously the management of the building of St. Peter's Church, he firmly opposed the clique of builders who had already been engaged, because in his opinion they were "ignoramuses and exploiters." From that moment he became an object of gossip, insult, and invective. This opposition is strange when we consider that as a private man he was timid and bashful; when insulted, or when he felt his position jeopardized, he fled instead of facing the danger. In his younger years he displayed a primitive fighting instinct which expressed itself in the tendency to bully and offend, to deride and to jeer. Biographers note his tactless and aggressive behavior toward Leonardo da Vinci. It may be that at the root of this was his jealousy and dread of rivals. It happened this way with Torrigiano (who broke his nose), Leonardo da Vinci, Bramante, and with Raffaello da Urbino. He had no rivals toward the end of his life.

As we see, the maturing personality of Michelangelo was characterized by the passage from ambivalent feelings and attitudes, from the struggle of these feelings and attitudes which were at one level, as it were (on the one hand, love and fine feelings, and malice and jealousy, high creative ambitions, and on the other, a meanness in certain matters), to a transcendental feeling of love, that is, a passage from unilevel disintegration to subordination of primitive attitudes and aims to ever higher ones through the process of multilevel disintegration. Creative unrest, gigantic aims and ideals, the need for transcendental values and the realization of the principles of justice, all these associated increasingly more intensely with his feelings of anxiety over himself, dissatisfaction with himself, and with his feeling of guilt. The activity of the third factor, with its work of negation, affirmation, and selection in the in-

---

[5]Papini, *op. cit.*

ternal and external environment, developed ever more intensely. The disposing and directing center localized at a higher and higher level, leaving the level of primitive instincts (primitive ambition, envy, offensiveness, need for recognition, covetousness) and linking increasingly more strongly to transcendental needs, namely, love of ideals, unselfish love of people, increasingly higher level of creative aspirations, compassion for people, and action based on this compassion.

A Brief Outline of His Shaped Personality

The turning point in the artist's life began about 1542. It was a period of unpleasant work in the Pauline chapel, a period which saw the deaths of the greatly adored Cecchino Bracci, Giovanni Simone, the artist's brother, and Vittoria Colonna, and a period in which Michelangelo himself was seriously sick. During this time his mystic experiences increased and his religious attitude attained the upper hand.

Thoughts about his death became the most real for him. Papini suggests that the paintings "Crucifixion of St. Peter" and "Vision of St. Paul," executed at that time, have autobiographic features. Paul, represented as an old man, possesses Michelangelo's features in his face. Michelangelo's disposing and directing center ascended. Eternity became the main object of his thoughts, feelings, and aspirations. He subordinated to it his art, thus far the central point in his personality. He wrote to a friend: "There is no thought in me left untouched by death ... I am so old that death often takes hold of my cloak, bidding me to follow her."[6] In the house where he died he drew death's picture under which he placed a funeral verset. The Christ of the last "Pietà" is "a heavy and very material body, who, not tearing away any more of the divine soul, descends to the grave, desiring to unite with the earth." As he shaped this corpse Michelangelo saw what he himself would become in several days (Papini). In a letter in 1557 to the prince of Florence, Cosima I, he wrote that he would gladly return to Florence, there to wait for his death. He also wrote that day and night he had been trying to familiarize himself with the thought of death. In the last years of his life he wished himself dead; the fear of death had disappeared. This wish was weakened by doubts as to his salvation. He saw death

---

[6]Papini, *op. cit.*

as an extension of creative life ("memory and brain have left in order to await me elsewhere"). The doubts changed into hope for unification with God.

How did the shaping of the various levels of Michelangelo's personality present itself in the last period of his life? We have already said that dominance was won by religious feeling in which he attained high transcendental values. His interests in art and work were consciously removed to the background. From manifestations of his behavior there developed solitariness, suffering of discomfort, and a loss of the remaining friendships after the death of his closest friends. There then grew the feeling of boundless solitude accompanied by the need for contemplation, elevation, and heroism. Michelangelo's ideals of beauty and strength became ever more spiritual. The development of his personality, which he revealed on a gigantic scale, was not finished in time. He lacked calmness, internal peace, and the harmonization of transcendental values with the earthly world. His estrangement from the world was accompanied by the highest development of artistic creation and religious experience.

St. Augustine

Introductory Remarks

The personality of St. Augustine presents a typical example of the development of positive disintegrative dynamisms, highly intensive dynamisms varying in form and in direction of activity. When we take a closer look at the life of the bishop of Hippo, from his early boyhood to the very end, we are struck by the incessant varidirectional multiplicity of the planes of the spiritual development of his personality. In addition, the intensity of development of the particular psychic processes (guilt, subject-object, perfection) is much greater with St. Augustine than with the average man. This was the cause of his constant struggle with himself and his selection of various contradictory ways of attaining the truth. Incessant struggle for better knowledge of himself, selection from among various forms of life, and final preference for the supernatural values over all others, these were the results of many years of deliberations, doubts, breakdowns, and spiritual ascents. This state is perfectly illustrated by many facts from St. Augustine's life which have been published in detail up to the present day. We shall here omit any systematic study of the course of St. Augustine's life from childhood to complete maturation. We merely want to make the reader, who can learn from biography the events that took place in St. Augustine's life, sensitive enough to be able to discover in these facts the manifestations of certain laws according to which the development of St. Augustine's personality took its course. For the theory of disintegration St. Augustine is, in some respects, its perfect illustration, although his life would not suffice to give the reader a complete reflection of the theory of disintegration.

As we shall see, St. Augustine in his last years of life had not yet attained a full harmonization of the contradictory tendencies which agitated him from his youth. Indeed, certain of his acts were in contrast with the ideal of a matured personality which he voluntarily imposed upon himself.

At the root of his positive disintegration lay the conflicting character of his psyche. A violent temperament, and an easily aroused sensual excitability inherited from his father, combined with a deep intelligence, gentleness, and goodness from his mother. This was most explicitly expressed by Papini:

> There was in him the sensualist of his father, and the tender-hearted mystic of his mother; the greedy lover of praises and the humble self-tormentor; with his sharp and subtle sensitivity he could perceive even the farthest figures of importance in the world, the most subtle movements of the human soul, and at the same time there was present in him harmony of mind, moderate and human wisdom; a tendency to the excessive erotic life early practiced, and at the same time a serenity, present often in him, which flourished in angelical and evangelical simplicity; pulsations of eager and explosive passions ... There was combined in him pedantry with mysticism, a high level of thinking, exact and systematic, with affectional fire, violence, disquietude, suffering joy. ... Abstraction and lyricism, logic and love of neighbor alternating but never contradicting and often complementing each other ... He is a sinner first and then saint, professor first and then shepherd, but at the same time he is a convert and a ruling man, a poet and rationalist, dialectician and romanticist, traditionalist, eloquent

rhetorician and popularizing orator.[7]

Such characteristics already show that the possessor of this personality was doomed to a life of constant struggle and suffering, which in effect did not bring him the appeasement he sought; in fact, as the same author writes:

> Augustine found happiness in nothing before he reached thirty years of age. ... Neither the first academic or stage triumphs of his youth, nor the Manichaean apostolate, nor philosophical researches, nor even a woman's love or his son's smile gave him the permanent joy of perfect happiness.[8]

His conversion, his discovery of truth, his changes in his mode of living, his scientific achievements, his deepening love for his nearest relatives and friends, all these and more St. Augustine owed to long, long inner struggle and meditation, to errors and to violent clashing with himself.

Beginnings of the Development of Personality

We may distinguish three periods in the shaping of St. Augustine's personality: its germination, formation, and full development. Let us briefly examine the first period, which embraces childhood and youth, namely from his infancy until he was 20 years of age.

As a child Augustine was fragile, and he remained sickly all his life. As a boy and a young man he displayed a very good memory. He was fond of amusements, shows, and sporting competitions. He was ambitious, recalcitrant, cheated in games, and was greedy; he lied and stole. Although he respected knowledge he did not like to learn and he had aversion to mathematics and Greek. On the other hand he willingly read poetry, particularly the *Iliad* and the *Aeneid*.

As a young man he set a high value on friendship; he was afraid of contempt; he was ashamed of his chastity before his companions, he was suggestive and voluptuous, and he wanted to be happy and famous. While studying in Carthage he acquired the knowledge demanded of a

---

[7]G. Papini. *Sant' Agostino.* Verona: A. Mondadori, 1964.

[8]Papini, *op. cit.*

rhetorician, but also took part in all the joys which this "city of Venus" then offered to its inhabitants (theater, amphitheater, circus, racing, "clubs"). At that time he fell in love, and remained faithful for fourteen years. ("In those years I had one, not in that which is called lawful marriage ... yet remaining faithful to her."[9]) The death of his father did not affect him much.

Although in the first period of his life he showed no great tendency for reshaping himself – he did no work upon himself in a broad sense, his behavior was controlled by the self-preservation and sexual instincts – nonetheless, the indicators of personality became rather marked in this period. They consisted in a manifold psychic hypersensitivity, uncommon intelligence,[10] ambition, exclusiveness of affections, love, a capability for introspection, a sensitivity to real greatness, and a peculiar faith in Christ.[11]

We may say, therefore, that the psychic structure of young Augustine was indeed primitively integrated, but there were inherent in it considerable possibilities for the development of personality. In the first period of Augustine's life, these germs of personality revealed themselves primarily in the area of feelings: unilevel disintegration of the emotional sphere. There were also weak manifestations of multilevel disintegration.

Augustine did not feel happy. He yearned for something great, boundless and unending. "I panted after honors, gain, marriage ..."[12] His disintegration deepened the moment he read "Hortensius," Cicero's philosophical treatise. There awakened in him fear as to the morality of the life he was leading; his ambivalence in relation to sensual pleasures increased; his intellectual disquietude arose, but "Hortensius" gave cer-

---

[9] *Confessions*, IV, p. 48. All quotations from St. Augustine are taken from *St. Augustine's Confessions*. Translated by Edward B. Pusey. ("Harvard Classics.") New York: P. F. Collier & Son, 1909.

[10] "...that, scarce twenty years old, a book of Aristotle, called the 'Ten Predicaments,' falling into my hands, and I read and understood it unaided ... read and understood by myself the books of those arts that are called liberal which I had an opportunity to read." *Ibid.*, IV, p. 62.

[11] E. Gilson writes that St. Augustine "never ceased to believe that Christ is ... the only way to happiness open to man." E. H. Gilson. *The Christian Philosophy of St. Augustine*. Translated by L. E. M. Lynch. New York: Random House, 1960.

[12] St. Augustine, *op. cit.*, IV, p. 62.

tainty to Augustine that wisdom and supreme good exist and they became a necessity for him, "... because even then I desired to be wise, and to grow from worse to better ..."[13] E. Gilson writes, "Wisdom, the object of philosophy was united in him with happiness. He seeks that good which satisfies all his desires and in effect brings appeasement."[14] He sought this wisdom in Christ, whom he worshiped from childhood, and found delight in reading the Holy Scriptures. He could not understand them, however, and this brought him to Manichaeism, which promised him a rational explanation of the Bible and not an anthropomorphic presentation of God.

This is the picture of disintegration in the first period.

The Period of the Formation of Personality

The disintegration of Augustine's psychic structure that began in the first period deepened markedly in the second period of his life. This period lasted about 13 years. The disintegration of the former period deepened and extended into the sphere of feelings, as well as into his intellectual, religious, and social life.

Augustine for the first time experienced the problem of death. A friend of his had died: "At this grief my heart was utterly darkened ... my native country was a torment to me, my father's house a strange unhappiness. ... Only tears were sweet to me."[15]

> I fretted then, sighed, wept, was distracted; had neither rest nor counsel. For I bore about a shattered and bleeding soul, impatient of being borne by me, yet where to repose it, I found not. I felt an uneasiness in my soul; not in calm groves, not in games and music, nor in fragrant spots, nor in curious banquetings, nor in the pleasures of the bed and couch; nor (finally) in books or poesy, found it repose. All things looked ghastly, yea, the very light; whatsoever was not what he was, was revolting and hateful.[16]

In these circumstances the ambivalence increased in relation to the problems of life and death, "... for at once I loathed exceedingly to live

---

[13] *Ibid.*, VI, p. 87.
[14] Gilson, *op. cit.*
[15] St. Augustine, *op. cit.*, IV, p. 51.
[16] *Ibid.*, p. 53.

and feared to die."[17] "... For I felt that my soul and his soul were one soul in two bodies and therefore was my life a horror to me because I would not live halved and therefore perchance I feared to die, lest he whom I had loved so much should die wholly."[18] There ensued, in a sense, a separation of intellect from volition: "To thee, O Lord, my soul ought to have been raised, for thee to light; I knew it; but neither could nor would seek the remedy."[19] Here we see appearing the "subject-object-in-oneself" dynamism: "I became unto myself an enigma, and I would ask my soul why it was sad, and why it afflicted me so vehemently, yet it could give me no answer."[20]

Experiences brought on by the death of his friend did not last long. His sensualism and primitive self-preservation instinct continued to be very strong. Augustine found new friends. After a quarrel with his mother he stayed at one of his friends and threw himself into an intemperate life. He did not, however, return entirely and forever to his former level of primitive integration, for he did not feel any happier, because always seeking truth he experienced disquietude.

There ensued further multidirectional development of the intellect (at about the age of 30). Multilevel disintegration manifested itself in this sphere. Its direct causes were contacts with the leading representatives of Manichaeism and Catholicism.

These contacts brought hesitation and uncertainty to Augustine. His trust in Manichaeism was shaken, and on the other hand there increased in him the need for a mathematical certainty as to the positive attitude of Catholicism. "For I desired to be assured of that which I did not see, as fully as I was certain that seven and three make ten."[21] This state caused skepticism to arise in him, and with it many rather unpleasant experiences: "Doubt, then, what to hold for certain, the more sharply gnawed my heart."[22] There then arose dissatisfaction with himself, "the more ashamed I was, that so long deluded and deceived by the promise

---

[17] *Ibid.*, pp. 53–54.
[18] *Ibid.*, pp. 52–54.
[19] *Ibid.*, p. 54.
[20] *Ibid.*, p. 61.
[21] *Ibid.*, VI, p. 86.
[22] *Idem.*

of certainties ..."[23] However, this was still not the feeling of guilt: "For I still thought that it was not we that sin, but that I know not what other nature sinned in us; and it delighted my pride to be free from blame; and when I had done an evil, not to confess I had done any ... But I loved to excuse myself, and to accuse I know not what other thing, which was with me, but which I was not."[24] Here we see the "splitting" of personality into observed and observing factors; that is, there developed the self-observation dynamism, which was not at the same time a self-educating factor.

In course of time the dissatisfaction with himself changed into shame, to which something near despair attached because of the loss of hope of the possibility of finding the truth. He sought further, however, and leaned toward Catholicism, but here new difficulties arose. The first concerned his apprehension of spiritual beings (Augustine was completely unable to apprehend immaterial things[25]) and the second concerned the question of solving the problems of personal life within the framework of Christian morality. The disintegration already embraced the intellect, the volition, and the feelings.

There are moments when Augustine felt tired of his inner disintegration.

> Meanwhile my sins were being multiplied and my concubine being torn from my side as a hindrance to my marriage, my heart which clave unto her was torn and wounded and bleeding. And she returned to Africa, vowing unto Thee never to know any other man, leaving with me my son by her. But unhappy I, who could not imitate a very woman, impatient of delay, procured another, though no wife. ... Nor was my wound cured, which had been made by the cutting away of the former, but after inflammation and most acute pain, it mortified, in time my pain became less acute but more desperate.[26]

He was then attracted by a calm and regular life.

> ... see it is no great matter now to obtain some station, and then what should we more wish for? We have store of powerful friends;

[23] *Ibid.*, V, p. 77.
[24] *Ibid.*, VIII, p. 147.
[25] Gilson, *op. cit.*
[26] St. Augustine, *op. cit.*, VI, p. 100.

if nothing else offer, and we be in much haste, at least a pres-
identship may be given us: and a wife with some money, that
she increase not our charges: and this shall be the bound of desire. Many great men, and most worthy of imitation, have given
themselves to the study of wisdom in the state of marriage.[27]

We may say that these were short-lived projections of primitive integration – what in modern terminology we would call relaxation in a too
intensive developmental process. However, the fear of death and its
consequences prevented his integration at a lower level.

> ... nor did anything call me back from a yet deeper gulf of carnal
> pleasures, but the fear of death and of Thy future judgment to
> come. ...[28]

This fear deepened disintegration and led to a valuation of his inner
attitudes, to a hierarchical structuring of his aims, to phenomena typical
of multilevel disintegration and to the beginnings of integration at a
higher level. It should be made clear that St. Augustine's apprehension,
resulting from a fear of justice and of punishment for his early life, was at
that time not the manifestation of pure selfless love toward the highest
Ideal; it was a fear of a lower level, which in later years changed into
selfless love. There developed an intense feeling of his own guilt and
the feeling of shame in relation to himself, which were lacking in the
former period.

> ... and I found myself in an evil way. And for this I grieved,
> and thereby I doubled my grief ...[29]
> ... where I had placed it [his soul] so that I might see it not ...
> that I might see myself, how deformed I was, how sordid, how full
> of spots and sores.[30]

The extant psychic structure was, however, not sufficiently disintegrated. The new and old dynamisms collided.

---

[27] *Ibid.*, p. 97.
[28] *Ibid.*, p. 100.
[29] *Ibid.*, p. 90.
[30] *Ibid.*, VIII, p. 135.

> ... my two wills, one old and the other new, one carnal and the other spiritual, fight, one against the other, and by their discord they drag my soul asunder.[31]

The results of this conflict were intensification of ambivalence toward higher values.

> Was it not I that willed, was it not I that could not will, when I was deliberating whether I should serve my Lord ...[32]
> I ... begged for chastity at Thy hand, and thus I said, "Give me Chastity and Continence, but do not give it yet."[33]

Kierkegaardean fear and trembling, the feeling of guilt, the struggle of rising to a higher level, slow crystallization of the third factor.

Finally the spiritual crisis came and Augustine was converted. Having overcome inner resistances he united unreservedly with his ideal, thus rising to a higher level and becoming more calm. Significant here is the scene described in the *Confessions*:

> ... And I cried out at large to Thee ... How long, how long? To-morrow and to-morrow? Why not even now? Why not even at this instant, make an end of my uncleanness? ... And lo, I heard a voice ... 'Take up and read. Take up and read.'

And – as he says himself – after he read the passage of the Gospel commanding him to change his way of life:

> No further would I read, nor was there cause why I should; for instantly with the end of this sentence, as by a clear and constant light infused into my heart, the darkness of all former doubts was driven away. ... I desired nothing more ... nor did I have any other ambition in this world.[34]

He slowly became a "new man." He became a self-affirming and self-educating personality in this second period of the development of positive disintegrative dynamisms. Ambitendencies disappeared and ambivalences weakened considerably. There appeared the attitude of moral vigilance, which prevents one from slipping to a lower level.

---

[31] *Ibid.*, p. 139.
[32] *Ibid.*, p. 140.
[33] *Idem.*
[34] *Ibid.*, pp. 141–142.

> ... rejoicing with trembling, in that which Thou hast given me,
> and bemoaning that wherein I am still imperfect ... a daily war
> by fasting, often 'bringing my body into subjugation' ... Placed
> then amid these temptations I strive daily against concupiscence
> in eating and drinking ... My evil sorrows strive with my good
> joys; and on which side is the victory, I know not ... And no one
> ought to be secure in that life ... that he, who hath been capable
> of worse to be made better may not likewise of better be made
> worse.[35]

There also appeared humility, a full opening to transcendental values.

> Thou calledst and shoutedst, and burstest my deafness. Thou
> flashedst, shinest, and scatteredst my blindness and [I] pant for
> Thee ... and I burned for Thy peace.[36]

In addition the feeling of guilt and love in relation to the highest ideal
appeared,[37] and finally his mystic experiences intensified.[38]

This transformation of Augustine's personality brought very useful
results to the whole range of matters to which he devoted himself. Having thought over his attitude toward life and his place in it, Augustine
became a useful man in the Christian community, and as a bishop fulfilled his duties successfully. He was wholly consistent in his attempts
to realize in his own life, and in teaching others, the goals of life which
he considered true. High intelligence and a deeply philosophical mind
led Augustine to create, as a consequence of the correct development
of his personality, the foundations of Christian philosophy for centuries
to come. Right up until the present time certain of his thoughts – for
instance, his conceptions of the world, of man, and of the spiritual life –
are ideas that are fertile for thousands of human minds. His philosophy
reflects the shaping of his personality by way of positive disintegration
and secondary integration.

---

[35] *Ibid.*, X, p. 191.

[36] *Ibid.*, p. 188.

[37] "Yet I, though in Thy sight I despise myself and account myself dust and ashes ..."
  Ibid., X, p. 173.

[38] *Ibid.*, p. 195.

A Brief Outline of His Shaped Personality

St. Augustine possessed all forms of excitability: sensual, affectional, psychomotor, imaginational, and mental. Sensual hyperexcitability is the ground for perpetual sensual hunger, continual and excessive satiation and dissatisfactions. Affectional hyperexcitability constitutes the ground for compassion, pity, anxiety about others and about one's own thread of life in connection with recollection and on analysis of the past. Psychomotor hyperexcitability, in conjunction with the other forms, is the main cause of violent reactions, motor unrest, and the need for action. Imaginational excitability plays a great role in forming the hierarchy of aims and in the development of prospection. Finally, mental excitability causes a whirl, a stream of problems, thoughts, multidimensional mental attitudes, and a richness of associations and methods of work.

His variety of feelings and interests made Augustine sensitive to everything human and to all the complications of life. Strong instincts, increased excitability, a variety of seemingly contradictory interests, all these caused his fluctuations in life, his tensions and depressions, his disquietude and enthusiasm. What we view here, therefore, is a violent process of disintegration.

The state of his continual sensual and affectional dissatisfactions, his instability of attitudes and variety of changing interests, his ambivalencies and ambitendencies did not yield the possibility of finding the center which harmonizes the other dynamisms and forms a hierarchy between them. This state of continual psychic fluctuation became unbearable for him. In these circumstances there gradually arose a tendency to depart from his early way of life that was based on the self-preservation and sexual instincts. His awareness of inner disorder increased; the tendency toward a more harmonious shaping of his spiritual self also increased. His "salvation" was at stake. The growing self-consciousness and yearning to transcend the present level combined with an increasing aversion for himself, with the feelings of inferiority and guilt, growing to self-hatred. The advancing process of disintegration introduced ever more fully the valuative or estimating factor.

The Manichaean dualism is solved by loving God as the highest good; skepticism is leveled by the introduction of the hierarchy of values and by the unification of free will with the will of God; sensual instincts transform into an enhanced sensitivity to beauty; affectional hyperexcitability transforms into a love of God and neighbor; imaginational hyperexcitability develops into a prospection in relation to goals. New attitudes and achievements lead to the discovery of the way to ecstasy. Secondary integration is thus attained. Ceasing to be the servant of contradictions and destroying nothing natural, but appraising and feeling them from the spiritual point of view, St. Augustine transformed his sexual drive into a love of beauty, transformed the species instinct into compassion, pity, sensitivity, and active love of his neighbor, thus creating a mature, self-conscious affectional attitude.

Can one say that St. Augustine's personality reached its fullness? Did it attain the highest development with respect to all fundamental qualities?

According to general opinion, the life of St. Augustine represents the process of toilsome harmonization of various tendencies. It seems to us, however, that with respect to certain qualities, this process did not fully come to its end. Excessive pride, for example, was not fully sublimated, because there remained some feeling of distance with respect to inferiors. Augustine also remained to the end of his life a man who loved external beauty, nature, motion, a man who found delight in seeing, seeking, and creating. Even when he was an old man he enjoyed himself like a boy, watching a dog chasing a hare, a lizard catching a fly, and a spider preparing its web to capture its prey. Papini is right in saying that Augustine calmed in himself and condemned, but did not annihilate, three fundamental concupiscences, namely, delightfulness, curiosity, and pride. It also appears that St. Augustine had no very close or devoted friends.

The tension between the kingdoms of God and Satan – reflecting on the one hand an earthly apprehension of himself, even including contempt for God, and on the other the love of God, to the point of contempt for himself – is represented in one of his chief works (*De Civitate Dei*) and is evidence of his keen mental and vital dualistic attitude.

However, notwithstanding this incompleteness and lack of achievement in certain areas, we may say that St. Augustine reached the highest development with respect to the majority of positive general human qualities.

J. W. Dawid

Introductory Remarks

J. W. Dawid, a Polish psychologist known for his numerous outstanding works, is a relatively rare instance of a fundamental typological and mental transformation which took place in the course of a few years under the influence of a great psychic injury. This injury brought about the disintegration of his former psychic structure and the replacement of it by a new structure of a different character, of different aspirations and attitudes toward life, and of a different world outlook and different hierarchy of values.

From his youth Dawid was interested in books and in theoretical deliberations. He revealed an introverted and probably schizothymic attitude. Those who knew him in his mature years maintained that he was characterized by a certain coolness in his affections or by great composure, an impersonal attitude, and a belief in the strength of his own intellect.

He was a representative of the school of experimental psychology; accuracy and clarity characterized his thinking and speech. As a young scientist he pointed out (at the International Congress of Education in Munich in 1896) the degeneration of analytic schools of psychology and pedagogy, and that the positivist movement had already won a clear victory over those movements characterized by spiritualistic trends. At that time Dawid displayed a tendency to base his thinking strictly on observed facts, and a reluctance to accept any obscure argumentation.

The whole of Dawid's work between the years 1881 and 1910 is characterized by stolidity and the accuracy of a scholar. He interprets life by physicochemical phenomena. All that which could not be subjected to an experiment was in his opinion not worth the effort of thought at all.

The last four years of his life present a completely different picture. It was a period of hard experiences, of deep sufferings, of the disintegration of his psyche, and of the development of faith in the existence of the supernatural world. These exceptional changes were caused by the suicide committed by his dearly beloved wife whom he could not or knew not how to protect against internal conflicts and their tragic solution.

A fundamental problem arises here, namely, what were the essential causal factors, what were the causal dynamisms in Dawid's psychic structure which were activated by this tragic occurrence, and which may throw some light on the deep changes in his psyche?

Indicators of Personality

In the period briefly outlined above, Dawid already revealed certain qualities and certain attitudes in which one could see some of the indicators of a fuller development of personality. That is to say, he revealed the need for formulating in himself not only the ideal of a scholar but also that of a man; he revealed wide scientific and social interests, courage, steadfastness, the need to realize ideals in everyday life, and creative unrest. He displayed a strong affectional engagement in the fight with directions of philosophical thought other than his own, and – as he himself confessed – it was impossible for him to accept a calm and indifferent attitude toward certain scientific and social questions which were of concern to him and in relation to which he adopted an attitude of protest.

The tendency to find not only the most proper system of philosophy but also a philosophy of life was – in our belief – a reflection of his need to shape his personality. Besides, Dawid had, as is known, a fundamental need for affectional, exclusive, and lasting bonds. These qualities and attitudes point, we believe, to certain disharmonious traits and nuclear dynamisms of positive disintegration – that is, to indicators of a fuller development of personality.

The Period of the Formation of Personality

The nuclei of personality, in the sense of the above-mentioned traits and dynamisms, had been activated, accelerated in development, and deepened through the greatest misfortune of Dawid's life. Under the influence of this misfortune he experienced the feeling of the complete disintegration of his structure, the dissolution of the foundations of his existence, the swaying and, strictly speaking, destruction of his thus far existing disposing and directing center, represented by his system of views and philosophical methods, as well as by attitudes toward life in living together and in cooperation with his wife.

We may assume that schizoid, introverted types, not too strongly tied to the external world, display attachment deeper than average to their next of kin, and the loss of one of their kin causes comparatively greater injury because of their retiring nature, exclusiveness of affections, their greater intensity and greater difficulty in adapting to new conditions. Excerpts from one of Dawid's letters throw light on this period of struggle and crisis:

> I loved my wife deeply, she filled the greater part of my life ... it scorches me to think that I did nothing to save her, that in the course of many years I contributed to this through my behavior ... I was always cocksure, conceited, strong and a rigorous judge ... Her death awakened in me a new organ, as it were, a capability to see and realize certain things in life ... now the only thing that is left to me is despair, which is an absolutely mortal disease. I just ask myself whether this is weakness? It may be so, but this depends on the point of view. I only know that in the last few years I learned more than in my whole life. I have never had such full knowledge about myself, such an awareness of the meaning of life, and of duty.[39]

These excerpts clearly point to the changes in Dawid's fundamental attitude, caused by his wife's suicide. According to Lukrec, friend and biographer of Dawid, there was a "deadly struggle" in him between an empiricist and a mystic: "a titan of accurate knowledge, demanding proofs and facts, and a despairing, lonely man aspiring for faith and life after death and for the possibility of uniting himself with his beloved wife."[40]

This struggle lasted for years and was accompanied by symptoms occurring in deep mysticism, namely, the feelings of inferiority in relation to others and oneself, the feeling of guilt, self-accusation, and asceticism. Before these shocks Dawid had no real reasons to feel guilty. Lukrec explains this in the following way:

---

[39] J. W. Dawid. *Ostatnie mysli i wyznania.* (*Last Thoughts and Confessions.*) Warsaw: Nasza Ksiegarnia, 1937.

[40] *Ibid.* Introduction by Lukrec.

This moral self-accusation is not a test of Dawid's moral value, but a test of his new spiritual life. Dawid's true moral picture is reflected by his works and ideas, by his highest demands on his own life, by his unselfishness, poverty, by his incessant protection of the weak and wronged, and by his strong fight for scientific, social, and political principles and convictions.[41]

His despair after the death of his wife ruined his physique and exhausted him mentally. Gradually a tubercular condition set in. Simultaneously with the weakening of the somatic functions, the need for a spiritual union with his wife grew in paroxysms of suffering, sharpness of intuition, and sometimes in hallucinations.

"Pain gave me new strength. One day, when I was in this state, I heard a voice: 'Don't cry, Wadysaw, it had to happen, I had to do it.' These words were uttered by myself, but at the same time they came from my lips involuntarily ... it came to my mind immediately that after all I may die, that I should die. This thought brought me contentment and relaxation. The first motive was the escape from pain, then other feelings and motives of punishment and expiation concentrated around this vision."[42]

In this new mental attitude, materialism was replaced by spiritualism; in psychological-educational methods intuition and inner experiment replaced natural experiment. Reshaping through personal experiences, and especially through sufferings and the conscious and active weakening and then the destruction of low impulses by a man capable of intensive life (the spirit of sacrifice, charity, and suffering) created new aims. In this process suffering, accepted by his own will, played a fundamental role. In his tendency to strengthen himself in spiritual reality Dawid – with all his possibilities and limitations – suppressed everything that connected him with his former life, and primarily with his sensual experiences and needs.

Suffering elevates a man, ennobles his spirit, but this takes place only in cases of active suffering, as a result of conscious will and an effort to sacrifice oneself in the name of a higher ideal. We see that the need here for suffering and its assessment were caused by the belief

---

[41]*Idem.*
[42]Dawid, *op. cit.*

that only in this way would it be possible to regain contact with the beloved person. What Dawid emphasizes several times in his statements about reshaping is the role of suffering in elevating love of a lower order into ideal love, love in another reality. Suffering which finds its expression in the feeling of guilt may be regarded, on one hand, as a process flowing from typological traits (introspection, self-sufficiency, introversion), which causes a feeling of excessive responsibility for one's deed, and on the other hand, as a mark of new values emerging, which act with extraordinary power and at the same time cause sorrow on account of the disappearance of the thus far strongly held values. If the suffering appears in the mind of a person living a new life as a condition sine qua non of obtaining new values (in this case the spiritual bond with the beloved person who had passed away), then the need for sacrifice is strictly connected with this dynamism.

> The deepest and the most essential trait of the mystical life is the need, the hunger for sacrificing oneself in this or that form, partly or completely. The highest and most perfect sacrifice is death and in fact one may say, from a certain point of view, that the essence of mysticism is the process of dying, including its last stage – death. Dying is not only a passive self-denying, but at the same time an active self-sacrificing. Every unselfish deed, every sacrifice, every effort made on behalf of others, is deathlike because it is a giving away of a part of one's body. Many must become impassive to hunger, to sensual pleasures, and to intellectual delights.
>
> We must lose these pleasures in order to gain others, we must renounce everything that is good in life to such an extent that later this renouncement becomes an integral part of us in our efforts, volition, and contemplation. Why are people brought up to face life but not death? He who does not know how to die, also does not know how to live. In order to acquire the capability for deeds such as those of heroism and sacrifice we must accept death beforehand and consider it as one of the most fundamental problems.[43]

His idealization of his wife, his feeling of guilt in connection with her suicide, the inclusion of suicide into his philosophy of life, and his own

---

[43] *Ibid.*, p. 157.

suicidal tendencies were a basis for the acceptance by Dawid of suicide as a positive phenomenon from the moral point of view. Suicide came into play here as a punishment, as a sacrifice, as a tendency for union with the beloved person, and as a reflection of the barrenness of life.

> In all great changes in moral crises, the idea of suicide arises almost always, at least as one of the alternatives. The mystics do not bind themselves to their bodies and senses, they reveal the need for death; conversion is very often accompanied by suicidal thoughts. This "other" person is outside of life, is transcendental and only in these conditions may he set himself against the empirical person. The will of death is the declaration of death, it is a protest and final harbinger of the victory of life over death, it is the suffering and despair, which belong to this world.[44]

In the last years of Dawid's life, therefore, there took place fundamental changes through the process of positive disintegration. Grievous experiences had, as we have already mentioned, activated his nuclei of personality and accelerated their crystallization. There arose and developed, very intensively, dissatisfaction with himself, feelings of guilt and sin, and the feeling of "otherness." There developed the awareness of the necessity of changes, of acquiring a new disposing and directing center which would take the place of the destroyed one, a new center formed from a set of feelings and aims which would bring about a new spiritual and transcendental being.

Through the denial of the majority of the thus far accepted values and tendencies in himself, through affirmation of new values and tendencies which arose in the process of positive disintegration, through the reconstruction and structuring of his relation to the environment, the so-called third factor was very clearly formed in Dawid's personality. All these dynamisms strengthened Dawid's attitude of love toward people and ideals, strengthened his courage, developed his self-awareness, formed a positive relation to the process of disintegration of many of his own values accepted thus far, and led to the shaping of a new personality in the process of secondary integration.

---

[44] *Ibid.*, p. 138.

A Brief Outline of Dawid's New Peronsality

Dawid's new personality is indeed a new personality and one can only find with difficulty the nuclei of this personality in the period preceding his tragic experiences. In the place of a life organized within a rather narrow framework of a philosophical system, exact scientific methods, selected contacts, and considerable assurance, there entered into the new personality strong internal conflicts, the feeling of inferiority in relation to himself, the feeling of dissatisfaction with himself, the feeling of guilt, and these gradually shaped a new disposing and directing center in the form of faith in transcendental reality, belief in the value of the mystical attitude and the contemplation method, as well as in a love for people, a capacity for self-sacrifice, and the will to face the unknowable. In place of his former scientific interests and tendencies arose – upon their negation – interests in the spiritual world and the tendency to realize its goals. In place of a physically lost loved one came the will to find her in the transcendental world.

There ensued the renouncement of the thus far affirmed values and the affirmation of thus far negated values both in himself and in the external world (the advent and development of the third factor). There arose, and then distinctly developed, a structuring of values with a grasp of the reality of the highest hierarchy of values, which is the ideal of personality. In this way Dawid's new personality was characterized by the traits of a gradually forming secondary integration through the process of positive disintegration and the emergence of a new disposing and directing center, a new hierarchy of values, and a new personality ideal.

What attitude should we assume toward those opinions which, despite his own statements, maintain that the second part of Dawid's life was less valuable, and even that in this period he suffered disorders of the function of reality and revealed many pathological symptoms? Of course, when one handles the matter schematically, such a complete loss of the desire to live, suicidal tendencies, the transformation of an empiricist into a mystic, the tendency to ecstasy, to talking to oneself in thought, and to extreme solitariness may suggest these opinions. It appears, however, that one may answer such an analysis by learning to know the fundamental developmental process of many outstanding personalities and by taking into consideration Dawid's statement that only the second phase of his life, the one subordinated to mysticism and the death-instinct, was meaningful. These opinions are also answered by the fact that his life was organized on new foundations in which he revealed creative abilities and great concern about the future of education.

Only on the basis of analysis of Dawid's new structure in all its aspects in relation to the former structure, and on the basis of the analysis of the whole story of his life, and of the last few years, may one, we believe, venture an opinion as to his mental health.

Clifford W. Beers

Introductory Remarks

The life and works of Beers are one of the examples of the distinct development of personality by means of mental shocks, unbalance, and mental illness. Beers also provides an example of an individual reaching a level close to personality through the development of social sensibility, creative syntony, insight into oneself, control of oneself, and development of the social ideal, which was one of Beers' main concerns.

The essence of Beers' reform, the preparation for which he had already started when in a hospital for the mentally ill and which he realized immediately after he left the hospital, may be shortly represented as follows:

1. Fighting against the prevailing treatment of the sick both in state and in private hospitals (the latter, seeking financial gain, employed irresponsible and untrained attendants for low salaries)

2. Working out the proper methods to care for the sick during their treatment

3. Attempting to change social attitudes toward the mentally ill and to remove the stigma connected with mental disease, thus facilitating the return of the mentally ill to society, by lessening the difficulties of their obtaining work and by treating their interrup-

tions in work in exactly the same way as interruptions due to
other diseases are treated

4. Preventing mental disorders and diseases

5. Organizing a central institution which would take care of these
   matters (Association of Mental Hygiene)

What properties and dynamisms, activated and enhanced by his stay
in a hospital, are revealed in Beers' childhood and youth, what shape
did they take, and how did they bring him to a mature personality? –
these are the questions for us to answer in this chapter.

Indicators of Personality

Beers already displayed in his childhood introvertive traits, enhanced
sentimentality, and excessive timidity, all of which he masked by laugh-
ter and wit. He took too much to heart the family's financial worries,
so much as to be afraid, without any ground, that his father would
commit suicide on account of them. In his boyhood he revealed "a
morbid overgrowth of an emphasis on justice"; in the years of his university studies a fear of a "public occurrence of his brother's epileptic
fits" (they occurred only at night).[45] After the death of his brother this
fear passed into a fear that he would become an epileptic himself. In
his autobiography he writes: "I considered myself condemned to death,
I thought and dreamed only about epilepsy, and during these six years
I thought innumerable times that I would take a fit."[46] The fear of a
fit "in the eyes of the lecture room" was as strong as that of taking an
examination. In such cases, although well prepared, he always said he
was not prepared. After a severe case of grippe there ensued a psychic
breakdown. Beers fell into a deep depression accompanied by delusions
as to the possibility of epileptic fits and fears of their being perceived
by others.

From that time Beers planned suicide. During the critical moment
of an "expected fit," due to his desire to hide it from his mother who

---

[45] C. W. Beers. *A Mind That Found Itself: An Autobiography.* New York: Doubleday,
1948, p. 3.

[46] *Ibid.*, p. 8.

was about to return to his room, he jumped from a fourth-story window. He did not kill himself, however. Aside from complicated fractures of his legs and light bruises on his head, Beers received no serious injuries. Epileptic delusions disappeared. There appeared instead delusions of persecution connected with his attempt to commit suicide. He considered the hospital, with its barred window, as an arrest; he took everything that happened around him, including medical intervention, as a shrewd inquisitorial procedure of the "third degree." He mistook his friends, members of his family, and even his own mother for spies, detectives, or "doubles." Letters which he received were, in his opinion, "falsified" and he did not open them for months. He claimed that he was under permanent police control and that everything was "the result of the misrepresenting tricks of the detectives." He was worried that his family would suffer "harm" and that he "had disgraced" Yale University, which he had attended. In order not to let the "final trial" take place, Beers sought an occasion to commit suicide, which never presented itself due to his constant fear of the "vigilant eye of the detective." Besides these persecution delusions Beers was plagued in the first period of his mental illness by various kinds of hallucinations auditory, visual, olfactory, gustatory, and tactile. He heard about him continuous murmurs and "false voices" which, for him, were "sounds" of hidden persecutors. He sometimes saw his own handwriting on the white bedclothes, moving pictures on the walls, unpleasant spots of maimed bodies, and so on. He smelled annoying odors, and the smell of burning human flesh. Food had for him the "smack of poison" and he sent it away untouched. He felt "millions of needles in his brain." Disorders of speech appeared (difficulty in finding the proper words to express thoughts, talking by single words), ending in complete dumbness. The state of silence and depression lasted for over two years.

What were Beers' personality indicators before his mental sickness and during it? We will mention, in the first place, the enhanced affectional excitability, the emotional and inhibitory timidity, regard for people's opinions, and the "morbid overgrowth of an emphasis on justice." Moreover, he displayed the need for and ability of concealing his states from other people, which reveals his insights into himself. Through his rather consciously prepared suicide he revealed the capacity for aggression in relation to himself, which is associated with the attitudes of dissatisfaction with oneself and with protest against oneself – very important dynamisms in the development of personality. His experiencing of refined and intellectually well-developed imaginative forms was probably connected to the coexistence of the feeling of guilt and the development of a refined social attitude.

The Period of the Formation of Personality

Beers revealed masked spiritual activity even in the phase of serious depression, and manic-depressive psychosis. He read newspapers, drawing conclusions of a personal character; he read books and closely observed his environment. Slowly he began to talk with the mentally sick, whom he did not suspect of detective-like tendencies. Gradually he regained his faculty of speech, the persecution delusions weakened. Then he came upon the idea of checking the identity of his brother; this idea – he writes – saved his life. He informed his brother in a letter that he had seen his double, but that if, however, this was not a double but the brother himself he should prove this by coming to him with the letter. If the visitor had been a double he instructed his brother to forget about the whole matter. His brother came to him, Beers convinced himself of his brother's identity, and from that moment he began to correct his delusions. The passage from the depressive phase to the maniacal phase was for him a period of enormous happiness. He calls this period his second birth. While formerly he felt in his brain "millions of needles," in the new phase he felt in it the "warm breath of the goddess of wisdom." The maniacal phase liberated and revealed in him capabilities which before his sickness he had never suspected that he possessed (literary and drawing capabilities). He spent many hours reading books in order to acquire efficiency in writing; he also wrote long letters and spent time drawing. These new creative efforts were not properly appreciated on the part of his physicians. A dull and malicious assistant physician ignored them and even prevented Beers from making them, punishing the patient by putting him in an empty prison cell when he did not heed his prohibitions. Even in those conditions Beers found his outlet in inventive ideas. He spent time thinking about the possibility of overcoming gravitation and building a "flying machine." From the first moment of the maniacal phase "plans to reform humanity" occupied Beers' mind. Delusions of greatness and enhanced feelings of God's providence gained strength. When taking part in religious services he interpreted Psalm 54 as a "call" for great changes and as an "order to engage in fighting." Caught in a mission of reform, he gave up his original desire to make humanity happy in all provinces and thought only about the reformation of hospitals for the mentally sick. To this end he purposely brought about his transfer to a division of violent patients in a state hospital (he had already been acquainted with such a division in a private hospital). He wanted to explore the methods of treating violent mentally ill patients. He learned the hard way the brutal methods that were used by hospital attendants and even by one of the physicians. For demanding his rights, for being unable to control his flood of words, and for defending other patients, he was starved, kept in an unheated room, beaten, strangled "till his eyes came out of their sockets," tormented by means of a "muff" or by being kept in a straitjacket for twelve hours or more. These torments resulted in a partial return to former delusions. He came to know the tortures of the "cattle cottage" where boisterous patients, those having hallucinations, or the physically weak, who required greater effort on the part of the attendants, were treated cruelly.

Beers informed the governor of the state about these inhuman methods in a 32-page brochure. Later, realizing that this method and also the method of "lecturing" the hospital personnel on every occasion about "what they should and what they should not do" would not be much help in changing the fate of the mentally sick, he assumed the rule of a meek patient in order to regain his freedom as soon as possible and to begin effecting his planned reforms.

What basic dynamisms are we able to single out, which arose or were developed during the period of positive disintegration – that is, during the formation of Beers' personality – and how did they influence the nuclei of the thus far formed qualities? Some of them stand out clearly. Primarily Beers developed through an active and well-prepared fight against the abuses of the hospital attendants in their relations with patients, through his feeling of justice and his sensitivity to the injustice done to others. Furthermore, he deepened his ability for self-observation through controlled experiments dealing with his capabilities for inquiry and observation. A very important dynamism in the development of his personality was the advent and growth in him of the capability for autopsychotherapy. Because of the existence and activity of these factors he did not passively succumb to the various phases of his illness but took a critical and prepared part in their course. It is most probable that these dynamisms were active factors in the advent and development of his new creative capabilities.

A very important dynamism in the shaping of his individual and social personality (realization of the ideal) was Beers' submission to hard and brutal experiences in order to obtain deeper knowledge of the bad treatment of patients.

A Brief Outline of His Shaped Personality

The main traits of Beers' shaped personality were the following qualities and dynamisms: a highly developed feeling of justice, a sense of social responsibility, a feeling of social mission (dynamic social ideal), a psychological insight in relation to himself and others, a considerable ability to control himself (for instance, by narrowing the scope of his activity), an ability for self-education and for autopsychotherapy, and creative capabilities (literary and painting). These dynamisms arose on the basis of nuclei revealed in childhood and youth which were enhanced many times and shaped in the period of the intensification of the positive disintegration process. With respect to enhancement, shaping, and reshaping there emerged as the most powerful such dynamisms as his highly conscious disposing and directing center, his personality ideal, and his insight into himself. Beers' new qualities included literary and painting capabilities. Among the relatively weaker dynamisms, those important for personality development were Beers' dissatisfaction with himself, his feeling of inferiority in relation to himself, and his feeling of guilt.

Jack Ferguson

Introductory Remarks

The life of Jack Ferguson, the American psychiatrist, is yet another example of personality development through dynamisms of positive disintegration. It is marked by a particularly intense development of unilevel disintegration in the way of psychomotor-sensual excitability and development of emotional life. This state lasted for a very long time and in fact made Ferguson's life useless to his closest circle of friends and to society in general. A small-town physician, devoted to his work, not able to stand contradictory tendencies which completely exhausted his activeness and energy, he stayed several times in a hospital for the mentally ill. At that time he committed a number of inconsiderate deeds, succumbed to excessive manias and even attempted to do harm to those dearest to him. However, a very strong disintegration of personality, along with a retained attitude of control – a disposition, at least, to control himself in very serious pathological conditions – permitted Ferguson to learn to know and to experience "the deepest pits of human experiences." He returned from the hospital cured of mental disease and enriched with new experiences, the existence of which he probably never before suspected. It is not only the curing of his disease that is significant in his case but also his retention and strengthening of the factors of self-control and self-education which regained dominance, with double might, in the subsequent period of his life. Elevation to a higher level resulted from a conscious selection by him of the highest values, and he regarded service to others as one of the highest values. This moving of life's ideal to the highest level to which a man may desire to climb points to the correctness of the course of the disintegrating dynamisms in Ferguson. As a consequence of this course his further life was marked by a conscious use of all his strength in order to realize the adopted ideal. As we shall see later, his works played a positive role in psychiatric therapy. The very process of disintegration, particularly when it came to intellectual development, was by no means ended, but there did ensue a calming down and self-education in the emotional sphere and in the self-preservation instinct.

Indicators of Personality in the First Period of His Life

During his medical studies and first years of practice Jack Ferguson displayed an increased affectional and motor excitability and increased feeling of his own importance. De Kruif writes that Ferguson's first years of life were very hard.[47] One might apply to him what Hemingway said, that the best school for a writer was an unhappy childhood. Given certain characteristic features of Ferguson, the influence of a hard childhood created within him, on one hand, the conditions of frustration, and on the other, a tendency to compensate for these conditions by passionate work and through his personal attitude toward his patients. He displayed these qualities in his work as a small-town physician. He never withheld his help from a patient, he never said No. According to De Kruif, Ferguson displayed certain paranoid traits. Being in a state of very strong tension, he began to suffer from insomnia and took excessive quantities of barbiturates, which only brought about the poisoning of his organism. Already several years before that time, in 1945, he had a severe attack of coronary disease.

After poisoning himself with barbiturates he was put in a hospital for the nervous and mentally sick, where he displayed delusions of grandeur, aggression, and the already mentioned paranoid characteristics. When he left the hospital his psychic state was improved but after some time he began again to show aggressive tendencies and displayed periodical paranoid tendencies; he wanted to kill his wife, who was his best friend, and suffered colored visual hallucinations and states of depression. These were to some extent the result of barbiturate poisoning. He was again put in a hospital. When he improved and obtained certain medical qualifications, Ferguson began to work as a medical practitioner in one of the small-town hospitals for the mentally sick. At that time he further displayed increased feeling of his own value, which was, however, compensated for by an opposite tendency, namely by the tendency to forget himself, to "deny himself" in a total devotion to work for others. He said that he was David and Goliath in one person – in whom the two constantly struggled. David represented his consciousness. He began to show a distinct need for perfection, and besides, in his inner experiences he associated his own mental sickness and that of other people with sins

---

[47]P. De Kruif. *A Man Against Insanity*. New York: Harcourt, Brace and Co., 1957.

committed and with feelings of guilt. Inner struggles intensified in him between the tendency to dominate and to fight and the tendency to deny himself and to help others. In his experiences the most important was his tendency to kill his excessive "I." Jack Ferguson was convinced that in order to "pass" through his own disorder, to pass the "Rubicon of the disease," it was necessary to "settle accounts with the past."[48]

The Period of the Formation of Personality

In spite of the growing alterocentric attitude and increased inner peace, Ferguson displayed further very strong motor excitability and an attitude of egocentric action. He then became an enthusiast of lobotomy and passed special courses and training. He was engulfed by an enthusiasm for psychosurgical treatment. However, his growing experience with his simultaneous increase of syntony in relation to patients, and his responsibility for them, led him to an increasingly more critical attitude toward surgical operations. After some time he accepted the opinion of one of the most outstanding American specialists in the field of psychosurgery, Dr. Walter Freeman, who maintained (according to De Kruif) that "lobotomy destroys psychotic demoralization, but does not rebuild morality."

Ferguson began, with all his passion, to seek the specific drugs which would replace the action of a lobotomy but which would not cause losses in the capabilities of an individual. He began to apply Serpasil; moreover, he went ever more deeply into the problems of the psychology of the sick, into their feelings of danger and into their anxieties. He was aware that a closer connection with the interests of a group rather than with oneself is one of the most proper attitudes toward the sick, and consequently toward their treatment. Such an attitude evoked emotional bonds between the patients and their physician. People ceased to avoid him. At the same time he found out that Serpasil has much better effect when associated with proper psychotherapy.

In that period he lost, as it were, his paranoia, he began to lift himself morally higher and higher, and he no longer resembled the man he had been several years before. In this way Ferguson passed through deep spiritual changes. His case has proved true the opinions of Meister

---

[48] *Ibid.*

Eckhart and the poet John Dryden, who maintained that one cannot attain a high level of development without the passage through certain periods of mental disorders.

Ferguson was ever more patient and cordial with his patients. He did not fall into states of excitation, and he was not disconcerted by the aggressiveness of the patients, their befouling, or exterior onerousness. He began to realize slowly a successful inner battle which was transposed to the area of his now great hospital, which contains 1000 patients. It was a further struggle between David and Goliath. In his work he was greatly helped by his staff of 107 nurses, most of whom possessed higher education. Slowly, with the help of his collaborators, he eliminated the monotony in the dress of the patients and eliminated the treatment of patients as lower creatures. At the same time he passionately sought the best application of newly invented drugs. Upon application of Largactil in conjunction with proper psychotherapy, he obtained good results in calming down patients and in eliminating their delusions and hallucinations. He observed, however, that many patients, after Serpasil and Largactil were taken, displayed further symptoms of excitation, fury, and aggressiveness. Ferguson then began to try a new drug, known as Ritalin. It acted fairly well on catatonics, bringing them partially out of their stupors. He came to the conclusion that, in the case of patients who were numbed after Serpasil, Ritalin gave good results. Patients began to smile and their eyes were expressive – no longer did they resemble the "eyes of a dead fish." He began to associate skillfully Serpasil and Largactil with Ritalin, forming very individual combinations. On the basis of these experiments Dr. Ferguson delivered in 1955 at the conference of the American Psychiatric Society a lecture entitled "Improvement of Forms of Behavior of the Hospitalized Mentally Sick." He stressed in the lecture that the "combinations of Serpasil and Ritalin brought new life into our institution and that they might become a tool that will help to change the hospital from a foster home to a communal medical center."

After this lecture opinions arose in certain circles that Dr. Ferguson's excessive enthusiasm reflected his arrogance. He knew about these opinions. He reacted to them calmly, explaining their advent in a matter-of-fact way, without displaying his former paranoid attitude.

In the meantime even greater changes took place in the ward. Influenced by their chief, the nurses were patient and gentle with the sick people and showed no disgust toward them at all. They helped them to come to a better realization of the true state of their disease. This led the patients to be more mindful of themselves, the way they dressed, more interested in themselves, and helped to increase their self-control. Interest in music and handwork gradually took hold of practically all the patients. Common celebrations and holidays were introduced, with the effect that not even one female patient would weep out of loneliness during Christmas. Slowly the patients became attached to the physician and to his deputies, who kept their head informed about all changes observed in the patients. In these circumstances, says his biographer, "the old paranoiac Ferguson died."

His victories did not lead him to an increased feeling of his own value. Engulfed by the problem of the mentally sick among old and very old people, he declined to accept degradation of such patients on the basis of general opinions that they suffer from atheromatous degeneration of the brain. After many years of study and observation he came to the conclusion that old patients have many symptoms close to those displayed by young patients, namely, disorders of behavior and an excess or an insufficiency of activity. It turned out also that application of Serpasil and Ritalin, and, above all, the way of managing very old patients, taking an interest in them, helping them to find meaning in their life, considerably improved the health of these patients. The help of nurses here proved to be invaluable. After some time Ferguson applied a new drug, know as Frenquel, derivative of ergotamine, which had positive effects on hallucinations and delusional symptoms. It turned out, after further trials, that Serpasil and Ritalin applied intravenously put the patients quickly out of the catatonic or similar states, calmed their states of excitation, and that Frenquel decreased delusions and hallucinations. Of course, in the middle of constant new trials there arose new difficulties. For example, new drugs from among those already mentioned tranquilized many patients, but also caused tremors similar to those found in Parkinson's disease. However, these symptoms could be weakened and often prevented from appearing by the proper combination of drugs. Besides, Ferguson introduced further care of the patients at home by nurses (under medical control) after they were discharged from the hospital. On the basis of all these experiments Ferguson came to the conclusion that prevention of mental disorders lies in the hands of the family doctor, who, with a better knowledge of psychiatry and a proper moral attitude, would be in a position to prevent the necessity of a considerable number of patients being handed over to a hospital for the mentally ill.

Dr. Ferguson continues his work by putting into practice his Samaritan ideal, as well as all his pharmacological and psychotherapeutic achievements in curing a patient.

A Brief Outline of His Shaped Personality

It is difficult to determine definitely the development of a living personality, as he can push this development ever forward. Jack Ferguson varies in this respect from the other examples, such as Michelangelo and St. Augustine. Therefore we cannot give here the characteristic features of the final stage of the development of his personality.

We just want to draw attention to the remarkable development of some qualities which have already been attained by Ferguson. Beyond a doubt the dominating quality in him has been intellectual passion harnessed by the high level of development of alterocentric feelings. In the first period of the development of his personality it was determined by morbid emotional and psychomotor excitability and excessive sensitivity. After the disintegration of the whole personality, the intellectual passion, subjected to control, passed into the service of the third factor and was subjected to the high ideal of service to other people. As a consequence of this development Ferguson obtained particularly good results in his knowledge of the organization of a hospital for the mentally sick, in working out complicated methods of pharmacological treatment, and primarily in improving psychiatric treatment by the application of drugs and psychotherapeutic methods. Thereby the role of psychotherapists was stressed – people who, to be effective in their work, must also pass through certain phases of internal disintegration and integration. As we have observed in the example of his attitude toward patients, Jack Ferguson has attained a very high degree of the attitude of love toward suffering people, of understanding, and of empathy. In the present period of his life, there ensues an equilibrium between the development of varidirectional and opposing attitudes. Excessive sensitivity subjected to the conscious dynamisms of the third factor and of the disposing and directing center, the nucleus of which is "service to man," and their cooperation with the intellectual sphere became the foundation of a new, increasingly more coherent personality.

Chapter 6

Conclusions Concerning the Concept of Personality

As we saw in the first part of this work, personality, from our point of view, is the principal aim of a man, the aim of his development, particularly of accelerated development. As we have also discussed, personality is, at the same time, an empirical, teleologico-normative, and historical phenomenon. Its development can be, and should be, evaluated with respect to those three aspects. This fact does not diminish, but rather strengthens, the objective evaluation of personality since it considers personality in all its dimensions, taking into account its unique, individual, unrepeatable composition and all its palpably human characteristics.

This approach permits us to "measure" not only personality traits common to many, but also its individual, multilevel characteristics in each person. Thus personality is considered empirically, equally in its measurable universal and individual characteristics and through comparison and unification of the main stages of its development, in its longitudinal aspect, in that or the other field, in relation to an individual's proposed objective program as well as to the development of other different selected individuals. Personality is also considered from the teleologico-normative approach, in accord with biological, social, and individual-personal models, in the process of transcending other models at a lower level and the realization of higher ones. Personality is further considered in the light of the role played by elements from the complete developmental history of the individual himself, objectively verified through analytic-synthetic comparison with the objectively evaluated development of eminent historical personalities.

It follows that a multidimensional synthetic approach to personality permits, as we mentioned above, objective consideration of the unrepeatable individual composition, that is, the autonomic and authentic personality.

We have stated that personality is the aim of man's development. This fact is particularly manifest in accelerated development. Such a development, in an individual, in all its main aspects, includes basic stressful elements, elements of disequilibrium, maladaptation, neuroses and psychoneuroses and all their dynamisms. Therefore development presents dynamic conflicts between what is "higher" and "lower" within an individual, between that which still exists and that which begins to be, between that which "is" and that which "ought to be." Such a development is a manifestation of the developmental instinct, the instincts of creativity and of perfection and appears, as a rule, in the process of positive disintegration, and especially in multilevel disintegration.

We see one aspect of this process in psychic overexcitability, in disequilibrium, in suffering, depression, anxiety states, obsessions, symptoms of "emotional immaturity," and so on. The second aspect is indissolubly connected, teleologically as well as in a cause-effect relationship, with the first. This second aspect includes all developmental elements, and especially the psychic inner milieu with its main dynamisms. Thus, the shaping of personality is a manifestation of the conscious incorporation of that which is conflicting, that which is "pathological," into the process of development. For this reason the principle of not rejecting "pathological" elements, but rather of grafting them onto normal and accelerated development, is the main tenet of the theory of positive disintegration. Thus, self-education and autopsychotherapy are emphasized in the shaping of personality. For the same reason, in psychotherapy, the accent is put on development and mental health rather than on rehabilitation and removal of "pathological" symptoms. In this way treatment is effected through development rather than development through "treatment." This is the manner in which the individual creatively elaborates so-called "pathological" dynamisms, in intimate connection to positive development. Thus each man's development of personality is a personal and social drama.

Only those individuals who have consciously and deliberately advanced along this road to personality development can help others, can shape their drama without introducing the danger of pushing toward negative disintegration those who otherwise would develop themselves positively through positive disintegration. The attitude derived from such a high level of knowledge and experience is accompanied by a great responsibility, however, for the introduction of elements promoting human dignity in "nervous" people, neurotics, and psychoneurotics. Such an attitude leads to the rejection of common pathological classification, accentuating rather the participation of such people in the creation of the highest human values through their own high level of development.

We then cease to cultivate the "treatment" of such individuals, but help them, with their collaboration, in their development. It is in this manner that a personality is shaped according to the theory of positive disintegration.

Supplement: Biographies of Kierkegaard, Beethoven, and Unamuno

Søren Kierkegaard

Threefold Causality in His Development

From early youth Kierkegaard manifested emotional, imaginational, and intellectual overexcitability and some symptoms of infantilism including capriciousness, obstinacy, and suggestiveness. In the area of emotional overexcitability he manifested emotional exclusiveness and idealism. Those innate qualities together with the saddening influence of his environment gradually developed into depression and even melancholy. He was a sad child.

From youth he disagreed with his father, who had a schematic religious attitude. Gradually young Kierkegaard began to disagree with the religious system of spiritual life, especially that of Christianity. In the course of time this attitude developed more strongly.[1]

In childhood he did not manifest special abilities and in his father's opinion he was incapable.

In 1830 he was a candidate for a baccalaureate. In this area we can read that: "Student Kierkegaard was childish for a long time without any distinct desire for independence and freedom, which impeded his progress in school."[2]

In 1846 Kierkegaard, recalling his own youth, writes: "It is awful when I think even for a moment about my miserable youth, about my fear for my father, about my own awful melancholy, and about all that which is even too painful to write down. I suffered also another

---

[1]K. Dabrowski. "Lincoln, Kierkegaard, and Kafka." In *Collected Papers* (forthcoming).

[2]Marguerite Grimault. *Kierkegaard par lui-même*. Écrivains de toujours, Paris: Éditions du Seuil, 1962, p. 17.

fear, namely in relation to Christianity, but on the other hand, I was attracted by it."[3]

Because of his short height, crooked backbone, and bad health, the opinion was held that he wasn't fit to join the national guard for students and he was withdrawn from the list of candidates.[4]

He had a distinct inferiority complex in relation to these traits, he wore glasses to conceal his eyes, he liked shadow.

He displayed irony, wit, derision, and criticism from childhood.

We can see that on the one hand he had hereditary and innate bases for an inferiority complex and overexcitability, especially emotional overexcitability. He lived also in sad, depressing, gloomy surroundings. On the other hand, he manifested independence and autonomy, disliked the atmosphere at home and the religion of his family.

His irony and derision were directed not only to others, but also to himself. It was, on the one hand, his reaction to the influence of his surroundings, and on the other hand, the expression of his keenness of intellect and mental independence.

Multidimensionality and Multilevelness in Development

In high school, especially in academic studies, he manifested various interests and more strongly multilevelness of attitudes. He was interested in the theater, opera, and music. He tried to compose himself.

He manifested early the ability of noting contrasts. His mental independence, irony, and even derision expressed his awareness of contrasts.

He writes in his letters: "Man cannot run away from fear because he loves it, while on the other hand – frankly – he doesn't love it because he runs away from it. Fear is congenial antipathy and antipathetic sympathy."

As we see, such an attitude harmonizes with his mental many sidedness, irony, awareness of contrasts, alertness of imagination and intellect.

On the other hand – as we mentioned – he manifested a distinct tendency to multilevelness. He manifested maladjustment to reality and adjustment to the ideal.

---

[3]*Ibid.*, p. 18.
[4]*Ibid.*, p. 21.

Formal Christianity was illusory for him; he looked for ideal Christianity.

Positive Disintegration, Neuroses, and Psychoneuroses

Idealistic tendencies of Kierkegaard found their expression in his imagination and in a search for truth through suffering and disruption. He rejected the reality of everyday life as well as many of his innate qualities. He distinctly exhibited the dynamisms of disquietude with oneself, inferiority feeling toward oneself, and "fear and trembling."[5]

He assumed that the attainment of the highest level of development, that is to say, the religious level, is possible only through suffering, disruption, choosing of oneself and choosing of a high level of external reality, choice in "fear and trembling." For the sake of realization of the absolute ideal he chose suffering, "fear and trembling." He came to terms with his disturbances, which he accepted as a positive case of mental illness.

We can say that he incarnates his mental illness and suffering in himself. This illness persecutes him incessantly. He calls it a melancholy; he is afraid of becoming mad. He thinks about suicide. He understands Christianity as a disruption, as a sharp awareness of contrasts.

Very often he is misunderstood by his acquaintances. His fiancée Regina cannot understand him and treats him as a mentally ill person. This cruelty causes facial tics. Medical advice is pessimistic because the doctor doesn't believe that the young man can conquer his sickness. In his own opinion, he has only God and the cross. In this case he derides himself because he doesn't want to make his fiancée unhappy.

Psychiatric diagnosis is: psychoneurosis of failure or mania, depressive psychosis or even schizophrenia. With these and simultaneously with a feeling of lack of sense in life, grows abnormal productivity which he accepts with passion and a feeling of creative necessity.

Melancholy becomes, according to M. Grimault, his greatest lover. He has gratitude for her because he becomes someone who is needed in the service of God. He lives intensively. He says he must live intensively and shove away extensiveness. His awareness of eternal responsibility is growing through crises in him, which shows that eternity really exists.

---

[5]Dabrowski, *op. cit.*

He accepts consciously the necessity of hindrances and persecutions. This consciousness of his own situation, full of contrasts, causes the union of genius and mental illness in him. He tells himself that it is a deadly sickness, and yet, at the same time, a creative one.

On the other hand he has sometimes a different opinion of his mental illness. At that time he asserts that he is not sick, because he can find help in himself. This illness is not hypochondria, because it gives him different religious tendencies – connected with a great satisfaction.[6]

He writes that when fear possesses the given individual it is its own reward and it can lead him back to faith. The individual will not find peace elsewhere because every other point of peace is only *"lary-fary"* even if for people it would be wisdom. Then if fear uses the individual for faith, it will eliminate that which is produced by itself.[7]

Infantilism and Positive Regression

From childhood Kierkegaard was desirous of calm, love, softness, and serenity; he desired love, but did not believe in it. He manifested ambivalences and ambitendencies. On one hand he expressed the above-mentioned tendencies, but on the other hand he ran away from them.

He becomes more egocentric, rejects extensiveness for intensity. It is based on his hereditary emotional sensibility and introvertive type, while on the other hand, it develops because of influence of his environment.

He is tender or hurtful; he can't find goodness and love in everyday life and so he turns back to the ideal world where it is possible to find them. In his opinions and feeling we can find regression to the world of dreams, to the ideal, and even to suffering.

Inner Psychic Milieu

Kierkegaard felt the fundamental discrepancy and disruption between his ideals and the much lower reality. It made him an ardent searcher for truth at any price, and a believer in the value of the subject in himself.

---

[6]Grimault, *op. cit.*, p. 135.

[7]*Kierkegaard: Wybor pism (Collected works)*. Lvóv: Polaniecki, 1914, pp. 113, 135.

Very early, as we mentioned, he felt the dynamisms of hierarchization. This strong dynamism of hierarchization permitted him to distinguish the stratification of developmental levels called by himself esthetic, ethical, and religious, which was the highest level.

The operation of autonomic factors is very pronounced in his thinking, feeling, and acting. Kierkegaard demonstrates clearly the action of higher dynamisms, especially, "subject-object" in oneself and the third factor.

He doesn't call them, as the theory of positive disintegration does, the characteristic dynamisms of the third level of development, but only names them. These are the dynamisms of astonishment with oneself, disquietude with oneself, dissatisfaction with oneself, and feelings of shame and guilt.[8]

The dynamism "subject-object" in oneself is decisive with regard to the significance of the subject. The choice takes place between the temporary "I" and the absolute "I," and between the temporary "you" and the absolute "you."

Kierkegaard saw sadness in joy and joy in sadness. Suffering was usually hidden in humor. He always underlined that man is different contrasts in tension that can't be adjusted. In sensual love he saw unfaithfulness or perfidy, in contrast to absolute love.

Psychic inner transformation – one of the main dynamisms of the inner milieu – was revealed in him in a remarkable way. He tells about "concentration on entering oneself and deepening oneself." This is the transformation of external stimuli. It is internal transformation operating in the area of the so-called own forces of the individual without the action of external stimuli.[9]

Positive Maladjustment, Transgression of the Biological Life Cycle and Psychological Type

Through reflection and the continuous choice of himself in suffering he tried to transcend his own psychological type. This transcendence is noticeable in his search for individual love and realization of his ideas by struggling, although struggling did not harmonize with his type. With

---

[8]Dabrowski, *op. cit.*
[9]Kierkegaard, *op. cit.*, p. XIII.

humility and courage he accepts depression and melancholy as necessary in his life, that is to say, in a sense, he consciously accepts his "mental illness."

In the opinion of all those who easily feel well adjusted Kierkegaard was strange, odd, mentally sick and a visionary. His life and works express the form of positive maladjustment.[10] He was critical, ironic, and sharp in his opinions, which made many enemies.[11]

1834 was a difficult year for him because he lost his mother and one sister. On the other hand in this year he was very intellectually active.[12]

This type of experience intensified his pain, depression, melancholy, and "fear and trembling." On the other hand, it determined his "developmental jumps," transgression of the biological life cycle and his psychological type, and the passing from the ethical phase to the religious one. Every form of the realization of multilevelness of reality is a proof of the transgression of the biological life cycle of man and his psychological type.[13]

As we see, these developmental jumps in proportion to the most painful and most upsetting problems, were the conditions for the transgression of the biological life cycle and his psychological type and they were the fundamental elements in his positive maladjustment to himself and his environment.

Authentism and Essence in Existence

According to Kierkegaard: "The esthetic choice founded on a changing hierarchy of values, is not a real choice."[14]

The individual chooses himself, according to Kierkegaard, in his eternal, absolute meaning. From among many great individuals, Shakespeare was the poet of his choice.

That which is subjective and elaborated by one's life history determines one's development. This subjective contains various tendencies, abilities, and talents.

---

[10]Dabrowski, *op. cit.*

[11]Grimault, *op. cit.*, p. 1.

[12]*Ibid.*, p. 24.

[13]Dabrowski, *op. cit.*

[14]Kierkegaard, *op. cit.*, p. XII.

Music for Kierkegaard is a value of the highest level. He is also fond of nature, he likes the sea, fields, and woods. He thinks, or rather, experiences ideas by thoughts.[15]

The most essential is that which we should do, not that which we should know. As we mentioned we wants ideal love.

> His passion for Regina became a pretext for his infinite meditation on love and marriage.[16]

He is connected with that which is individual, unrepeatable, and subjective. According to him: "Becoming of subject is most important for every man, and at once it is the highest reward for him; it is eternal happiness which exists only for a subjective man. This state expresses eternal value for oneself."[17]

According to Hegel's conception, eternal is higher than internal and the moral purpose of man is a manifestation of himself in the global. Contrary to this, Kierkegaard says that each individual contains an unspeakable secret and also that faith is a paradox, according to which internal is higher than external.[18]

Using a superficial approach to the handling of this subject, we would say that Kierkegaard is egocentric, but if he was, he was a positive egocentric. He agrees with Pascal, according to whom, subjectivism expresses potential awareness through passion.

According to Kierkegaard, the essence of Christianity is a paradoxical Christianity. It is the religion of absolute suffering, intellectual and moral passion, spiritual perfection.[19]

This essence of Christianity relies on searching for one's own truth, being oneself, and only oneself; it relies on living and acting without compromises; on living through passionate faith.[20]

Now we can see that in the opinion of Kierkegaard, essential was that which was unique, unrepeatable, chosen, individual, and which is

---

[15]Grimault, *op. cit.*, p. 32.

[16]*Ibid.*, p. 48.

[17]*Ibid.*, p. 70.

[18]*Ibid.*, p. 74.

[19]*Ibid.*, p. 103.

[20]Kierkegaard, *op. cit.*, p. XVI

conquered through a difficult history of development with suffering, depression, "fear and trembling," and constant heroism in the realization of ideal.

Personality

The prevailing opinion is that Kierkegaard – repulsed in his lifetime and many years after his death – gave people the highest forms of the philosophy of life. At present he belongs to the most attractive, popular, and very authentic philosophers.

It would seem that his extreme idealism and his absolutism cannot contain the attractive elements of life. His extreme idealism never accepted the majority. He always asserts that millions of people (where everyone is the same) destroy the ideal and factor of individualism and the relation between "I" and "you." When an individual appears different from those millions, there appears "two," that is to say, "I" and "you."[21]

Kierkegaard is an outstanding example of the process of positive disintegration which discovers and rejects superficial matters. This individual attitude is irreconcilable with regard to the low level of press articles and propaganda.

Kierkegaard transfers reality into the world of ideals; his love and friendship are possible only on the level approaching to the ideal. Regina thinks about union in this world, but Kierkegaard stands off from reality and lives in the world which is more subtle, "ethereal," than the real world.[22] He expresses internal worlds and has difficulties in the external world. He did not get the chair of philosophy. It was given to someone who was less suitable than Kierkegaard.

Only after 20 years was his monument built. Bishop Mynster in his funeral speech said about him: "Everyday he received an excess of persecution which became his daily bread. To him the problem of career and promotion did not exist, but what did exist, on the contrary, was the problem of more and more degradation."[23]

---

[21] Dabrowski, *op. cit.*

[22] Grimault, *op. cit.*

[23] *Ibid.*, p. 179.

This is in accordance with Kierkegaard's opinion that choice itself determines essence of personality. This is a choice repeated many times. First it is an ethical choice, and secondly, a religious one because according to him, ethical man does not choose. However, the religious choice is an absolute choice.

He writes about himself as follows: "When all around a man sinks into silence, when everything becomes festive like a starlit night, when the soul feels alone in the universe, then arrives not the white knight but the eternal celestial Power and 'I' chooses himself or rather begets himself."[24]

He writes also that: "We choose ourselves not in our directness, not as a casual individual, but we choose ourselves in our eternal importance."[25]

Self-selection, according to him, expresses freedom. It seems to us, that the above sentence expresses, according to our terminology, a secondary birth or birth of personality. It is a process close to a high level of autonomy and authentism.

And now here are Kierkegaard's ideas on the attitude of a mystic and the attitude of an individual valuing the concrete, which is very close to the theory of positive disintegration:

> A mystic's mistake is that in selection he does not become concrete before himself and before God; he chooses himself abstractly. He does not have transparency because anybody who thinks that abstract is transparent, is wrong; abstract is dim and foggy. His falling in love with God has the highest expression in feeling, in the mood at dark, in fog; he joins with his God with vague motions.[26]

And further: "Real, concrete choice not only removes me from the world but also brings me back in the same moment."[27] "The eternal value of man depends on the fact that a man can have his own history."[28]

---

[24] Kierkegaard, *op. cit.*, p. VII.

[25] *Ibid.*, p. XII.

[26] *Ibid.*, p. XXXVI.

[27] *Ibid.*

[28] *Ibid.*, p. XL.

And further: "Who chooses himself ethically, chooses himself concretely as a definite individual; the individual is conscious of himself, that means, he is conscious of this definite individual with his several gifts and inclinations, impulsess and passions which are dependent on some surroundings. He is conscious of this definite individual as a definite product, definite world. But if a man realizes himself in this way, he accepts all this and takes the responsibility for it."[29] Here Kierkegaard expresses one of the fundamental dynamisms of personality according to our conception.

And now here is Kierkegaard's conception of purpose: "A man living ethically sews purposes everywhere. He does not destroy the esthetic life but makes a spiritual life."[30]

> What is general can easily coexist with the individual without destroying it, like the fire which burnt without destroying the bush. ... even so with man who is an aim in himself, yet this aim is at once different because sameness as an aim is not an abstract sameness existing everywhere, and therefore nowhere, but a concrete sameness. A particular individual is not general, and if this is demanded of me, this demand is wrong ... if this is not accepted, then personality becomes abstract, its attitude towards duty is abstract, and its immortality is abstract.

Kierkegaard even more strongly stresses the separate individuality of a person in relation to the highest being: "it is less terrible to fall on one's face when the mountains tremble when God speaks, than to sit next to Him as with an equal; and yet it is God's concern to have us sit thus next to Him."

---

[29] *Ibid.*, p. XLI.
[30] *Ibid.*

Ludwig van Beethoven

Fourfold Causality in His Development

Beethoven had four exceptional characteristics which favored the development of his unique inner life. These characteristics, or life circumstances, were his faithfulness to his experience, his lack of malleability, his deafness, and his emotion isolation from the world.[31]

As a youth, Beethoven was forced to study music even to the point of having to travel and live away from home for long periods of time. His father, who thought of Ludwig as a prodigal son, was a complete incompetent and cared little of the family. Ludwig looked to his mother for comfort but was unable to do so when he was sent away to school. As he grew older it was necessary for him to take over most of his father's job, which left him little time for practicing his music, and no time for the pleasures of life. In other words, he lived most of his younger years in poverty and retained few pleasant memories of those years.

Ludwig was impervious to criticism; his manners were atrocious; he ignored conventions; and he was permanently subject to no social passions, not even sexual love.[32] He seemed to feel that other people were quite common and of no real match to him. This seemingly was proven in all of his musical competitions with other pianists, which generally were of no match to him. Although his level of education was low, he proved, at least to himself, that he was of considerable intelligence in that whenever he so felt he was able to pass all exams placed before him. In Beethoven's youth his father had been extremely harsh concerning his music lessons, but outside of music, his father cared nothing for the boy's education.[33] This possibly was the cause of his great naiveté in matters of life, love, and manners.

In 1798, it appears that he first noticed the symptoms of deafness. His first reaction to this was rage at the senselessness of the hideous affliction and that he, of all men, should lose that particular sense, must, indeed, be the most abominable of ironies. This knowledge of

---

[31] J. W. N. Sullivan, *Beethoven: His Spiritual Development*, New York: Knopf, 1936, p. 224.

[32] *Ibid.*, p. 66.

[33] *Ibid.*, p. 77.

his growing deafness was the cause of his emotional isolation from the world, along with his unbelievable feeling of superiority. In a letter to his doctor friend Wegeler, he wrote: "... I have avoided almost all social gatherings because it is impossible for me to say to people: I am deaf."[34] At times his doctors prescribed visits to the country, which again took him away from the public and even more made him an isolationist.

Multilevelness in Development

Beethoven exhibited in his life the feelings of both shame and disquietude. The main reason for his feeling of shame stemmed from his increasing deafness. This resulted in an increase in shyness and a great tendency to retreat from society. For two years he avoided almost all social gatherings because of the nature of his profession, which he felt sounded unnatural when connected with his deafness.[35]

His extreme feeling of disquietude also was a result of his increasing deafness. He felt an intense responsibility to himself of having to complete all of the pieces of music possible even though he felt hindered by his infliction. He felt that he must assert his will in order not to be overcome. He had to summon up all his strength in order to go on living and working in spite of his fate. He once said, "I will take Fate by the throat."[36]

Of Beethoven's religious beliefs we know very little except that they were not orthodox. That Beethoven, towards the end, came to possess a mystical apprehension of life is indisputable, but it is probable that this mystical outlook would have been, in his case, more recalcitrant even than usual to exposition in words. But, so far as these things may be expressed in words, we may conclude, from his own remarks, that he believed in an ultimate, benign and intelligent Power, and that he believed that existence was planned and purposeful. This was shown quite well in the musical expressions used in his Mass in D and also in his habit of writing down such Eastern phrases as, "I am that which is. I am all that was, that is, and that shall be."[37]

---

[34] *Ibid.*, pp. 102–104.
[35] *Ibid.*, p. 107.
[36] *Ibid.*, p. 108.
[37] *Ibid.*, pp. 212–213.

Positive Disintegration, Neuroses, and Psychoneuroses

Beethoven possessed an almost boyish idea of fate. To him Fate was the name for a personified conception of those characteristics of life that call out the heroic in man. But in this idea of Fate it is something external. The inner state witnessing to its existence is heroism or, it may be, fear. In talking of Fate, Beethoven was not talking of an experience, but of something that conditions experience. A feeling of the need and importance of the heroic principle persisted in Beethoven up to the end.[38]

In his younger years, he felt the fear of losing his ability to compose due to his increasing deafness. He never conceived of Fate as the blind, cold, indifferent, impersonal order of the universe, but as an enemy. His deafness was a creation of that maleficent, external power he called the "Creator," or rather Fate, which he had "often cursed for exposing his creatures to the merest accident." His capacity for a deep and passionate realization of suffering necessitated, if he were not to be reduced to impotence, a corresponding capacity for endurance and an enormous power of self-assertion. To Beethoven the character of life as suffering became a fundamental part of his outlook. The deep sincerity and naiveté of his nature, combined with the circumstances of his life, made this knowledge inevitable.[39]

Due to his inability to work with others, he soon developed an almost paranoiac character. He was so sure of his superiority over others in composing music that when Haydn gave an unfavorable opinion of one of a set of three trios, he was convinced that Haydn's action was actuated by envy, jealously, and malice. However, one main source of this problem was his inability to handle money and his lack of knowledge of business matters which always made him suspicious of his publishers and others with whom he did business. At times he was justified in his fears, as when he was not paid by his patrons, which only helped to strengthen his already strong emotions of distrust of others.

The intense fear of deafness caused him in his younger years to look for marvelous cures. It seemed as though he'd lost even the slightest hope of improvement so that now he clutched eagerly at any chance of

---

[38] *Ibid.*, p. 142.
[39] *Ibid.*, pp. 64–65.

a cure. When one doctor's treatment would show no immediate results, he would quickly accuse the doctor of negligence. In his attempts to explain why he, a great composer, should be inflicted with deafness, he attributes it to his bowels, which had bothered him all his life.

Infantilism and Positive Regression

After his mother died, Beethoven had no one to turn to for love. As for the death of his father he cared little, since there had been no love between then. Up until the age of forty, he had been content with his small triumphs with women but now he was financially set and he felt the need to settle down, to have order in his domestic affairs, and to satisfy his craving for companionship. Nevertheless, marriage without love was impossible to Beethoven, and his attitude towards love was essentially romantic. He had, as we have seen, very little understanding of men, and it is probable that he had even less of women. A beautiful face was very likely, for him, to seem the index to a noble mind. A wife, to a man of Beethoven's nature, was absolutely essential to this full human life and even more so while deafness threatened him with a terrible isolation.[40]

After having been rejected several times, e.g., proposal of marriage to nineteen-year-old Therese Malfatti, Beethoven reconciled himself to the fact that he would never know the state of marriage. It is evident also that the first years of Beethoven's non-productive period coincided with this time of restless and unsatisfied yearning for sexual love and for the peace of marriage.[41] We find then his regression to the idea of an ideal married life which he can only visualize in his mind.

Inner Psychic Milieu

Beethoven's deafness and solitariness are almost symbolic of his complete retreat into his inner self. No "external storms" could now influence his work; at most they could only interrupt it.[42] He came to realize that his creative energy, which he at one time opposed to his destiny,

---

[40] *Ibid.*, p. 173.
[41] *Ibid.*, p. 181.
[42] *Ibid.*, p. 220.

in reality owed its very life to that destiny. It is not merely that he believed that the price was worth paying; he came to see it as necessary that a price should be paid. He believed to be willing to suffer in order to create is one thing; to realize that one's creation necessitates one's suffering, that suffering is one of the greatest of God's gifts, is almost to reach a mystical solution of the problem of evil, a solution that it is probably for the good of the world that very few people will ever entertain.[43]

His earlier, almost boyish idea of Fate became a much profounder conception. Fate, to him, is no longer personified as some sort of powerful enemy that sufficient courage can defy, even if hopelessly. It was now a truly universal destiny, too complete to evoke any thought of resistance. The brooding mystery from which it merges is, like the primeval darkness that preceded creation, something that conditions the human world, but which is not part of it. And this extra-human power has nothing benevolent about it, necessary as it may be for the molding of the human soul. Beethoven now resigned or submitted himself to his destiny of the solitude of deafness and realized he could still compose even with this abominable affliction.[44]

Positive Maladjustment, Transgression of the Biological Life Cycle and Psychological Type

The opinion of others concerning Beethoven's character was diversified but on one thing there was a general agreement, and that was on his musical genius. In one letter written by Goethe to Zelter, Goethe complained, "His talent amazes me; unfortunately he is an utterly untamed personality, not altogether in the wrong in holding the world to be detestable, but who does not make it any the more enjoyable either for himself or for others by his attitude."[45]

Beethoven had many enemies whose vanity he had injured but then too he had many friends who simply put up with his contemptuous lack of restraint. The following quote from Ludwig's diary of 1814 shows quite well his feelings towards others: "Never show to men the

---

[43] *Ibid.*, pp. 232–233.
[44] *Ibid.*, pp. 215–216.
[45] *Ibid.*, p. 100.

contempt they deserve, one never knows to what use one may want to put them."[46] Beethoven's rapid alterations of feeling for one and the same person are comic, and seem to testify to a complete lack of insight on his part.

To most women, he appeared as ugly, poor, ill-bred, and terrifyingly impulsive and self-willed. Perhaps this fact, being repulsed by most women, caused him to try to break up the marriage plans of his brother Johann to a woman of loose character. Even by using violent and tactless measures he was unable to stop the union, and perhaps even hurried the outcome. This episode is a good illustration of Beethoven's extraordinary lack of understanding of normal people. In trying to override his brother as he did he was treating him with the same contempt he had for most men, but this time it was violent and passionate.[47]

Beethoven's violent need for an outlet of his unleashed love and unbearable solitariness led him to pour a wealth of emotion into his nephew Carl; from Carl he demanded the love and sympathy that had been denied him. This idolatrous love was mixed with so much suspicion that it led to his nephew's attempting suicide. His love was merely a blind, irrational, pitiful attempt to make at least one point of contact with that warm human world from which he was shut out. Deep within himself the artist in him knew that his isolation was irretrievable. Personal relations, that should give him a sense of completeness and satisfy his hunger, were impossible. Beethoven's relations with his nephew caused him, almost continually, great anxiety.[48]

During these periods Beethoven was at the very height of his creative power. Although he produced his greatest music at that time, he worked very slowly. The states of consciousness with which he was concerned contained more and more elusive elements, and came from greater depths. The task of creation necessitated an unequalled degree of absorption and withdrawal.

---

[46] *Ibid.*, p. 98.
[47] *Ibid.*, p. 193.
[48] *Ibid.*, pp. 204, 219.

Personality

As a younger man, before deafness set in, Beethoven as a whole man was intensely alive and lived in a vivid world. Everything interested him. He was eager for society, and for anything that contributed to the wealth of impressions that poured in upon him every day. His art was not yet a refuge to him, a mystery to be served, the only region in which his soul could escape all trammels and become completely free, but a glorious vehicle for the oppression of the vivid experiences life presented to him.[49]

By the end of the summer of 1802, after his deafness had increased appreciably, Beethoven had found that his genius, that he had felt called upon to cherish and protect, was really a mighty force using him as a channel or servant. With Beethoven, so extraordinarily creative, a state of more or less unconscious tumult must have been constant as a result of his feeling of being possessed by a power of genius. But only when the consciously defiant Beethoven had succumbed, only when his pride and strength had been so reduced that he was willing, even eager, to die and abandon the struggle, did he find that his creative power was indeed indestructible and that it was its deathless energy that made it impossible for him to die.

Beethoven's Heiligenstadt Testament of Autumn, 1802, marks the crisis in his life. Never again was his attitude towards life one of defiance, where the defiance was an expression of what is called his "strength of character." He had no such need of defiance, for he no longer had any fear. He had become aware within himself of an indomitable creative energy that nothing could destroy. He is no longer afraid for his art. He no longer fears that "the most beautiful years of his life must pass without accomplishing the promise of his talent and powers."[50]

His solitariness was one of the things Beethoven found it hardest to accept. He may have known, with the profound instinctive knowledge of genius, that solitude was necessary to the highest development of his creative power. But to know is not the same thing as to accept, and the full acceptance of his irrevocable and profound loneliness was one

---

[49] *Ibid.*, p. 101.
[50] *Ibid.*, pp. 108–109, 113–114.

of the last and greatest of Beethoven's victories.[51]

Beethoven realized early in his life of his superiority over others in his field. His lack of knowledge in dealing with others certainly made him many enemies, most of which, however, respected him for his genius. He had an almost supernatural need for love which perhaps many took to be mental illness on his part, but which showed only more of his full personality. In most of his attempts to show his love, he went beyond what the average person would consider natural love; and therefore was shunned. He was an idealist in most matters, but, to reach the ideal personality one must stand above all others.

---

[51] *Ibid.*, p. 184.

Miguel de Unamuno

Threefold Causality in His Development

From his early childhood Unamuno was considered a pensive child. He was really gifted and liked to set off contrasts. This special aptitude appeared very soon, even during the period of his infancy. Perhaps this was linked with introversion and taciturnity which, already in that time, were prevalent in his character. So, we may say that the genetic endowment of Unamuno seems to have been a preparation for deep understanding of contrast.

As a teenager, Unamuno began to elaborate his own philosophical system based on contrariety between different problems of life he was thinking about. He was a glutton for books, spending many evenings on reading by candlelight.

All this looks as if the influence of external milieu played little part in his particular development. He early began to act on the basis of his autonomous and authentic tendencies, and consequently presented clear signs of *third factor* as we define it. We shall elaborate all these traits in following chapters.

Multidimensionality and Multilevelness in His Development

During his life, Unamuno fought against French intellectualism and German pedantry, because he considered them as the propagators of an *illusive objectivism*. He manifested anger and disgust towards the use of so-called positive methods in relation to humanism. As an example, the history of sociology and psychology appeared to him as a cemetery of dead and abortive ideas.[52] He rather believed in the value and necessity of close contact with concrete reality in ethics and all humanistic fields. He felt the *taste of Absolute* hidden in the love of concrete things.

Unamuno also fought against the idea of intellectual specialization in science, especially in humanistic science. For him, intuition, emotion, and action are the primordial forces for understanding and living life: the true human being should say *I feel, this means I am,* or *I will, this means I am,* and not *I think, this means I am* (Descartes) because cold

---

[52]R. M. Albérès. *Miguel de Unamuno*. Paris: Éditions Universitaires, 1957, p. 65.

and dry thought is very poor. Man is often proud of his thinking, but in reality he hides himself inside his intellectually coherent systems. True thought should rather express basic contrarieties, in order to take into account the contrarieties of complicated, tense, and tragic reality.

The Christ has contained in himself all contrarieties and maladjustments of a human being which cannot be resolved in this world. His life proves, in the opinion of Unamuno, that intellectualism has nothing to do with spiritualism, and may even kill it. Thus, the doctrine of Christianity may overcome Christian faith which is not sure of itself. This coming phenomenon is the triumph of rationalistic theology. It alienated Unamuno from Christianity because he lacked, not of respect for individual thinking, but of belief in any rationalism.

Many times Unamuno thought that he had little knowledge, and even that he would never have much; but he felt the necessity and wanted to know, and this was sufficient to him. In his opinion, the philosopher is a rationalizing animal who tries to elaborate a conception of cosmos and life which he could enter in his logical system.[53] It is too easy to include spirit in the matter, or matter in the spirit: we may say that all is matter, or all is idea. It is easy also to reduce the unknown to apparently beautiful and logical concepts ... but it does not change our incompetence.

In conclusion, we may say that Unamuno avoided the danger of intellectualism. He presented multidimensional and multilevel development on one hand, concreteness on the other. The taste he developed for a representative act like theater – which needs as much emphasis as life – points out the great tension that has subtended his development.

Positive Disintegration, Neuroses, and Psychoneuroses

In his works and emotional life, Unamuno revealed his great sense of tragedy and agony. As an example, even existence as such is for him a tragedy. This comes from the definition of *tragedy* in itself. Indeed, this term expresses the relation to a certain reality which transcends the individual and in front of which his mind is powerless.[54]

---

[53] *Ibid.*, p. 60.
[54] *Ibid.*, p. 68.

According to Unamuno, the great tragedy of existence is the strong fight between life and death. In a human being, the sense of life should be clearly related with sense of death, because we live only in contrarieties and for contrarieties. Life is a tragedy, an eternal fight without victory, and even without a hope of victory; it is a true essential controversy.[55]

Through this perception of existence, Unamuno was near to the personality of Kierkegaard, whom he called *the man of mystery who lived in continuous eternal despair.* It is obvious that this name is in strict concordance with the aim of a human being which is for him the continuous fight to his mystery until his death. It is also in strict concordance with the title of one of Unamuno's works: *Feeling of Tragedy of Human Life.*[56]

In the opinion of Unamuno, knowledge creates such sham problems as objectivism to hide the basic agony of life; but in his opinion knowledge will never be able to give true satisfaction to our emotional and volitive needs, nor to our thirst for immortality.

Unamuno always wanted to go towards true problems of life. He believed and hesitated without interruption. So he fixed the truth in contrarieties and great tensions. This decision resulted from his love for concrete life: his philosophy of break is based upon contrarieties between some theoretical attitudes and living reality. In front of such contrarieties, he thought that we can have a much more existential approach to reality through poetry, drama, arts, and religion than through knowledge. As an example, he quotes the Christ who came nearer and nearer the essence of life by essential speeches, hyperboles, and parables.

If we resume, we see that Unamuno's attitude towards problems of life was based on disintegrated reality in the sense of contrarieties, fights, and paradoxes together with anxiety, depression, and agony.

Infantilism and Positive Regression

We do not see in the work of Unamuno and in his attitudes towards life any typical trait of infantilism and positive regression. However we may find some marginal traits of these phenomena in his personality.

---

[55] *Ibid.*, p. 97.
[56] *Ibid.*, p. 30.

According to many psychologists and psychopathologists, the great predominance of Unamuno's imaginative and emotional life over the place he sacrificed to the function of knowledge is a clear sign of infantilism. We disagree with this opinion.

We nevertheless admit that he presented an animistic and even mystic approach to reality which he considered as permitting a deeper experiencing of reality than other methods.

His opinion that we should mature throughout all of our life could also be interpreted as an infantile trait, but this judgment would have no other basis than statistical data concerning so-called normal attitudes towards reality. So we may say that Unamuno presented the tendency to appropriate penetration in the Vivid God which characterizes continuous maturation of individual and humanity in their tragic but true attitudes towards transcendental sense of life.

Inner Psychic Milieu

Unamuno gave in all and each of his works much of his personal experiences. He was very vigilant and criticizing in relation to all human phenomena and especially with those he considered as mistaking the true sense of human life. In the same way he criticized himself and his own reactions. As we already know, this attitude comes from his deep perception of contrarieties and their basic role in life and thinking.

One of Unamuno's opinion was that it is necessary to be defeated, to suffer because of our own errors. He was sure that he would no more be human if he ceased presenting the highest disquietude and eternal fear hidden in the eyes of sphinx. He understood and accepted the opinion of Kierkegaard according to which it is necessary to live in continual distress. For him, it is impossible to live *in pax*, he must live in war: the smaller joys he gets from life are at once faded by need for eternity.

In the opinion of Unamuno, any Christian or mystical virtue contains in its essence the true paradox of life and eternity. This is the reason why Saint Teresa of Jesus had as a characteristic exclamation the following expression: *I die because I cannot die!*[57] This is also the explanation of Christ's attitude including all difficulties of this life which could not be resolved in this world.

---

[57] *Ibid.*, p. 98.

According to Unamuno, even thought – i.e., true thought – can be reached only through pain and suffering. In this sense the true intellectualist should be the one who is never satisfied with himself and others.

Now, if we translate the attitudes of Unamuno into the terms of the theory of positive disintegration, we must conclude that Unamuno presented a vivid, dynamic, multidimensional, and multilevel inner psychic milieu. He manifested such symptoms as disquietude towards himself, subject-object in himself, and fight with himself – this means action of third factor with hierarchy of values and ideal of personality. He made the necessary bondage between emotional, intellectual, and instinctive functions, subordinating them to the highest intuitive functions.

Positive Maladjustment, Transgression of the Biological Life Cycle and Psychological Type

We see in Unamuno clear characteristics of positive maladjustment to the reality throughout his active and authentic acceptance of contrarieties as an essence of life, and his acceptance of great difficulties as a way to find the truth.

Unamuno understood very well that all those contrarieties and difficulties could not be resolved in this world but only in another transcendental world. By this we see that he was maladjusted to *what is* and perhaps adjusted to what *ought to be*. He presented also maladjustment towards intellectualism and all systems of knowledge.

As we know, contrarieties created in Unamuno the feeling of tragic sense of life. For him, this sense of life is the transgression of one-sided reality that must be carried on, even in spite of absence of evident result. So we may talk in Unamuno of a hierarchy in which *what is*, is subordinated to what *ought to be*. This hierarchy manifests a tendency to transcend his own biological life cycle and psychological type.

This tendency to transcendence is shown in Unamuno's personality and works through his following distinct but inseparable traits: first he evinces in his concreteness a highly developed love for existence, and second, he suffers at the same time a great distress. He suffers because he cannot be sure that his life will be eternal. Therefore it is the margin between beauty of life on one side and its lack of eternity on the other that is the basis of pain and suffering.

This genesis of Unamuno's agony permits us to understand why *Don Quixote* was for him a vivid work of literature, rather than a dead work: Cervantes seems to have transposed in mythology the transcendental reality he lived through.

From all this, we may clearly see the way and realization of Unamuno's transcendence of his own biological life cycle and psychological type. This way is the one of adjustment to higher reality and to ideal of personality, with maladjustment towards lower reality.

Authentism and Essence in Existence

Many human beings affirm that they can explain and justify their existence. Unamuno did not present that pretension. In many of his works, he states that we are born without any possibility of asking why. In this field, we cannot discover life as a basic reality; we cannot describe and control that reality. We even cannot state that it is impossible to define it anywhere and in any time.[58] And most of all, we cannot define the beginning and the end of this adventure which we call *life.*

As we may see, Unamuno had a very authentic attitude towards life which was for him a paradox. Among other things, he saw this paradox in intellectual affirmations, in the attitude of many so-called scientists who express fanatic ideas against any affirmation, but who themselves affirm with great strength that nothing could be affirmed.[59] As for himself, Unamuno never created any elaboration in his creativity. He liked concreteness and its complex contrarieties. He wanted to be a lover of concrete human beings in his emotional and instinctive life. He was of the opinion that Anglo-Saxons showed too much utilitarianism and German abundance of pedantism.

In conclusion, we may tell that Unamuno revealed himself in his works and life attitude as very different from most of his contemporaries. He was authentic, courageous, and fully aware of essentials in his attitudes towards knowledge, concrete everyday life, social life, politics, etc.

---

[58] *Ibid.*, p. 13.
[59] *Ibid.*, p. 69.

Personality

Is it justifiable to say that Unamuno has reached the level of personality as defined in the theory of positive disintegration? It is very difficult to answer this question, but we may affirm that Unamuno surely approached very near to the level of personality. He presented a clear hierarchy of values, with true human values on the highest levels; this means with individual and common essence. The individual essence was for him the preservation of concrete, exclusive, and unrepeated human values, the consciousness in relation to those values, and the highest interest in multidimensional and multilevel fields of experience. The common essence was made of understanding, empathy, and responsibility in relation to human individuals and large social groups.

His multidimensional and multilevel – this means hierarchical – attitude is expressed in the following opinion: "The life is absurd, but it is such an absurdity which gives a hope of sense beyond our knowledge."[60]

It is also absurdity that makes Unamuno see much more authenticity in Catholicism – in spite of all his criticisms towards it – than in Protestantism. Indeed the first is much more connected to hope and the second is clearly linked with justification of actual problems; this means, according to Unamuno, that Catholicism is more transcendental and Protestantism more adapted to actual life.

Unamuno was very authentic when he said that a human being fulfills his destiny only when he can think about death and experience it and, as a consequence, when he can think about life and feel it. On the highest level of realization of human beings, he places love and empathy. In his opinion, God should be sensitive towards love, heart, and never be a God of theologians.

---

[60] *Ibid.*, p. 36.

Appendix: Personality, Outstanding Abilities, and Psychoneuroses in Children and Young People

As an addition to this work we wish to present the results of our systematic investigations, carried out under the author's direction at the Institute of Mental Hygiene and Children's Psychiatry of the Polish Academy of Sciences, which throw light on a considerable section of our inquiries. These investigations concern personality and its development in correlation with outstanding abilities and psychoneuroses in children and young people. Thus, they represent preliminary experimental confirmation of the main hypotheses advanced and statements made throughout this text. It is nevertheless desirable, even necessary, that further experimentation be carried out, not only concerning the specific hypotheses tested here, but also many other hypotheses found throughout the text.

Subject and Scope of the Investigations

The problem of outstanding abilities in a given field of science, art, or endeavor has been, for some years now, the subject of some interest to many specialists. Particularly valuable, from the point of view of social usefulness and pedagogical practice, is the knowledge of the mental and physical development of gifted children and young people. In the Soviet Union, as well as in the United States, a great deal of research work is done in this direction. This work was also started in Poland, for the first time on an extensive scale, in the Department of Mental Hygiene and Children's Psychiatry of the Polish Academy of Sciences. In this work we were greatly helped by the Polish Society of Mental Hygiene.

When studying outstanding abilities, one encounters numerous difficulties both in the course of studies and when one attempts to systematize their results. The difficulties of the first kind concern the methods of study, which should permit the acquisition of exhaustive data on the physical and psychic development of the individual; the difficulties of the second kind appear when one tries to determine the correlation between examined abilities and somatopsychic qualities, indissolubly connected with all other qualities of the individual.

We selected, from a very great number of problems, several of weighty and practical importance. These were problems concerning personality, outstanding abilities, and psychoneuroses. These conceptions are known to the reader and we shall omit here their detailed definition. We would like, however, to call attention to their correlation and arrangement in the children and young people examined by us. We have not found in literature any attempt to discover and compare the correlations between these three qualities.

Of course, one should keep in mind that both our investigations and conclusions are no more than the initial phase of further, widely planned studies of outstanding abilities, that in our conclusion we endeavor only to indicate directions, the "tender" points of the problem, and that therefore these conclusions should not be regarded as fully elaborated and permanent schemes and generalizations. On the contrary, it is our wish that the themes touched upon should encourage other institutions to cooperate with us in our study of outstanding abilities, and also to examine critically some of the correlations indicated here.

Herein we will give the results of experimental investigation of a group of gifted children and young people, aged 8 to 23. Conclusions are based on the examination of 80 children, of whom 30 were generally intellectually gifted (from elementary schools), and 50 were children and young people from art schools (drama, ballet, and plastic art schools). One of the first control groups was a group of 30 mentally deficient children; among them were 10 examined at the same time as the gifted children, and 20 diagnoses were taken from the card register of the author. Every child was examined by means of the best available and best-developed psychological methods (personal inquiries, questionnaires, tests, talks, observations) and was subjected to detailed internal neurological and psychiatric examination. Every child was subjected also to a medical inquiry extending back to the prenatal period and including his hereditary make-up. The examinations were carried out in the autumn of 1962, in

Warsaw schools, by a dozen or so physicians and psychologists.

Definition of Our Main Concepts

Since we shall dwell here on the correlation between outstanding abilities, personality, and psychoneuroses, we will briefly recall what we mean by these concepts.

The term *outstanding abilities* denotes abilities (in any field of a man's life) which permit him to achieve results considerably surpassing the average standard accepted for individuals of the same age, education, and so forth. In our examinations we came into contact with two kinds of capabilities: general and special. Outstanding general abilities were noted in children from elementary schools who were able to attain higher than average results in general learning on tests (though in school they did not always attain these results). The I.Q. of this group (general ability) ranged from 120 to 146. General abilities were divided into humanistic, mathematical, and natural. Outstanding special abilities were possessed by children attending art schools. Manifestations of these abilities differentiated into theatrical, dancing, plastic art, and finally into musical abilities. All the examined children who possessed special abilities had an I.Q. rating of between 110 and 155, that is to say they were, at the same time, generally intellectually capable.

By the term *personality* we mean that self-conscious, self-affirmed, and self-educating unity of the fundamental qualities of a man, the unity which includes among others the faculties of interests, thinking, higher drives, feelings, temperament, and so on. The main components of the internal environment of a developing personality are multilevel dynamisms and conflicts, a more or less high degree of insight into oneself, an ability to control and reshape one's psychic structure, and the presence of creative and perfective dynamisms. The internal environment is the better developed the more the individual is characterized by that so-called "psychic richness," which includes a plurality of interests and capabilities, an intense emotional life, and finally the ability for accelerated development.

The terms *neuroses* and *psychoneuroses* have not been precisely defined. We employ them here in their generally accepted sense, that of symptomatic sets occurring primarily in the nervous system (neuroses) or in the psychic area (psychoneuroses). We also employ here the traditional symptomatic units of psychasthenia, neurasthenia, anxiety neurosis, neurotic depression, hypochondria, sexual neurosis, and vegetative neurosis.

Within any one particular type of neurosis (e.g., systemic, obsessive, compulsive, etc.) we assume, in general, three different stages of intensity.

1. The most serious stage – one of distinct neurotic or psychoneurotic illness, causing very strong disorders (for instance, distinct disorders of the function of reality, strong aggressive or suicidal tendencies, difficulties in conducting normal study, or distinct psychosomatic disorders)

2. The medium stage, of passing symptoms of nervousness or neurotic or psychoneurotic disorders, often not noticeable externally, and which do not leave permanent traces in the psyche (for example, symptoms of increased psychic excitability, passing motor unrest, slight symptoms of showing off, impulsive actions, mood-lability)

3. The light stage on the borderline of normality, evidenced by psychic overexcitability, some symptoms of anxiety, and so on

General Characteristics of the Children Examined

Every one of the investigated children showed considerable vegetative, sexual, affectional, imaginational, and intellectual hyperexcitability which constituted a foundation for the emergence of neurotic and psychoneurotic sets. Moreover, it turned out that these children also showed sets of nervousness, neuroses, and psychoneuroses of various kinds and degrees of intensity, from light vegetative symptoms, or anxiety symptoms, to distinctly and highly intensive psychasthenic or hysterical sets. The arrangements of these sets allowed very rich descriptive diagnoses, varying with each particular child.

With the children and young people investigated certain definite psychoneurotic sets predominated, namely those of about 30% medium-degree anxiety neurosis, 25% medium-degree hysterical sets, 25% light-intensity neurasthenic sets. The examination also revealed a considerable amount of hypochondria, psychasthenia, and vegetative neurosis to the extent of about 10% each. Of course, each of these sets greatly differs in particular cases, depending on the child's age, kind of interests and abilities, type of school, environmental conditions, and so forth. There are multiformed connections between these sets. The pictures of the neurotic and psychoneurotic sets are very rich and differentiated. Below we give an example of a set of anxiety neurosis with neurasthenic and hypochondriacal components:

> Boy, aged 8, in third grade of an elementary school, good educational conditions. Doing very well in school subjects, 136 I.Q. Wechsler test. Creative ability in drawing. Theoretical interests, humanistic.
>
> Quite wide pupils, strongly trembling eyelids and trembling of hands. Increased abdominal reflexes. Increased psychomotor excitability of a constricted type. Tic-like movements. Increased muscular tension. Dreams about fears and persecutions. Distinct waxy suppleness (*flexibilitas cerea*).
>
> Apparently good contact with his environment. Recommended for social action. Avoids people. Timid in new situations. Looks for help from adults. Lacking self-dependence. Strong fear of suffering injustice, fears the possibility of losing his mother, fears the school teacher's castigation, fears sickness, hospitalization and physical effort. Afraid to be late for school. Leaves much too early. Afraid to sleep alone, or to remain alone in a room. Inhibited, helpless, and uncertain. Periodic opposition and outbursts of aggression leaving him very tired. Impatient, gets angry easily and cries. In school work he is uncertain of himself, trembles, gesticulates, loses his head and forgets. Has great difficulty in concentrating. Gets discouraged easily, has an inclination to pessimism and believes he will never succeed in doing things. Sadness and the feeling of inferiority dominate. Diligent and systematic in work to exaggerated extent. Avoids sad books and emotional films. Affectionate.

An example of hysterical sets with psychic emotional overexcitability and anxiety follows:

Girl, aged 20, with good home background; 116 I.Q. Outstanding ability in all general subjects, and in dancing and acting.

From early childhood has had fits of bad temper, of whims, and made suicidal threats; blackmails those closest to her.

Presently suffers from headaches, giddiness and heartaches without apparent reason; disorders in breathing, difficulties in falling asleep; nausea when caught by emotion; allergy to the odors of ether and benzine; easily faints when in anger; her bodily extremities cool; her hands and feet moist. Accelerated psychomotor drive and process of thinking. Cannot concentrate. Plaintive. Smokes cigarettes. Uneven appetite. Claustrophobia. Fears loneliness.

Nervous, touchy, noisy. The tempo of work and the behavior dependent on mood. Outbursts of joy and periods of shyness. One-sided interests, spends her time seeking sensations. Lazy in doing her duties, chats easily. In states of nervous tension beats those nearest to her.

As one may see from the above examples the psychoneurotic symptoms were often displayed by great tension which caused frequent conflicts with the environment. They often lead to a dissipation of the positive developmental qualities, together with an upsetting of the possibility of the development of exceptional abilities.

The Internal Environment and Kinds and Levels of Psychoneuroses

One may inquire as to the cause of the increased tendency among gifted children who have good conditions of life and learning to become subject to states of nervousness or psychoneuroses. Probably the cause is more than average sensitivity which not only permits one to achieve outstanding results in learning and work, but at the same time increases the number of points sensitive to all experiences that may accelerate anomalous reactions revealing themselves in the psychoneurotic sets.

The reason why children and young people are inflicted with some and not other psychoneurotic sets is another problem. Most probably the cause lies in the individual personality of the child, which is specifically shaped by the multifarious influences of his particular environment.

In an attempt to show the causes of the tendency to a give kind and level of psychoneurosis we will use the term *inner milieu.* The inner milieu which arises with the development of the individual differs greatly with particular persons. With some it is in its initial phase, in which the individual has merely the disposition to build the personality at a higher level. Often however, even with older youths we do not observe any attempts at self-education or at the self-direction of one's own qualities and abilities with a view to attaining higher individual or social values.

Among the children and young people we examined, about half did not possess the distinct rudiments of a rich internal environment. It turned out that the quality of the structure of this environment was clearly correlated to the development and level of psychoneurosis.

With the existing developing internal environment the neurotic sets appeared in the following sequence:

In theatrical schools: first psychasthenia, then anxiety neurosis, neurasthenia, hypochondria, hysteria. In plastic art schools: psychasthenia, anxiety neurosis, neurasthenia, oppressive neurosis. In ballet schools: vegetative neurosis, anxiety neurosis, neurasthenia. In general education schools: anxiety neurosis, hypochondria, neurasthenia, psychasthenia.

When a developing internal environment was lacking, there predominated:

In theatrical schools: neurasthenia, hysteria, infantile neurosis. In plastic arts schools: hysteria, neurasthenia, oppressive neurosis, and vegetative neurosis. In ballet schools: hysteria, anxiety neurosis, vegetative neurosis. In general education schools: hysteria, anxiety neurosis, hypochondria.

Summing up these results we may state that, with all those examined, independent of the type of school, with the presence of a rich and developing internal environment, the number of anxiety and psychasthenic sets increases, but when such an environment is lacking, hysterical and neurasthenic symptoms dominate.

Such a state of affairs may be due to multifarious causes. Probably there is a positive connection between the lower set in the hierarchy of psychoneurotic symptoms (e.g., hysteria) and the weak degree of insight into oneself, which is connected with the conscious reshaping dynamisms. Of course, this cannot be the only connection. Which symptoms are primary in such a set? For example, is it intense psychic richness that is primary, a richness which at the same time allows the possibility of increasing the degree of self-reflection and automatically evokes symptoms of disorders at these higher levels (e.g., excessive subtlety, disorders in the reality function)? Or is it the other way – is it the disposition to psychoneurosis that disorders the highest qualities of the psyche and allows the possibility of realizing these hierarchically higher qualities of the personality?

Further analysis showed that not only the kind but also the level of a given concrete neurosis is conditioned, not only by the presence of a more developed internal environment but also by the level of this environment. Numerous examples indicate that the same neurosis or psychoneurosis shifts and becomes localized at a higher level if at the same time the internal environment arises and develops.

The problems raised in these pages require further elaboration. At this point, however, we would like to add several detailed conclusions concerning the kinds and seriousness of psychoneurotic sets:

1. When the organizing structure of personality is lacking, the degree of intensity of neurotic sets increases distinctly. Sets of a more intensive course but also of a lower level of disordered functions then appear.

2. Anxiety neurosis, in cases where the developed internal environment is lacking, may be light but it appears as a neurosis with more serious symptoms when the internal environment is developed, and then it is a disorder of the higher level function (existential anxieties). Moreover, it is a neurosis which has the tendency to appear whether the developed internal environment is lacking or present.

3. Hysteria, with very intensive symptoms and at a lower level of disordered functions, occurs most frequently when the internal environment is lacking, and vanishes almost completely when the internal environment is developing. The stronger the hysterical sets, the weaker the symptoms of other psychoneurotic sets. And likewise inversely. Hysteria occurs to a great extent irrespective of one's age.

4. With older youths the degree of neurasthenia increases when the internal environment is lacking.

5. Psychasthenia tends to associate with more serious neurotic states of the following type: obsessions, neurasthenias, and anxiety neurosis.

6. Anxiety neurosis is the most "sociable," the light symptoms of which associate with the stronger degrees of neuroses of the lower type, namely with vegetative neurosis and with hysteria. More serious anxiety neurosis associates with an increased intensity of psychoneuroses at a higher level.

Internal Environment and General and Social Abilities

When dealing with the internal environment one should refer to other qualities which, together with it, go to make up the concept of personality. We have in mind here, primarily, outstanding abilities, interests, thoughts, and manifestations of one's relation to the external environment – all encompassed in the internal environment – as related to the level and kind of psychoneurosis. Due to lack of space we shall give only some of the correlations.

The lack of development of an internal environment (and therefore, indirectly, a greater tendency to psychoneurotic sets of the hysteric and neurasthenic type) is connected with certain attributes of thinking, such as the predominance of practical intelligence, a weak ability for the mechanical memorization of numbers, weak abstract and symbolic thinking, rigidity of intellectual content, stereotyped thinking, fastidiousness, weak conceptual analysis and thinking, chaos, an agglutinative character of thinking, an inability to concentrate, such qualities as criticism, correct judgment of the situation, visual-motor coordination, artistic intuition, the dominant role of impressions in artistic thinking.

The arising internal environment, in which the sets of psychasthenia and anxiety neurosis appear frequently, is associated with such qualities as the tendency to confabulate and to make generalizations, gaudiness, originality, richness and plasticity of intellectual contents, an ability for abstract thinking, the less frequent occurrence of stereotyped and chaotic thinking, correct logical thinking, a good knowledge and vocabulary, good mathematical and symbolic reasoning, magical thinking, perseveration, and difficulties in concentration.

With older youths, having one-sided interests which concern only their study curriculum (e.g., interests in dancing or in plastic arts) neurasthenic sets dominate. The remaining young people develop interests and abilities in various forms of social and personal life by further education of themselves, by studying the problems of art, extracurricular plastic works or paintings, by collecting museum pieces, by ballet and singing, by learning to know nature, or by sports and traveling.

The development of interest and abilities – in fact the whole inner richness of the examined children and youths – was accompanied by creative abilities. These abilities were very numerous and differentiated, depending on the age, kind of school, and so on. They were revealed in special creative abilities, such as spontaneous literary creativity (writing in rhymes or writing drama), in one's own interpretation of a dance, in an original painting or drawing, in composing songs, in sculpture, in a disposition for pantomime, and so on.

Among older youths the majority of creative abilities were possessed by individuals with a very advanced development of their internal environments, by individuals characterized by excessive sensibility and subtlety, by a weakening of social contact, by a richness of the associative apparatus, a strong need for evaluation, a strong artistic imagination, and a tendency to confabulation, difficulties in concentrating, a tendency to be tired, and peculiar vegetative reactions to psychic experiences.

Neuroses with Oligophrenic Children

Let us now mention the neurotic symptoms of oligophrenic children. A very weak, or rather no development of the internal environment, is here associated with specific symptoms of nervousness. These children are unable to control their thinking. They experience anxieties because of primitive external causes (beating, abuse, physical injury, and noise). The hierarchization of values takes place in the world of sensual experiences (the best things in life are the favorite dish or a person from whom one gets something). Moral concepts are accepted according to standards set by the environment with respect to internal behavior (e.g., when one sits properly one is good). Their feelings are more shallow, there is a lack of consonance with those close to them, and tragic accidents are presented in a lighthearted form. As may be seen from the above, these children do not show symptoms of the hierarchy of values. The kind of neurosis connected with such psychic underdevelopment is typical. Namely, vegetative neurosis and very marked psychomotor and sensual hyperexcitability predominate exclusively. They reveal themselves frequently among oligophrenic children and there appear tendencies to increased muscular tension, to limb reflexes, to hand trembling, to dermographism, to perspiration, onychophagia, a disposition to tiredness, tearfulness, noisiness, a remarkable mobility, and very strong tic like symptoms. Moreover, they are characterized by primitive manifestations of anxiety, lightheartedness, euphoria, by a light susceptibility to suggestion, a lack of shyness, excessive courage, and undue loquacity.

We see, therefore, that in the case of oligophrenic children the picture of neuroses has a specific character. Further correlations will not be considered here.

Conclusions

In order to sum up we wish to stress once more that:

1. All gifted children and young people display symptoms of increased psychoneurotic excitability, or lighter or more serious psychoneurotic symptoms.

2. In general the presence of all-around interests in children and young people coincides with complicated forms of psychoneurosis, with psychoneuroses of higher hierarchical system of functions (psychasthenia, anxiety neurosis, obsessive neurosis) or with a higher level of the same kind of neurosis.

3. Psychoneurosis becomes more complicated with the development

of the internal environment, but at the same time there appear autopsychotherapeutic dynamisms.

4. The development of personality with gifted children and young people usually passes through the process of positive disintegration, which is connected with the already mentioned complexity of neurosis, and on the other hand it leads to self-control, self-education, and autopsychotherapy.

5. The lower the level of the development of personality and intelligence, the more primitive the forms of psychoneurosis observed (up to its absence in more serious cases of mental deficiency).

At this point we would like to turn our attention to certain of our own reservations with respect to the material presented. The weaknesses, among others, are the relative brevity of the study and the insufficient number of control groups. This deficiency is partly compensated for by the group of oligophrenic children and by the author's experiences gained from the study of children of average mental level. The possible objection that the detected symptoms of nervousness and psychoneurosis constitute normal developmental symptoms would be groundless, since the described and analyzed symptoms are identical with the accepted sets of symptoms in neuroses and psychoneuroses.

Therefore, the best conclusion seems to be the thesis that there is a positive correlation between abilities and nervousness and psychoneurosis.

We think that we shall have reached our goal if this work will focus attention on the positive relation between the structure of personality and susceptibility to being afflicted with psychoneuroses. The practical conclusions should be drawn primarily by psychiatrists, psychologists, pedagogists, and all those dealing with the problem of outstanding abilities. It may be that in the future it will be the gifted, internally rich children who will start the process of lowering psychic tension and the process of liquidating the manifestations of nervousness by developing their internal environment, that is, by the development and shaping of personality.

Glossary

Abdominal Reflex Contraction of the muscles of the abdominal wall in response to stroking the overlying skin.

Abulia Loss of will; inability to decide on anything.

Accelerated Development Type of development characterized by multiple forms of psychic overexcitability (primarily emotional, imaginational, and intellectual), strong creative instinct, and strong autonomous factors. Accelerated development tends towards organized multilevel disintegration and secondary integration. It, thereby, tends towards transcending the psychological type and the biological life cycle. See *Transcending the psychological type, Transcending the biological life cycle.*

Adjustment See *Negative Adjustment, Positive Adjustment, Negative Maladjustment,* and *Positive Maladjustment.*

Affective Perseveration A tendency toward exploration and development of deep emotional relations and interests. It leads to few but very close relationships of love and friendship, or to a very profound dedication to one's vocation. It occurs in individuals who are both emotional and introverted. They experience deeply and strongly, they remember their experiences vividly because of enhanced affective memory. Affective perseveration is related to the development of such attitudes as faithfulness to principles, loyalty in friendship, and constancy of interests. This quality is developmentally positive.

Ambiequal Type A type of personality differentiated by Rorschach. On the inkblot test it gives a balance of response between internal movement and sensitivity to colors. It corresponds somewhat to the balance between introversion (emotional self-sufficiency and exclusivity, self-reference for norms and values), creativity, dependence on the external world, and sensitivity to it (need for emotional contact with environment, conformity with others, relative lack of self-reference).

Ambitendencies Contrary drives which are struggling for dominance yet never gaining it for an extended period of time. For example, greed and the accumulation of money may conflict with the desire to spend it all and have a good time, a death wish (suicidal tendency) may conflict with the drive to self-preservation. As in Ambivalences these are conflicts between drives of the same level, therefore they are unilevel, and as such are characteristic of unilevel disintegration.

Ambivalences Conflicting attitudes as of obedience and rebellion, inferiority and superiority, love and hate, etc. Ambivalences are characteristic dynamisms of unilevel disintegration. The sense of higher and lower values is absent, the conflicting feelings are of equal value, therefore, they represent one and the same level.

Amphotonia See *Autonomic Disequilibrium.*

Animism The belief that objects in nature, or natural phenomena, are endowed with their own consciousness, or are inhabited by souls or spirits.

Arrhythmia A change in the rhythm or force of heartbeat. Arrhythmia may be caused by organic changes or by an alteration in the control of heartbeat without physical impairment (it is, therefore, a functional disorder).

Asthenia Weakness, also tendency towards depression as in psychic asthenia (psychasthenia).

Asthenic A type of body build characterized by small trunk and long limbs, also tending towards feelings of inferiority, weakness, passivity. Underestimates himself, is uncertain in his behavior and gives way.

Astonishment With Oneself The feeling that some of one's mental qualities are surprising and unexpected. It is one of the earliest developmental dynamisms, and is mainly cognitive in nature, though not exclusively. It is active at the time of transition from unilevel to multilevel disintegration, usually accompanied by disquietude and dissatisfaction with oneself.

Authenticity, Authentism Authenticity denotes a high degree of unity of one's thinking, emotions, and activity. Authentism involves conscious activity in accordance with one's "inner truth," i.e. one's autonomously developed hierarchy of values; it is a developmental force.

Autism (or Autistic Thinking) Mental activity serving to gratify the thinker without respect to actual reality. Portrayed by Thurber in "The Secret Life of Walter Mitty."

Automatic Dynamisms Mental processes stemming from constitutional typological factors lacking conscious inner transformation, e.g. the "spontaneity" of action painting or "happenings."

Autonomic Disequilibrium Amphotonia, Dystonia, or Vagosympathetic Dystonia. Lack of balance between the activity of the sympathetic and the parasympathetic nervous systems, characterized by quick switches of dominance from one system to the other (see *Autonomic Lability*). Autonomic disequilibrium is characteristic of the lower neuroses.

Autonomic Disorganization The most evolved stage of Autonomic Disequilibrium (q.v.). It is expressed in the alternating strength of activity of the two autonomic systems: the sympathetic and the parasympathetic. It is observed as a prevalence of activity of the sympathetic nervous system in one field (e.g. digestive, or circulatory) and at the same time a prevalence of activity of the parasympathetic system in another field (e.g. genito-urinary, or respiratory).

Autonomic Lability A tendency to sudden transfer of tension between the sympathetic and the parasympathetic nervous systems. These reactions have disturbing consequences, as for instance, sudden drop of blood pressure and fainting spells, or the reverse when a sudden rise in blood pressure is spontaneously compensated by bleeding from the nose or mouth.

Autonomic Nervous System A system of neurons controlling the involuntary activity of the viscera: digestive organs, heart, lungs, kidneys, glands, etc. It has two parts, the sympathetic and the parasympathetic. The stimulation of the sympathetic system mobilizes the organism by quickening respiration, heart rate, raising the blood pressure, etc. The action of the parasympathetic system is for the most part functionally reciprocal. The excitation of one system results in the inhibition of the functions controlled by the other, for instance, the increase of respiration and heart rate suspends digestion.

Autonomic Somatization The transformation of acute psychological tension into nervous somatic symptoms under the control of the autonomic nervous system. For instance, an increase in the pulse rate, blushing, or growing pale, growing tense, hysterical paralysis, etc., occur as a result of a severe emotional experience. The symptoms and syndromes may grow from very weak to very strong. It is believed that in autonomic somatization the disturbance is due more to the lability of the autonomic nervous system rather than to the intensity of psychological processes. Cf. *Psychosomatization*.

Autonomy A dynamism of inner freedom. It signifies a consciously developed independence from lower drives and from the influences of the external environment.

Autopsychotherapy Psychotherapy, preventive measures, or changes in living conditions consciously applied to oneself in order to control possible mental disequilibrium.

Babinski Reflex Spreading of toes when the sole of the foot is scratched. A sign of pathology in the nervous system.

Catatonic Schizophrenia (or Catatonia) Type of schizophrenia characterized by slowness of movements, or prolonged immobility, sometimes by muscular rigidity and inflexibility.

Chwostek Reflex Local contraction of facial muscles in response to being struck by a mallet or to other stimulus.

Coenesthesia The totality of internal sensations by which one perceives one's own body. Coenesthesia is increased when emotional processes are converted into the processes controlled by the autonomic nervous system, and vice versa, and are experienced as numbness, fornication, or internal oppression. Disturbances of coenesthesia take the form of vertigo, palpitation, nausea, etc. Marked coenesthesia is frequent at the stage of unilevel disintegration and may represent an initial phase toward control of the autonomic nervous system by the growing personality.

Confabulation More or less unconscious creation of imaginary experiences, often in great detail, to cover up memory gaps or other lacks of own material.

Contact Introversion Introversion combined with conscious need for external contact. It results from the transformation of rigid introversion into a mixed introvertive-extrovertive type. It is an example of the transformation of a one-sided psychological type to a richer one less delimited by constitutional factors. Thus it represents an expression of the developmental potential. Contact introversion is connected with the dynamism and process "subject-object in oneself."

Conversion A mental mechanism by means of which an emotional reaction is expressed in an alteration of a function of the body, e.g. paralysis of a limb as an escape from a threatening or painful situation, or as an extreme affective identification with a paralyzed beloved person. Conversion reaction is characteristic of hysteria.

Creative Dynamisms Different abilities and talents finding their expression in a search for "otherness," for non-stereotype facets of reality. All developmental dynamisms are creative by their power of transforming the individual and his perception of reality.

Creative Instinct An assembly of cohesively organized forces, often of great intensity, oriented toward a search for the new and the different in the external and the internal reality. Creative instinct is associated with accelerated development.

Cutaneous Reflex Wrinkling of the skin or gooseflesh upon mechanical stimulation of the skin.

Cycloid Refers to a person who shows relatively marked but normal swings of mood between excitement and depression, less strong than in the cyclothymic (q.v.).

Cyclothymic Exhibiting alternating moods of elation and depression, activity and inactivity, with mood swings out of proportion to apparent stimuli. A mild form of manic-depressive behavior.

Defense Through Development With the progress of development the defensive (i.e. protective) forces localize themselves at a high level toward the service of individual growth. Mental development is the best protection against mental disorder. It is the lack of mental growth, or its stalemate, that favors mental illness.

Delusional Center A disposing and directing center identified with a delusion (of persecution, jealousy, etc.) which controls behavior.

Dermographia Sensitivity of the skin to local mechanical irritation. When pressed or scratched the skin produces a reddish, or sometimes white, raised mark which may stay for a short while or a long time, in which case we have a prolonged and more intense dermographic response.

Developmental Instinct The source of all mental developmental forces of the individual. It is absent in mental retardation and psychopathy.

Developmental Potential The constitutional endowment which determines the character and the extent of mental growth possible for a given individual. The developmental potential can be assessed on the basis of the following components: psychic overexcitability (q.v.), special abilities and talents, and autonomous factors (notably the Third factor).

Disintegration Loosening, disorganization or dissolution of mental functions and structures. See *Unilevel Disintegration, Multilevel Disintegration, Negative Disintegration*, and *Positive Disintegration*.

Disposing and Directing Center A center which controls behavior over a short or long period of time. At a low level of human development this center is identical with either one or a group of primitive drives (e.g. self-preservation, sexual, aggressive, etc.). At higher levels of development this center becomes an independent dynamism working towards harmonious unification of personality.

Disquietude with Oneself The feeling of uneasiness with oneself; one of the earliest dynamism marking the beginning of multilevel disintegration.

Dissatisfaction (or Discontent) with Oneself An early form of the dynamism of valuation (the third factor). A potent motivator of conscious development.

Drive A concrete instinctive need of great intensity demanding satisfaction.

Dynamic Insight (or "Prise de Conscience") Strong, global, momentary states of self-awareness. They tend to generate dynamic understanding of one's behavior with the consequences of changing it.

Dynamism Biological or mental force controlling behavior and its development. Instincts, drives, and intellectual processes combined with emotions are dynamisms.

Dystonia See *Autonomic Disequilibrium*.

Ecstasy Extreme absorption of attention resulting in a semi-trance as a consequence of intense contemplation of a limited field; a state characteristic of mystical experiences.

Ekklisis A term introduced by von Monakow to describe one of the two biopsychic vectors of behavioral patterns of living beings: approach and avoidance, attraction and repulsion, syntony and dislike, flight and aggression. Ekklisis is the name for the outward movement, Klisis is the name for the approach movement.

Emotional Immaturity The persistence of emotional and intellectual qualities characteristic of children and youth past a young age. Associated with tendencies to Positive Regression (q.v.) it is an essential component of creative development.

Emotional Retardation A negative form of Emotional Immaturity; lack of emotional development characterized by primitiveness and rigidity of affect, very low level of syntony and emotional sensitivity. Associated with psychopathy and some forms of mental retardation.

Empathy High level of Syntony (q.v.).

Erythema Pudicum The tendency to blush because of feelings of shame, timidity, or inhibition. An indicator of emotional overexcitability. It is often due to periodic heightened sensitivity to the opinions and judgments expressed by others. It is combined with somatopsychic sensitivity.

Evolution A development which proceeds from lower to higher levels of organization. Positive disintegration is the type of process through which individual human evolution occurs. See *Involution*.

Existential Anxiety Anxiety states on a very high level of development involving the awareness of the fact of one's existence and the responsibility that follows from it. Fear for others prevails over fear for oneself. Existential anxiety arises on the basis of psychic overexcitability (q.v.) of alterocentric nature. It embraces empathic and intellectual components on a very wide range with the emphasis on the human dilemma of existential choice. It is also related to the awareness of the universality of human experience as expressed by St. Paul: "If anyone is weak, do I not share this weakness? If anyone is made to stumble, does not my heart blaze with indignation?" (II Cor. 11, 29).

Existential Hysteria A psychoneurosis at a high level of development arising on a background of existential experiences and actions prompted by empathy (alterocentric preoccupations). With hysteria it has the following similarities, though expressed at a higher level: intense affects, strong dramatization, attitude of gesture, demonstrativeness, tendency toward ecstasy or contemplation.

Existential Psychoneurosis Psychoneurosis on a high level of development which involves a dominance of existential preoccupations. These existential components are peculiar to each kind of psychoneurosis-depressive, anxiety, infantile, obsessive, etc.

Extravert A type of personality exhibiting strong interest in external reality, inclined to rely in his judgments and experiences on the opinions of his environment; inclined to syntony and adaptation to others, does not tolerate solitude.

Flexibilitas Cerea See *Waxy Flexibility*.

Functions The instruments of mental and emotional equipment, e.g. reality function, empathy, identification, responsibility, intuition. See *Levels of Functions*.

Hebephrenic Schizophrenia (or Hebephrenia) Type of schizophrenia characterized by shallow inappropriate affects, unpredictable behavior, silly mannerisms.

Hierarchization The process of developing or activating different emotional levels. It stems from conflicts of value which reflect the existence of feelings corresponding to higher and lower values (i.e. more preferred vs. less preferred choices). A hierarchy of values is a hierarchy of higher and lower levels of emotions.

Hyperkinesis Excessive restlessness of movements.

Hypertonia (or Autonomic Hypertonia) High tension of the autonomic nervous system (q.v.).

Hypobulia Lowered ability to act or to make decisions. Less severe than Abulia.

Hypomanic Refers to mild manic conditions, characterized by restlessness, flight of ideas, distraction.

Hypotonia (or Autonomic Hypotonia) Low tension of the autonomic nervous system (q.v.).

Infantilism A combination of infantile mental qualities. In its positive form it is associated with plasticity and emotional sincerity characteristic of children. In its negative form it is associated with general lack of developmental potential as in mental retardation.

Inferiority Toward Oneself The feeling consisting .in the experiencing and awareness of the disparity between the level at which one is and the higher one toward which one strives. It is the shock of realization of one's unfaithfulness to the ideal of personality, to the hierarchy of values which begins to take shape but as yet lack stability, followed by a desire and actions to transform oneself.

Inhibition Means of control of physiological or mental processes at any level of activity by reducing or stopping the flow of a given process

Inner Psychic Milieu (or Internal Mental Environment) The totality of mental dynamisms of a low or high degree of consciousness. The inner psychic milieu may be hierarchical, as in multilevel disintegration, or ahierarchical, as in unilevel disintegration. The inner psychic milieu as a ground for positive development must be hierarchical, and it is this type which is normally understood under the term.

Inner Psychic Transformation The process by which the work of developmental change in man's mental structure is carried out. It makes possible the transcending of the psychological type and of the biological life cycle (see *Transcending*).

Integration Consists in an organization of instinctive, emotional and intellectual functions into a coordinated structure. See *Primitive Integration* and *Secondary Integration*.

Interneurotic Levels Psychoneurotic syndromes characteristic of different levels of development. For example, phobias, organ neuroses and hypochondria are limited to Level II (unilevel disintegration), while paranoid and catatonic schizophrenias can occur at Level II and III and thus are disorders of higher level representing greater complexity and greater possibility of growth. Psychoneurotic anxiety and depression are still higher because they do not occur below Level III. Correct and precise diagnosis of a syndrome helps to identify the developmental level of a patient.

Intraneurotic Levels Levels of functions differentiated within the same psychoneurotic syndrome. Lower levels are characterized by predominant somatic control while higher levels by predominant mental control. For example within the category of psychasthenias neurasthenia represents a higher level than hypochondria, but lower level than psychasthenia, all three involving the same group of functions.

Introvert A type of personality having difficult contact with his environment, inclined to base his behavior on his own judgment, imagination and experience; inclined to solitude, avoids other especially at times of grave difficulties.

Involution Negative development. Opposite of evolution (q.v.). Development which proceeds from higher to a lower level of organization. It tends toward severe disorders (psychosis, psychopathy, mental retardation), and may lead to the dissolution of mental organization.

Kinaesthesis The sense of movement derived from receptors in skeletal muscles, joints, etc. In the Rorschach – a movement response.

Klisis A term introduced by van Monakow to describe the approach tendency as one of the two main behavioral vectors. See *Ekklisis*.

Level I Primitive integration (q.v.).

Level II Unilevel disintegration (q.v.).

Level III Spontaneous multilevel disintegration (q.v.).

Level IV Organized multilevel disintegration (q.v.).

Level V Secondary integration (q.v.).

Levels Of Functions The qualitative and quantitative differences which appear in mental functions as a result of developmental changes. Lower levels of functions are characterized by automatism, impulsiveness, stereotypy, egocentrism, lack or low degree of consciousness. Higher levels of functions show distinct consciousness, inner psychic transformation, autonomousness, creativity.

Lability See *Autonomic Lability.*

Magical Thinking An emotional, imaginational, and intuitive type of thinking based on the assumption (most often unconscious) that some phenomena may operate exempt from the causality of the laws of nature. Magical thinking explains different phenomena in a miraculous or fantastic way.

Meditation Practice of mental concentration leading to inner calmness and sense of well-being.

Meditative Empathy An expression of sympathy towards another person but with strong reflective, and even meditative, components. It is a high level of syntony of closely integrated intellectual elements. The intellectual elements do not diminish such empathy but rather enrich and develop it: "I know you and I always refine this knowledge; yet this does not diminish my feeling for you but differentiates it."

Mental Health Development towards higher levels of mental functions, towards the discovery and realization of higher cognitive, moral, social, and aesthetic values and their organization into a hierarchy in accordance with one's own authentic personality ideal.

Mental Illness The absence or deficiency of processes which effect the development of emotional and instinctive functions. It takes the form of either (1) a negative, nondevelopmental disintegration which may end in dissolution of mental structures and functions, or (2) a strongly integrated, primitive, psychopathic structure.

Migratory Neurosis An organ neurosis with a tendency to periodical quick migration from affecting the function of one organ to affecting another, or from one system of organs to another.

Multilevel Disintegration Multilevel disintegration is a process of developing an authentic hierarchy of values from conflicts between higher and lower levels of instinctive, emotional and intellectual functions. The conflicts are conscious since they involve the awareness of valuing one level over another, therefore, they are conflicts of value.

Multilevelness Division of functions into different levels, for instance, the spinal, subcortical, and cortical levels in the nervous system. Individual perception of many levels of external and internal reality appears at a certain stage of development, here called multilevel disintegration. See *Levels of Functions*.

Negative Adevelopmental, involutional. Refers to factors which arrest development or act against it either by making mental organization rigid, or discomposing it (involution).

Negative Adjustment Nondevelopmental adjustment. Unqualified conformity to a hierarchy of values prevailing in a person's social environment. The values are accepted without an independent critical evaluation. It is an acceptance of an external system of values without autonomous choice. An adjustment to "what is."

Negative Developmental Potential A constitutional predisposition to psychosis, psychopathy, or mental retardation, or other severe disorders preventing development or leading to the dissolution of mental life.

Negative (or Involutional) Disintegration A process characterized by the operation of dynamisms dissolving the organization of mental structures and functions. Its end is chronic mental illness. It occurs almost exclusively at the stage of unilevel disintegration.

Negative Maladjustment Rejection of social norms and accepted patterns of behavior because of the controlling power of primitive

drives and nondevelopmental or pathologically deformed structures and functions. In the extreme case it takes the form of
psychosis, psychopathy, or criminal activity.

Negative Regression Thinking, experiencing, and acting resulting from
regression to lower and more primitive levels of behavior.

Nervousness Enhanced psychic overexcitability in the form of excitability of movements, senses, affect, imagination, and intellect. Nervousness does not in any way entail the impairment of mental
functions.

Neurasthenia A type of psychoneurosis characterized by cycles of excitation followed by excessive fatigue, even exhaustion. Lower
level of psychasthenia, frequently associated with obsessions and
phobias.

Neuropsychic Processes Mental and emotional processes occurring at
the neurological level intimately connected with somatic functions
and primitive emotional and instinctual functions.

Neurosis Psychophysiological or psychosomatic disorders characterized
by a dominance of somatic processes. There are no detectable
organic defects, although the functions may be severely affected.

Nuclei Incipient forms of developmental factors which may or may not
develop.

Oculocardiac Reflex Reflex obtained by lightly pressing on the eyeballs
(closed eyelids) and measuring the pulse. The reflex is said to be
positive if fluctuation in the pulse rate is observed.

One-Sided Development Type of development limited to one talent
or ability, or to a narrow range of abilities and mental functions.
In such development the creative instinct and empathy appear
absent. In exceptionally capable individuals their one sided development may come under the control of a primitive disposing
and directing center and in the extreme case may take the form
of psychopathy or paranoia.

Organized Multilevel Disintegration Developmental level IV. A stage of development when a high level of self-awareness makes possible a greater degree of self-direction and self-determination. External conflicts disappear, and internal conflicts become less overwhelming and intense.

Overexcitability See *Psychic Overexcitability.*

Paranoid Schizophrenia Type of schizophrenia characterized by delusions of persecution, or delusions of power, or both.

Parasympathetic Nervous System See *Autonomic nervous system.*

Partial Disintegration Disintegration within, one or a few related dynamisms. It may lead either to reintegration at a previous level, to reintegration at a lower level (primitive integration), to partial integration at a higher level, or to global disintegration. Partial disintegrations followed by partial integrations at a higher level characterize the developmental pattern of people with average developmental potential. In contrast, global disintegration and global secondary integration (if any) are the privilege of people with rich endowment for accelerated development.

Partial Secondary Integration A cohesive organization of some of the emotional and instinctive functions at a higher level. It comes about as a result of partial multilevel disintegration.

Pathological Hereditary Endowment The occurrence in the family tree of psychoses, psychopathy, mental retardation, or other forms of mental disorder.

Pathological Rumination A type of obsession characterized by the tendency to dwell on the same problem without seeking to find a solution to break the "vicious circle." It is typical of unilevel processes of disintegration.

Perseveration Persistent and recurrent thought or image; compulsive repetition of the same phrase or word over and over again. See also *Affective Perseveration.*

Personality A self-aware, self-chosen, self-affirmed, and self-determined unity of essential individual psychic qualities. Personality as defined here appears at the level of secondary-integration (q.v.).

Personality Ideal An individual standard against which one evaluates one's actual personality structure. It arises out of one's experience and development. At first the ideal may be an imitation, nevertheless, with the growth of individual awareness it becomes authentic and autonomous to eventually become the highest dynamism in the development of personality.

Perversion Neurosis A neurosis resulting from a very strong attraction and repulsion and internal conflict in relation to uncommon sexual urges such as fetishism, necrophilia, homosexuality, or severe masturbation. Internal tension and self-awareness are acting strongly and simultaneously, because there is the awareness of the strength of the impulses and their aberrant nature together with a refinement which removes the possibility of hurting or shocking a sexual partner.

Polarity Existing between two opposites, as in emotional fluctuations between pleasant and unpleasant, between joyous and sad.

Positive Developmental or evolutional. Also used to refer to development with emerging direction of growth from lower to a higher level of functions (process of hierarchization).

Positive Adjustment (or Developmental Adjustment) Conformity to higher levels of a hierarchy of values self-discovered and consciously followed. It is an acceptance of values after critical examination and an autonomous choice. It is an adjustment to "what ought to be." Such hierarchy of values is controlled by (or developed from) the personality ideal.

Positive Disintegration A process of development involving characteristic dynamisms and some degree of awareness of development. It releases the creative powers of the individual, it enriches his psyche, and it carries his growth toward a higher level of psychological functioning. There are four stages of positive disintegration forming an invariant sequence: (1) unilevel disintegration, (2) spontaneous multilevel disintegration, (3) organized multilevel disintegration, (4) transition to secondary integration.

Positive Maladjustment A conflict with and rejection of those standards and attitudes of one's social environment which are incompatible with one's growing awareness of a higher scale of values which is developing as an internal imperative.

Positive Regression Regression in the service of the ego. Temporary regression to an earlier emotional period, or withdrawal from current activities in search of isolation. It is caused by a need for saturation with the carefree and warm experiences of childhood, or by a need to have psychic rest, or a time off to accommodate an experiential load. Positive regression allows an individual to prepare more fully the unfolding of his creative potential, to prevent mental disorders, to preserve and develop his autonomy. It is common in people with emotional and imaginational overexcitability.

Prespasm A prespasmatic state. A state of "preparation" for psychic spasm (q.v.) resulting from painful external or internal stimuli and tension. These stimuli evoke unpleasant reactions and result in fear or flight (avoidance) in acute, unconscious forms.

Preventive Mechanisms See *Protective Mechanisms*.

Primitive Drives Drives (q.v.) operating at the level of primitive integration. Their action is characterized by great intensity, inflexibility, automatism, egocentrism, biological control. They lack the conscious components of reflection, empathy, inhibition. For instance, sexual drive at the primitive level precludes personal involvement with the sexual partner, precludes considerations of discomfort or hurt sustained by the partner.

Primitive Functions Emotional and instinctive functions (q.v.) operating at the level of primitive integration. They are characterized by automatism, impulsiveness, stereotypy, egocentrism, lack of inhibition, lack or low degree of consciousness.

Primitive Integration (or Primary Integration) Developmental level I. An integration of all mental functions into a cohesive structure controlled by primitive drives.

Prise de Conscience See *Dynamic Insight.*

Prospection An ability to temporarily transpose one's thoughts and feelings into the future, usually associated with rich imagination and fantasy. It may also have a strong intuitive component as a sense of timing of the development to come. Characterizes not only dreamers but also dynamic individuals given to construction of hypotheses or long-range planning.

Protective Mechanisms Psychoneurotic processes and dynamisms which by their relatively mild disintegrating power protect against mental breakdown or suicide. The richer the hereditary endowment the stronger are the protective dynamisms. Cf. *Defense through development.*

Psychasthenia A type of psychoneurosis characterized by lowered biopsychic tonus, especially in regard to primitive functions and adjustment to actual reality. Psychasthenia is characterized by feelings of inadequacy, obsessions, anxieties (especially existential), depressions.

Psychic Overexcitability Higher than average responsiveness to stimuli, manifested either by psychomotor, sensual, emotional (affective), imaginational, or intellectual excitability, or the combination thereof.

Psychic Spasm Psychic state analogous to a physiological spasm. It is the sudden arrest in an unpleasant way of ongoing mental activity as a result of new and unfamiliar experiences. It may also be evoked by the sudden appearance of an uncontrollable impulse.

Psychic Spasmophilia Condition analogous to the "spasmophilic" constitution (see *Spasmophilia*). Psychic spasmophilia does not depend on the physical spasmophilic constitution but may, when present, function together with it. The characteristic traits are excessive sudden responses to positive and negative psychic stimuli. Psychic spasmophilia is an expression of susceptibility to frustration or to being hurt. It acts also as a psychic defense against too strong stimuli by giving a warning signal to consciousness about impending emotional danger or overwhelming joy, which may upset the balance. This mechanism serves the role of delaying or "diluting" negative and positive stimuli of an intensity higher than the system can handle.

Psychomotor Crisis Acting out of psychic tension through temper tantrums, destructive behavior, running away, or hysterical conversion. Psychomotor crises are frequent in cases of psychomotor and emotional overexcitability not combined with other enriching components of the developmental potential which in this case is rather limited, and due to the absence of a multilevel inner psychic milieu does not offer the possibility of a positive release.

Psychoneurosis A more or less organized form of growth through positive disintegration. Lower psychoneuroses are predominantly psychosomatic in nature, higher psychoneuroses are highly conscious internal struggles whose tensions and frustrations are not anymore translated into somatic disorders.

Psychosomatization An excessive tendency for transposition of intense psychical experiences onto somatic processes. The high tension is absorbed by somatic functions thereby altering their course. This can be manifested as paresis, paralysis, hysterical numbness, etc. In psychosomatization the genesis of a disturbance is believed to he in the psyche. Cf. *Autonomic Somatization.*

Reality Function A function which guides the behavior of the individual in his testing of internal and external reality. It adapts his behavior to the demands of those levels of reality which he perceives as the more vital. Reality function at a low level deals with the basic needs of everyday living. Reality function at a high, level deals with the experiences and processes of inner creative reality.

Regression See *Negative Regression* and *Positive Regression.*

Schizoneurosis A psychopathological syndrome on the borderline of psychoneurosis and schizophrenia (psychosis).

Schizophrenia Simplex Type of schizophrenia characterized by withdrawal, apathy, indifference. It progresses slowly but irreversibly.

Schizothymic Showing tendency to an uneven, diffuse, inconsistent behavior with weak syntony and poor adjustment to the environment, often with symptoms of queerness.

Secondary Integration Developmental level V. The integration of all mental functions into a harmonious structure controlled by higher emotions such as the dynamism of personality ideal, autonomy and authenticity. Secondary integration is the outcome of the full process of positive disintegration.

Self-Perfection Instinct The higher form of the creative instinct (q.v.). It appears in accelerated development when the individual's primary concern is his self-growth.

Simple Schizophrenia See *Schizophrenia Simplex.*

Somatopsychic Refers to the lowest level of psychoneurotic processes, i.e. those occurring without any participation of consciousness. At the somatopsychic level mental processes are almost entirely under the control of biological processes. The next higher level is the psychosomatic where psychological tensions are transposed to somatic processes via the autonomic nervous system.

Somnambulism Sleepwalking. Walking and carrying out complex activities while in sleep, or a hypnotic or related state.

Spasmophilia The tendency toward muscular twitching, spasms, or convulsions from even slight mechanical or electrical stimulation. Psychic Spasmophilia (q.v.) is a metaphor used here to describe easily mobilized strong and sudden involuntary emotional reactions, tensions, which are experienced not unlike internal convulsions.

Spontaneous Multilevel Disintegration Developmental Level III. The stage of development which occurs with the emergence of a direction of development and a sense of "higher" and "lower." These two phenomena are strictly inter-dependent. They are the result of intense emotional experiences and spontaneously developing conflicts of value (see *Hierarchization*).

"Stuttering" of Somatic Functions A tendency toward spastic psychophysical activity. It is observed as sudden blushing or growing pale, as pharyngeal spasms, or "stuttering" of urination. It is the manifestation of the transformation of very strong somatopsychic (q.v.) tension to spastic symptoms.

Subject-Object in Oneself One of the main developmental dynamisms which consists in observing one's own mental life in an attempt to better understand oneself and to evaluate oneself critically. It is a process of looking at oneself as if from outside (the self as object) and of perceiving the individuality of others (the other as subject, i.e. individual knower).

Sympathetic Nervous System See *Autonomic nervous system.*

Sympathigotonia A state resulting from high tension in the sympathetic nervous system manifested by accelerated pulse, high blood pressure, dilated pupils, or hypoacidity of the stomach.

Syntony Responsiveness to the environment, chiming in with. Primitive syntony is impulsive behavior and is not much different from gregariousness. Higher levels of syntony involve insight into other people's feelings and experiences. More conscious and deliberate forms of syntony combined with an attitude of helpfulness we call empathy.

Tetanoidal Personality Personality type differentiated by Jaensch and characterized by muscular twitching, spasms, tendency to convulsions, etc., as in tetany. The activity of the parasympathetic nervous system is prevalent. Psychologically a tetanoidal individual shows somewhat uncoordinated behavior; his responses are not harmonized and are not integrated.

Third Factor The autonomous factor of development. The first factor is the constitutional endowment, the second factor is the social environment. The third factor is the dynamism of conscious choice (valuation) by which one affirms or rejects certain qualities in oneself and in one's environment.

Transcendental Obsession Obsession with problems of transcendence, i.e. with problems of supersensory reality. It is not much different from a scientist's obsession with an unsolved problem, or an artist's obsession with the search for new means of expression.

Transcending the Biological Life Cycle Replacement of somatic determinants of maturation, aging, or disease, by mental determinants of rich psychic development (accelerated development), continued creativity in spite of aging, continued psychic growth past maturity, etc.

Transcending the Psychological Type Introduction of traits of opposite type to one's original type, e.g. an extravert becoming to some extent an introvert. This developmental change occurs as a consequence of the dynamism of inner psychic transformation and is characteristic of accelerated development.

Unilevel Disintegration Developmental Level II. Protracted and recurrent conflicts between drives and emotional states of similar level and of similar intensity appearing as ambivalences and ambitendencies (q.v.), e.g. changing and alternating states of attraction and repulsion, love and hate, joy and sadness, excitement and depression, moodiness. The conflicts may not be consciously experienced. When they are they are experienced as pulls of equal value, in contrast to multilevel conflicts, and, therefore, do not tend towards a solution but seek immediate palliatives like alcohol, drugs, or suicide.

Vagosympathetic Dystonia See *Autonomic Disequilibrium.*

Vagosympathetic System See *Autonomic Nervous System.*

Vagotonia Excessive excitability of the vagus nerve. A state resulting from high tension in the vagus nerve manifested by slowing down of pulse, arrhythmia, low blood pressure, constricted pupils, peripheral vascular disorders.

Value See *Hierarchization.*

Waxy Flexibility A passive response by which a person's arm or posture retains the position in which it has been placed. Usually thought to be characteristic of catatonic schizophrenia this response is easily obtained from normal individuals.

Index

About the Author

Kazimierz Dabrowski (September 1, 1902–November 26, 1980) was a psychologist, psychiatrist, educator, and prolific writer, publishing over 30 books and 250 papers in various languages during his lifetime. He received degrees in medicine (University of Geneva, 1929) and psychology (Poznan, 1931), certificates in psychoanalysis (under Wilhelm Stekel in Vienna, 1934) and public health (Harvard University, 1934), and habilitations in children's psychotherapy (University of Geneva, 1934) and psychiatry (University of Wrocław, 1948), among other honours and achievements. In addition to Stekel, Dabrowski studied under some of the most prominent figures in his field, both in Poland and abroad, including Jean Piaget, Pierre Janet, Édouard Claparède, and Stefan Blachowski.

In 1935 he founded the Institute of Mental Hygiene in Warsaw, Poland, which he directed until 1948. Under Nazi occupation, he and his colleagues used the facility to hide Polish resistance soldiers, refugees, doctors and priests involved in the underground movement. He was arrested by the Gestapo in 1942. In 1950, the communist authorities arrested him and his wife, and he was incarcerated for 18 months. After his release, strict restraints were placed on his activities until he was declared 'rehabilitated' in 1956.

Throughout his career he taught and lectured at many universities around the world, including a professorship in experimental psychology at Warsaw in 1956 and, from 1964 on, the position of Professor and Director of Clinical Research and Internship at the University of Alberta. He also served as Visiting Professor at Laval University in Quebec from 1968. He passed away in Warsaw in 1980 after suffering a heart attack in 1979.

CPSIA information can be obtained at www.ICGtesting.com
Printed in the USA
LVOW10s0023070416

482446LV00023B/559/P